GLOBAL HEALTH GOVERNANCE:
INTERNATIONAL LAW AND PUBLIC HEALTH
IN A DIVIDED WORLD

Global Health Governance

International Law and Public Health in a Divided World

Obijiofor Aginam

UNIVERSITY OF TORONTO PRESS
Toronto Buffalo London

© University of Toronto Press Incorporated 2005
Toronto Buffalo London
Printed in Canada

ISBN 0-8020-8000-6

Printed on acid-free paper

Library and Archives Canada Cataloguing in Publication

Aginam, Obijiofor, 1969–
     Global health governance : international law and public
health in a divided world / Obijiofor Aginam.

     Includes bibliographical references and index.
     ISBN 0-8020-8000-6

     1. Public health laws.   2. Public health laws, International.
     I. Title.

     K3570.A45 2005   344.04   C2005-900560-2

This book has been published with the help of a grant from the Canadian Federation
for the Humanities and Social Sciences, through the Aid to Scholarly Publications
Programme, using funds provided by the Social Sciences and Humanities Research
Council of Canada.

University of Toronto Press acknowledges the financial assistance to its publishing
program of the Canada Council and the Ontario Arts Council.

University of Toronto Press acknowledges the financial support for its publishing
activities of the Government of Canada through the Book Publishing Industry
Development Program (BPIDP).

This book is dedicated to Chichi, Ikem, Nwando, and to the blessed memory of Oranyelugo Aguolu and Ivan L. Head

Contents

Foreword

The issue of global health is of increasing concern as one of the areas requiring urgent international attention. International law has an important role to play in the promotion of public health, and in this regard it needs to harness the resources which a variety of disciplines have to offer. In this book Professor Aginam performs this task admirably, bringing to the aid of international law interdisciplinary perspectives from human rights law, medicine, history, political science, philosophy, economics, and sociology, among others.

Aginam's thoughtful analysis of how the problem of global health needs to be addressed includes a consideration of colonialism, underdevelopment, globalization, South-North relations, and the activities of non-state actors. The community of international lawyers must draw on all the perspectives and insights available to it in handling the problem of global disease, which, as the author points out, has resulted in greater loss of life than the world wars. Yet global health receives little attention compared with most of the other issues with which international law concerns itself.

The world is being unified in many ways, and one important aspect of this is 'microbial unification.' Microbes know no national barriers, and the traditional distinction between national and international health regimes is obsolete. Intercommunication through easier transport, the free movement of goods and services, tourism, and other factors contribute to the spread of communicable diseases. The world is fast becoming a single germ pool in which there are no health sanctuaries or safe havens. All of humanity is vulnerable and needs protection. Apart from the health-related human rights aspects of globalization, there is the enormous problem of globalization of poverty and the gap that is visibly growing between the South and the North. When vast numbers live at a level of basic poverty, problems of public health, malnutrition, infant mortality, preventable diseases, and their communication across all national boundaries demand a multicultural and multidisciplinary approach.

International law also has a special role in relation to global strategies, their coordination through all available agencies, and their synchronization into practical working programs. This calls for a synthesized and liberal extension of international law principles beyond their traditional confines. The conditions of impoverishment, deprivation, and rightlessness wherein the great majority of the global population lives call for a wider application of international law if world health is to be significantly advanced.

This book presents a pioneering and wide-ranging survey of the problem of global health in all its complexity. The author brings to it a practical vision, based on broad personal experience and scholarship, which will be of value to all individuals, agencies, and governments involved in the promotion of public health.

Apart from its discussion of the consequences of multilateralism and globalization, the book contains an important case study of traditional medical therapies for malaria in Africa. This is a prototype of similar studies that can be undertaken in regard to traditional medical therapies for various diseases in other global regions. There is a vast range of knowledge to be explored in this field, which has enormous potential to contribute to global welfare.

Through its many-faceted approach this work adds an important dimension to the discipline of international law, which is the primary tool we have for establishing the global society of the future. It is a vital contribution to international law and will no doubt be treated as a landmark study. I congratulate the author on this innovative and authoritative work. It opens up new frontiers and greatly enhances the practical value of international law in ameliorating the conditions of the vast bulk of humanity.

Judge C.G. Weeramantry
Former Vice President
International Court of Justice
The Hague

Acknowledgments

I am indebted to a long list of persons and institutions for their support as I explored this important issue of our time: the governance challenges of the globalization of public health. I thank God for sustaining me with good health in the course of writing this book, especially his grant of journey mercies as I travelled to many parts of the world. I am immensely indebted to my wife, Chichi; my son Ikem; my parents Osodieme and Ezeonyekachi; my two brothers and three sisters; my parents-in-law, Egbueziora and Margaret; and to my immediate and extended families, particularly all the Aginams, Ezeuzoekwes, Uzoatus, Aguolus, and Nwezes, for their emotional support. I developed the conceptual framework for this study during my tenure as a doctoral candidate in law at the University of British Columbia, Vancouver and Professors Ivan L. Head, O.C., Q.C., S. Salzberg, both of blessed memory, and Karin Mickelson deserve my sincere thanks for their detailed and critical comments on earlier drafts of the various chapters. I should like to thank the Faculty of Graduate Studies, University of British Columbia, for their generous financial awards of University Graduate Fellowship and Theodore F. Arnold Graduate Fellowship to me in the period 1998–2001. Without these fellowships, my research may not have been possible. I am also indebted in many ways to the Rockefeller Foundation and the Institute of International Studies, University of California at Berkeley, for the travel grants that funded my participation in the African Dissertation Workshop at Berkeley and the Health and Society in Africa Conference at Stanford University in early 1999. The meetings introduced me to social science research methodologies and opened a channel of communication with a number of scholars working on health-related issues in Africa.

I should like to thank the World Health Organization (WHO) for generously funding my tenure as Global Heath Leadership Officer at their headquarters in Geneva, Switzerland, 1999–2001. It is a gross understatement to say that this book benefited from my two-year stay at the WHO headquarters. My time in

Geneva provided me with the enviable privilege of personally observing the annual sessions of the World Health Assembly, the WHO Executive Board, and a series of important meetings aimed at forging consensus among WHOs 192 member states on a number of global health issues. I also travelled to many countries for WHO meetings, an experience that shaped the thoughts I have explored in this book. It was a rare privilege to have worked closely with top policy makers at the WHO on the Framework Convention on Tobacco Control and the revision of the International Health Regulations. I thank particularly Douglas Bettcher, Derek Yach, Sandy Cocksedge, and Nick Drager, all senior WHO staff during my tenure, and Professor Johan Giesecke of the Karolinska Institute of Public Health, Stockholm, Sweden (formerly of the WHO) for making my stay at the WHO an experience to be treasured for life. I should like to thank the International University of Peoples' Institutions for Peace, Rovereto, Italy, and its director, Professor Guilliano Pontara, for giving me the opportunity to attend their international training program in 1998, and also for inviting me as visiting/guest lecturer on 'Globalization and Health' in May 2002.

Also on the list of institutions that deserve my thanks is the Academic Council on the United Nations System (ACUNS), which funded my participation in their annual summer workshop on 'International Organisation Studies' at the Centre for Globalisation and Regionalisation, University of Warwick, Coventry, U.K., in summer 2000. I presented draft chapters of this book at the ACUNS meeting and received detailed comments from the workshop directors: Paul Wapner (School of International Service, American University, Washington, D.C.), Christine Chinkin (London School of Economics), and Jan A. Scholte (University of Warwick). I also benefited from comments made by fellow ACUNS workshop participants, especially Ralph Wilde (then of the University of Cambridge), Kent Buse (London School of Hygiene and Tropical Medicine), Raphael Njoku (University of Kentucky), Mark Drumbl (Washington and Lee Law School), and Tim Murithi (United Nations, Geneva). At Warwick, I received overwhelming support from the then executive director of ACUNS, Jean Krasno (Yale University). I am grateful to my Geneva circle of friends and fellow scholars: Dr Edward Kwakwa (World Intellectual Property Organization), Dr Omar Ahmed (World Health Organization), Professor Obioma Nwaorgu (World Health Organization), Dr Patrick MaCarthy (United Nations Institute for Disarmament Research), Geoffrey Onyeama (World Intellectual Property Organization), Beryl Carby-Mutambirwa (International Union for Research on Cancer), Chinedu Osakwe (World Trade Organization), Uche Gwam (World Meteorological Organization), Kingsley C. Moghalu (Global Fund to Fight AIDS, TB and Malaria), William Onzivu (World Health Organization), and Collin Archer (International Peace Bureau). I should like to acknowledge the intellectual inspiration I have received over the years from the scholarship of Obiora C. Okafor, David P. Fidler, Lawrence Gostin, George Alexandrowicz, Richard Falk, I.P.S. Okafor, Nick Drager, Anthony Anghie, Makau wa Mutua, Jutta Brunnee, Maurice Iwu, Rebecca Cook, and James Thuo Gathii. My thanks are also due to my friends most of whom are scholars in their own right: Clement Adibe, Joel Ngugi, Pius Adesanmi, Ikechi Mgbeoji, Paul Ocheje, Chika Onwuekwe, Chinedu Ezetah, Ray Onyegu, David Mackenzie, Russell Jutlah, Ucheora Onwuamaegbu, Femi Elias, Chinonye Obiagwu, Gerald Heckman, Patrick Osakwe, Reginald Nnazor, Romanus Ejiaga, and Chidi Oguamanam. I wish to express my gratitude to my employers, Carleton University, Ottawa, for their support since I joined the faculty in July 2001. Finally, I acknowledge the 'unquantifiable' support of my foremost mentors, A.R.K. Saba, Lawan Marguba, Chris Nduka (KSM), Olisa Agbakoba (SAN), and Oranyelugo Aguolu of blessed memory, who taught me that hard work was a shortcut to success in most human endeavours.

GLOBAL HEALTH GOVERNANCE:
INTERNATIONAL LAW AND PUBLIC HEALTH
IN A DIVIDED WORLD

Introduction

My mother gave birth to me in the late 1960s, during the Nigerian civil war. My parents lived in a small rural village in the Eastern Region of Nigeria – then the breakaway Republic of Biafra – that came under heavy shelling by Nigerian federal troops. Biafra was completely cut off by an economic blockade, and in the villages it was widely believed that the Nigerian federal authorities were pursuing a war of genocide. Bombs hit both military and non-military targets, fell on innocent civilians, and completely destroyed social infrastructure. Massive hunger and starvation set in, resulting in uncontrollable malnutrition, deplorable medicare, and excessively high infant mortality. It was in this difficult and hopeless situation that my mother's labour pains started. Because of the acute shortage of gasoline in war-ravaged Biafra, there was no car to take my mother to the nearest medical clinic then managed by Irish Catholic Missionaries, about a twenty-minute drive from her home. Providence had it that I was born on a highway without any medical assistance whatsoever. My father, who was a teacher at the time, became my mother's emergency midwife, nurse, and obstetrician, all in one.

The scenario of my birth reveals the contemporary health divide between the industrialized and developing worlds. Even in times of peace and normalcy, more than half of the world's population routinely faces difficult and turbulent health challenges. In many developing countries, access to clean water, food, housing, nutritious diets, and sanitation is a luxury. Medical clinics are many kilometres away and inaccessible and the cost of medicines is prohibitive, placing them beyond the reach of the majority. There is one physician to thousands of people. Babies are not vaccinated against leading killer diseases, and public health budgets are a tiny fraction of spending compared to other sectors like defence and foreign affairs. Strategies for primary health care, health protection, and health promotion lack effective policy interventions that would facilitate the delivery of public health dividends to the populace as a public good. This dire situation is now compounded by the emergence and re-emergence of diseases that constitute a global threat.

History is replete with epidemics and pandemics that decimated a sizeable percentage of humanity the Plague of Athens in 430 B.C.; the Black Death (Bubonic Plague) in fourteenth-century Europe; smallpox, measles, scarlet fever, chicken pox, and influenza in the Americas in the sixteenth and seventeenth-centuries; and global swine flu in 1918–19. At the dawn of the twenty-first century, natural disasters and environmental calamities, food insecurity, wars and civil conflicts, globalization, forced and intentional migrations, travel, trade and tourism, poverty, and underdevelopment combine to propel the emergence and spread of diseases and pathogenic microbes across the geo-political boundaries of nation states. With the recent outbreaks of ebola haemorrhagic fever, lassa-fever, hantavirus, West Nile virus, and Severe Acute Respiratory Syndrome (SARS); the re-emergence of multi-drug-resistant tuberculosis; and the global pandemic of HIV/AIDS and other diseases that transcend national boundaries humanity is now repositioned for a decisive battle with the microbial world. The transnational spread of epidemics and pandemics serves as wake-up calls for nation states, multilateral institutions, and civil society to rise to the challenges and vicious threats posed to humanity by disease. Because the interaction between humanity and diseases is almost as ancient as human history, and because infectious diseases have killed more people than have wars, the challenge of protecting humanity's health against microbial threats should catalyse a coordinated multilateral policy response to facilitate the 'epidemiological transition'[1] required across societies.

The definition and parameters of public health differ across societies, cultures, and disciplines. It has been observed that

> Human health is a derivative of multiple circumstances, not all of them fully understood or subject to accurate measurement. Because health is a relative term, both its measurement and its indicators assume varying interpretations within and among societies, cultures, and geographic regions. Any endeavor to examine the health environment on a global scale – as distinct from a compound of statistics gathered from individual states – must therefore be sensitive to attitudinal variations. Not all societies place the same value on health; not all individuals accept the validity of even the most basic of health determinants.[2]

Public health has become analogous to the proverbial 'road traversed by many pathways.' Almost everyone has a view of what health means, what it does not mean, how to protect or promote it, its parameters and determinants, its linkages with other socio-economic factors, and the paradigms – legal, legislative, and social – for its promotion and progressive realization. An interdisciplinary discussion of public health or even a discussion by scholars of the same discipline can easily become a cacophony of the discordant voices reminiscent of the biblical Tower of Babel,[3] or what one scholar refers to as 'characteristic of a dinner party conversation that endeavors to recall the plot of *The Two Gentlemen of Verona*.'[4] Most legal scholars confuse the terms public health, health care, primary health care, medical services, and medicare. In *The Right to Health in the Americas*,[5] Roemer argued that the phrase 'right to health' is an absurdity because it implies a guarantee of 'perfect health.'[6] She opted for the phrase 'right to health care,' which encompasses 'protective environmental services, prevention, health promotion and therapeutic services as well as related actions in sanitation, environmental engineering, housing and social welfare.'[7] Leary has pointed out that 'such an extensive definition seems contrary to common understanding of the phrase 'right to heath care.'[8] The editors of *The Right to Health in the Americas* similarly recognized that the phrase 'right to health' may be conceptually misleading and suggested 'a right to health protection' comprised of two components: a right to health care and a right to healthy conditions.[9]

In the absence of any consensus on the definition and basic components of public health by legal scholars, this study charts a fuzzy landscape of multilateral health challenges in a paradoxically interdependent/globalizing and sharply divided world. Notwithstanding the raging debate between the 'positive'[10] and 'negative'[11] schools, it combines the tenets of 'health promotion,'[12] 'primary health care,'[13] and 'determinants of health'[14] to explore the multiple dimensions of public health in a world polarized by socio-economic inequalities. Because these approaches are supportive of a 'positive' definition of health, it explores public health broadly from an international legal perspective, and creates critical linkages between health and human rights, poverty, underdevelopment, globalization, and South-North relations.[15]

There are many good reasons why the promotion of public health in a multilateral context deserves heightened interest and attention from scholars, national policy makers, multilateral institutions and civil society in an emerging 'global neighbourhood'. Prominent among them is the increased global interdependence between nation states and populations. As people, goods, and services cross national boundaries in volumes hitherto unseen, disease pathogens permeate geo-political boundaries to threaten populations in distant places with unprecedented speed.[16] The phenomenon and process of globalization and the consequent vulnerability of national boundaries have altered the traditional distinction between national and international health.[17] Exploring the politics along the 'domestic-foreign Frontier,' Rosenau identifies a response that treats the emergent frontier 'as becoming more rugged and, thus, as the arena in which domestic and foreign issues converge, intermesh, or otherwise become indistinguishable within a seamless web ...'[18] 'While foreign policy still designates the efforts of societies to maintain a modicum of control over their external environments, new global interdependence issues such as pollution, currency crises, AIDS and the drug trade have so profoundly changed the tasks and goals of foreign policy officials.'[19] One consequence of globalization is the mutual vulnerability of populations within the 'global village'[20] to the transnational spread of deadly infectious diseases and other non-communicable threats. Microbes carry no national passports, neither do they recognize geo-political boundaries or state sovereignty. Propelled by travel, trade, tourism, the phenomenon of globalization, and a host of other factors, public health threats occasioned by an outbreak of a disease in one remote part of the world can easily transcend national boundaries to threaten populations in distant places.

The world is fast becoming a single germ pool in which there are no health sanctuaries or safe havens from pathogenic microbes. This study explores the concept of mutual vulnerability and juxtaposes it with the 'South-North health divide': disparities and unequal distribution of disease burdens between industrialized and developing worlds and the implications of these disparities for multilateral health governance. It also makes policy recommendations to narrow the apparent regime deficit between multilateral health policies and the realities of public health programs on the ground, especially in the developing world. In our interdependent yet divided world, all of humanity is vulnerable to the prevailing, emerging, and re-emerging threats of disease. This vulnerability calls for enlightened self-interest as nation-states grapple with the challenges of using legal-governance mechanisms to forge a humane and effective multilateral/global health order. Although the scope of this inquiry is interdisciplinary in that it draws from seminal works in public health and epidemiology, history, international relations, and the social sciences, it falls substantially within the parameters of international law. Its primary domain is law, its focus is multilateral institutions, and its subject of analysis is the international legal response to the globalization of public health.

Chapter 1 sketches the parameters of the research problem(s), reviews the literature, and identifies the clusters of research questions and methodology for the study. To explore the complex ramifications of the multilateralization-globalization of public health I juxtapose the terms *mutual vulnerability* (mutual threats posed by disease to all of humanity in an interdependent world),[21] and *vulnerability of multilateralism* (the challenges of forging multilateral consensus on cross-border spread of disease in an interdependent world). The two challenges are inexorably linked, and the interaction between them paradoxically highlights the intriguing tenets of self-interest (multilateralism and mutual cooperation) and the frustrating dangers of isolationism (protectionist national policies). Chapter 1 argues that international law has been at the margins in multilateral health discourse for two main reasons. First, a few lawyers who explore the vast terrain of global health challenges focus narrowly on segmented issues instead of taking a more holistic approach that radically problematizes or theorizes the relevance of law in multilateral/global health governance. Second, lawyers and public health scholars have yet to forge symbiotic ties on multilateral health discourse and governance. Exploring the relevance of law in the protection and promotion of public health multilaterally, I argue for increased collaboration between international lawyers, epidemiologists, and scholars of other disciplines relevant to public health.

Chapter 1 further explains the methodology employed to answer the research questions posed by the study; a hybridization of critical, analytical, and descriptive analyses of interdisciplinary literature as well as policy documents of relevant multilateral health institutions, especially the World Health Organization. The study relies on social science qualitative interviews to explore ethno-pharmacological and indigenous malaria therapies of rural populations in the developing world. These therapies, as well as the interviews, are used to assess the effectiveness of global malaria control strategies of the WHO.

Chapter 2 explores the strange paradox of a 'global village in a divided world,' and assesses how socio-economic inequalities affect the health of populations in the developed and developing countries. The chapter explores two levels of inquiry/analyses under the rubric of the *globalization of poverty*. The first level of inquiry deals with the limits of international treaty provisions on the human right to health, especially the importance of financial and technical resources in realizing the right to health under the International Covenant on Economic, Social and Cultural Rights (ICESCR) (1966). The second level of inquiry deals with the health-related impacts of structural adjustment programs (SAPs) prescribed by the international financial institutions, especially the World Bank, for most of the developing world. This inquiry explores the emerging perspectives aimed at closing the contemporary South-North health divide by focusing on paradigms that are better suited to promote public health in a multicultural world. In this endeavour I draw on the works of Falk,[22] Nader,[23] Trubek,[24] and Snyder,[25] all within the progressive schools of legal anthropology and law and Third World development. Although public health is complicated by vulnerabilities that lie outside the South-North health divide – for instance the deprivation of women and other marginalized groups of full access to public health services – this book focuses primarily on global health governance in contemporary international relations.[26]

Chapter 3 explores the boundaries, ramifications, and complex dynamics of mutual vulnerability in an era of globalized epidemics: the erosion of geo-political boundaries by pathogenic microbes and the increased susceptability of humans to microbial threats in an interdependent world. Historically, humans across cultures have dealt with disease and illness in a variety of ways. Although mutual vulnerability has been with us at least since the Plague of Athens, the use of international law as a governance mechanism against mutual vulnerability is comparatively recent. France did not convene and host the first International Sanitary Conference until 1851. Cholera outbreaks in Europe in 1830 and 1847 were the catalysts for the earliest public health multilateralism and infectious disease diplomacy. These outbreaks compelled European states to convene successive international sanitary conferences and to use international sanitary conventions/ regulations as governance mechanisms against the cross-border spread of disease. To explain the dynamics of mutual vulnerability in the present era of multilateral crisis of emerging and re-emerging infectious disease (EIDs), the study looks at the re-emergence of tuberculosis and 'airport' or 'imported' malaria in the industrialized countries of the global North. Arguing that the distinction between national and international health has become obsolete, chapter 3 examines the potential of self-interest to promote humane public health multilateralism. Malaria and other diseases may have heavier mortality and morbidity burdens in the developing world, but they are no longer solely the exclusive problems of developing countries. The distinctions between 'our disease' and 'their disease' have become anachronistic in multilateral health discourse and policy making.

Because combatting mutual vulnerability is beyond the capabilities of any one country or group of countries, chapter 4 discusses the necessity of increased and sustained multilateral approaches that could potentially check the globalization-transnationalization of diseases under the rubric of vulnerability of multilateralism. To better understand the gaps in contemporary multilateral public health diplomacy, the politics of law and public health among sovereign states in nineteenth-century European-led infectious disease diplomacy must first be explored. Economic, strategic, and other interests of European nation states, all noticeable phenomena in the nineteenth century sanitary conferences, remain serious impediments to effective multilateralism in the present era. South-North politics at the World Health Organization and the acrimonious tone of the nuclear weapons debates at the World Health Assembly are recent examples of the contemporary vulnerabilities of public health multilateralism.

Another important feature of nineteenth-century infectious disease diplomacy was the use of international law (sanitary treaties and conventions) as mechanisms to share epidemiological information on outbreaks and cross-border spread of disease. In the nineteenth century, international law was engaged in complex manoeuvres with colonialism and colonized peoples across the world. This study explores the colonial and post-colonial legacies which nineteenth-century public health diplomacy (the international sanitary conferences) bequeathed to the contemporary international health order. This analysis repositions international law as a post-ontological discipline that plays, or could potentially play, a key role in the governance of globalized/multilateral health threats. I explore two legal mechanisms used by the World Health Organization to govern global health issues: the International Health Regulations (IHR) (on infectious diseases) and the recently adopted Framework Convention on Tobacco Control (FCTC), with a focus on the gaps in the enforcement of the IHR and the likely potential of the FCTC. Although the World Health Organization has innovative treaty-making powers under Articles 19–21 of its constitution, this study argues that extreme reliance on legal strategies in global health governance by the WHO, while necessary, may not on its own deliver the ultimate dividends of health as a public good, especially in the developing world. In public health, law is only a means to an end, and not an end itself. An effective combination of legal and non-legal strategies is required to facilitate epidemiological transition across a range of societies. Because the WHO has no history of enforcing legally binding treaties, we need a comparative study of the multilateral treaties that govern global environmental issues: the Montreal Protocol on Substances That Deplete the Ozone Layer and the World Bank's Global Environmental Facility. The World Health Organization, in its renewed efforts to use international legal strategies and interventions to pursue its global health mandate, must learn from the effectiveness (even if limited) of these environmental regimes.

Chapter 5 explores the interaction between traditional African malaria therapies and the WHO's multilateral malaria control strategy: the Roll Back Malaria Campaign (RBM), a major partnership between governments, multilateral institutions, corporations, and foundations. The RBM campaign must be assessed against the behavioural practices of rural populations in malaria-endemic parts of the world to discover the extent to which such global partnerships respond to the local constituencies they purport to serve. Traditional medical therapies employed by indigenous societies in most parts of Africa have often been dismissed as witchcraft, quackery, sorcery, magic, or unscientific barbarism that is unfit to be integrated into the multilateral/global health policy framework. This study argues that traditional African herbal medicine used by local communities to treat malaria can be synthesized with, or integrated within, multilateral malaria control strategies. Contemporary multilateral governance of transnational public health challenges is witnessing a vicious tension between a coalition of nation states and another coalition of civil society and non-state actors. Policies incubated at multilateral forums by states as repositories of state power are increasingly viewed as harmful to a range of public goods: the environment, public health, and human rights. As a result of the tension between these policies and the realities on the ground, global/multilateral policies are often characterized as 'globalization-from-above.' Applied to the interaction between indigenous malaria-therapies used by populations in malaria endemic societies of the Third World and the WHO's RBM campaign, would the contemporary multilateral malaria control strategy be viewed in this light? Field interviews conducted with traditional healers, rural populations and Western-trained physicians practising in rural communities in Nigeria suggest that there is a regime deficit between the global malaria control policy of multilateral institutions and ethno-pharmacological practices of rural populations in malaria-endemic African societies. Traditional medicine, which is not an integral part of the WHO's RBM project, is popular among rural populations in such societies. Despite the popularity of traditional medicine, the phenomenon of globalization, however, has started to erode traditional medical therapies in most of the developing world at an alarming speed, while simultaneously doing little to place Western medicines within the reach of these Third World populations. This conundrum necessitates a multifaceted dialogue across cultural, disciplinary, and theoretical schools, a dialogue leading to policy recommendations to alter the global burden of disease that is presently distributed unequally between populations in the industrialized and developing worlds.

Chapter 6 discusses these multilateral policy recommendations. It coins and uses the term *communitarian globalism* to focus on the active participation of every important actor in multilateral health governance: multilateral institutions, nation states, civil society, and other non-state actors. Because underdevelopment and poverty breed diseases, and because enormous resources are needed to rebuild decaying public health infrastructures across the Third World, there is an urgent need for collaboration between the World Bank (because of its immense resources) and multilateral institutions within the United Nations system, especially the World Health Organization and the United Nations Children's Fund (UNICEF). The World Bank has been criticized for its obsession with extreme neo-liberal policies, some of which I assess in chapter 2, in discussing the impact of structural adjustment programs. Therefore, it is important to search for commonalties between the World Bank's vision of health and the WHO's public health mandate along the lines of equitable policies such as the Alma-Ata Declaration on Primary Health Care, which command near-universal acceptance by almost all the member states of the World Health Organization. These commonalties pave the way for a disease non-proliferation facility: a modest proposal for a multilateral funding regime very similar to the Montreal Protocol on Substances That Deplete the Ozone Layer and the Global Environmental Facility. This proposal has recently received its most visible multilateral imprimatur in the form of the Global Fund to Fight AIDS, Tuberculosis and Malaria proposed by UN Secretary-General Kofi Annan, the G-8 Summit, and the United Nations General Assembly as one way to curb the global threats posed by these diseases. Chapter 6 discusses the problems and prospects of the Global Fund to Fight AIDS, Tuberculosis and Malaria regime and argues that its *modus operandi* must recognize divergent national and socio-economic contexts. In accordance with multicultural approaches to health, governance of the fund must draw on both available expertise within civil society organizations, the United Nations system and sustainable practices of populations that live with the morbidity and mortality burdens of these diseases. The Global Fund must be transparent and accountable to constituencies where the burdens of these diseases are heaviest. Its governing instruments must reflect equity, justice, and fairness, and must be sensitive to the unequal disease burdens between the global South and the global North.

This study argues that the distinction between national and international health has become obsolete with the advent of globalization, and that mutual vulnerability demands multilateral approaches to the transnationalization of disease. It does not, however, postulate that nation states will wither away and become irrelevant within the reconfigured normative boundaries of global health governance. Our present world order is still composed of sovereign nation states, and communitarian globalism consequently envisions certain key roles for nation states in the scheme of global health governance. The onus of basic curative, protective, preventive, and promotional health care services lies substantially on governments in national jurisdictions. These services have multiple dimensions: basic sanitation and hygiene, resource-allocation decisions, poverty alleviation, food security, regulation of health insurance, and other policy, legal, and administrative interventions. It is only when governments begin to address these basic and essential health services within national jurisdictions that the transnational spread of disease and microbial threats in an interdependent world will start to diminish. Notwithstanding the continued relevance of the nation state, communitarian globalism, poses a serious challenge to the Westphalian system of multilateralism. The promise of non-state actors in global health governance is boosted by the persistent exclusion of a sizeable portion of humanity from the protective structures of the nation state, from the ascendancy of the state from the Treaty of Westphalia, 1648, to the present day.[27] Thus, the emergent multilateral-global health governance is, paradoxically, a fragmented but unified fabric involving a multiplicity of actors within the realm of state actors and transnational networks of civil society actors. Commitment to the health of humanity in an interdependent, globalizing world requires enormous sacrifices, critical choices, and multilateral approaches. Accidental or intentional tolerance of disease in any part of the global neighbourhood constitutes a threat to populations in distant places. What ought we do to protect populations in the emergent global village from microbial threats? Neither isolationism nor protectionism has the capacity to provide any defences against advancing microbial forces. Enlightened self-interest must now guide both state and non-state actors to forge multilateral ties and consensus on globalized health challenges in a divided world. This study therefore explores the prospects and potential offered by self-interest for disease non-proliferation in our emergent global neighbourhood.

Chapter 1

Conceptual Framework and Methodology

A The Conceptual Framework of the Study

I The Research Problem(s)

That the world is a 'global village'[1] or a 'global neighbourhood'[2] is a truism that metaphorically underscores the increasing interdependence of populations, markets, and nation states. From the mid-seventeenth century, multilateralism has grappled with the multiple dimensions of the economic, health, social, and environmental vicissitudes of global interdependence. A plethora of globalizing forces has emerged in the form of complex international airline networks, flows of foreign direct investment, ecological tourism, religious pilgrimages, international sports festivals, regionalism, and free trading blocs.[3] But, almost simultaneously, the emergent global village is threatened by a surge in the number of refugees fleeing civil wars and conflicts, environmental and natural disasters, and South-North disparities, as well as the emergence and re-emergence of infectious and non-communicable diseases.

In the twenty-first century, very few, if any, urgent public health events remain solely within the purview of national jurisdictions. An obvious consequence of globalization is the increased risk of the transnational spread of pathogenic microbes, communicable and non-communicable health threats. People and goods are crossing national borders in massive numbers unparalleled in human history. In the field of global public health, it has been argued that the powerful impetus of globalization undermines state sovereignty, as power flows out of the formal structures of the nation state into the hands of non-state actors. The pervasive impact of globalization, which is apparent in telecommunications, manufacturing strategies, international trade, and global capital flows, has shattered the traditional distinction between national and international health. Globalization has enabled pathogenic microbes to spread illness and death globally, with unprecedented speed.[4] The fact that an outbreak of an infectious disease anywhere in the world poses a threat to populations everywhere repositions multilateralism as an option in the battle against diseases and pathogenic microbes. The World Health Organization argues that infectious diseases now constitute a 'world crisis.'[5] Leading epidemiologists and other scholars agree.[6] As observed by John M. Last, 'dangers to health anywhere on earth are dangers to health everywhere. International health, therefore, means more than just the health problems peculiar to developing countries ... There are many good reasons why we should be concerned about world health. The most obvious is self-interest: Some of the world's health problems endanger us all ...'[7] If 'self-interest' must catalyse effective and humane multilateral health cooperation, why has so little been achieved in this regard? Put another way, why have nation states largely been reluctant to act together to protect the global neighbourhood from the calamities of cross-border disease spread? The utility of these questions is twofold. First, a strange paradox currently confronts international scholars and multilateral institutions: the paradox of a global village and a divided world. One extreme of the paradoxical frame projects a humane global neighbourhood, in which all of humanity is part of a global compact united by the immutable bonds of human life and dignity. The other extreme projects a turbulent neighbourhood marked by unequal distribution of global disease burdens on the populations in the South and the North; and by the poverty and underdevelopment of over 70 per cent of the world's nation states and populations, mainly in the global South.

Second, these questions hypothesize the apparent apathy and indifference of most of the industrialized world towards global health challenges.[8] This apathy is evidenced in the weakness of the contemporary international normative order on public health and remains a major contributor to underdevelopment and heavy disease burdens in most of the developing world; it is also conspicuous in the bias, limited scope, and colonial origins of the international sanitary regimes, from the first sanitary conference in 1851 to the formation of the WHO in 1948. Bias is glaringly manifest in present-day public health multilateralism and diplomacy. There is an imbalance in the priorities of multilateral institutions, including the United Nations organs and specialized agencies with a mandate on protection and promotion of global public health.

As argued in the introduction, the vicious threat posed by diseases and pathogenic microbes to the emergent global neighbourhood is predicated on two slightly different but linked concepts: the *mutuality of vulnerability* and the *vulnerability of multilateralism.*[9] Mutual vulnerability refers to the traditional, emerging and re-emerging threats that South-North disparities and the globalization of public health pose to populations in the global neighbourhood irrespective of whether they live in the developing or industrialized worlds. The emergence of new diseases and the re-emergence of old ones across the world constitutes a global crisis of complex magnitude.

Vulnerability, which first affected national boundaries through the globalization of markets, now has a marked impact on populations through the globalization of infectious and non-communicable diseases. From Thucydides's account of the Athenian plague of 430 B.C.[10] through cholera outbreaks in mid-nineteenth-century Europe, down to contemporary epidemics and pandemics, the mutual vulnerability of populations across national boundaries has become the dominant concept in global public health discourses and policy-making agendas. Related to this is the twin concept of vulnerability of multilateralism – the gaps, limitations, shortcomings, and politicization of early and contemporary public health multilateral health initiatives.[11] The politics of nineteenth-century public health diplomacy, which culminated in the International Sanitary Conference of 1851,[12] are still conspicuous in twenty-first-century public health multilateralism, and vulnerability of multilateralism, in the form of South-North politics, remains a dominant phenomenon in the work of the WHO – the specialized agency of the United Nations with a mandate to 'act as the directing and coordinating authority on international health work.'[13]

This study relies on two levels of inquiry to assess how the vulnerability of multilateralism has either advanced or impeded the mandate of the WHO. The first level of inquiry deals with selected issues of South-North politics at the proceedings of the World Health Assembly; the second offers a critical assessment of the WHO's Roll Back Malaria campaign. The first level of inquiry assesses the extent to which the South-North health divide impedes the legitimacy or effectiveness of a multilateral institution like the WHO, while the second explores the extent to which traditional medical therapies and bio-medical practices indigenous to malaria-endemic societies (especially in Africa) are integrated as a core component of the RBM campaign. Following Richard Falk's critique of contemporary market-driven global civilization as 'globalism-from-above,'[14] my assessment of the RBM campaign focuses on its incorporation (or not) of indigenous medical therapies.

The complex interaction of the mutuality of vulnerability and the vulnerability of multilateralism leaves indelible fingerprints on global health discourses and policy making and has continued to shape the contours of contemporary public health diplomacy. Far from being effective or humane, public health multilateralism has remained at a crossroads. As nation states navigate the Scylla of protectionism, driven by what they perceive as strategic/national interests, and the Charybdis of multilateral protection/promotion of public health, the South-North health divide continues to widen alarmingly. This epidemiological apartheid takes its toll on millions of lives across the globalizing world. Mutuality of vulnerability and the vulnerability of multilateralism provide the catalysts for a reform of multilateral-global health governance. In exploring these two inter-twined concepts, this study charts the future of multilateral-global health gover-nance that would be humane and responsive to the health needs of vulnerable populations in the global neighbourhood, what Falk has identified as global part-nership that 'fulfills the vision of unity and harmony.'[15]

The first task is to explore mutual vulnerability in a way that induces genuine self-interest. If populations in the United States or Canada were in real danger of a fatal attack of ebola haemorrhagic fever from Democratic Republic of Congo or Chagas' disease from Bolivia (through global trade, travel, and tourism), would this induce sufficient self-interest to engage these North American countries in developing the surveillance capacity of public health facilities in either Congo or Bolivia? Would the perceived threat compel a *quia timet*[16] transfer of resources from an industrialized to a developing country through multilateral health initia-tives? Exploring mutual vulnerability from this perspective paves the way for a 'reconstructive' inquiry, an inquiry that strives to reshape the normative bound-aries of contemporary global health governance. As a response to the vulnerability of multilateralism, this 'reconstructive' mission, inter alia, searches for alternatives and makes an argument for fairness, equity, and humanistic approaches to multi-lateral cooperation in the global public health arena. In this endeavour, with some caveats, this study draws on Thomas Franck's fairness discourse,[17] Falk's[18] humane world order, and John Rawls'[19] theory of justice.[20] If populations within the geo-political boundaries of nation states, developed or developing, South or North, were viciously threatened by disease with a comparable uniform degree of lethal propensity, mutual vulnerability would reconfigure the normative bound-aries of global health governance in the twenty-first century. Although this initia-tive is beginning to receive some attention from multilateral institutions involved in the RBM campaign,[21] greater efforts and resources are required to protect the global neighbourhood and its endangered populations from the threat of disease.

II Literature Review

Public health falls within the scientific discipline of epidemiology.[22] As such, what is its relation to international law? Of what relevance is an international covenant, treaty, or regulation to cross-border threat or spread of disease? Can public health effectively be the subject of global normative governance mechanisms? Can an international lawyer and an epidemiologist forge a collaborative alliance on global health policy making and scholarship? Most regrettably, the failure to address these questions has stultified scholarly progress and academic inquiry on a plethora of multilateral-global issues where international law and public health intersect. Evi-dence from the available literature indicates that international lawyers have remained largely passive within the scholarly edifice of global public health. Multilateral public health institutions have also discarded international law as a useful operational tool in the evolution of global health policies. Epidemiologists, on the other hand, have often complacently analysed global health issues from the narrow parameters of medical science. Notwithstanding these shortcomings, law and public health in the global arena can be compared to the proverbial 'mansion with many rooms' or 'road traversed by many paths.' International lawyers have traditionally confined themselves to the peripheries, opting either to sit in one of the rooms in the mansion or simply to stand on one of the paths. In exploring the vast terrain of multilateral health, most lawyers adopt segmented approaches to public health challenges. Overly legalistic, the bulk of seminal works by lawyers on bioethics, the human right to health, the human right to a healthy environment, the health implications of war and use of nuclear weapons, and international trade and public health often displays an obvious disregard for holistic and interdisciplinary approaches. Even within 'mainstream multilateral health scholarship and policy-making,'[23] extreme legalism remains a dominant analytical feature in the works of the very few international lawyers who have explored the interaction of global public health and international law with intellectual rigour.

In her discussion of the mandate of the World Health Organization, universal access to conditions for health, and the role of international health regulations in global infectious disease surveillance, Taylor relied on the WHO's statistics on disparities in health standards between rich and poor countries.[24] Her critique of the WHO's reluctance to utilize law and legal interventions to facilitate its global health strategies implies that the essence of law and legalism in global health policy making is teleological; that law can contribute to a significant reduction of disease burdens within and among countries.[25] Fidler, one of the most prolific contemporary scholars of international law and public health, canvasses similar arguments for the increased use of international law in multilateral health strategies.[26] His recent treatise, *International Law and Infectious Diseases*,[27] sketches an international legal paradigm for globalization of public health. Employing theoretical, analytical, and historical frameworks, Fidler explores critical linkages between global public health and human rights, international trade, environmental issues, war and weapons. According to Ian Brownlie, 'Fidler has used international law as a framework within which to organise his study of the normative and institutional techniques employed by the international community in order to control and prevent the spread of disease. His legal expertise is infused by his knowledge of international relations thinking and techniques. The outcome is a successful study of considerable originality.'[28]

Fidler's treatise posits the challenge of emerging and re-emerging infectious disease threats as a challenge for the international community.[29] His historical account of multilateral health cooperation after mid-nineteenth-century transboundary outbreaks of cholera in Europe underscores the centrality of mutual vulnerability to disease and pathogenic threats in an interdependent world, which in turn elevates public health within the agenda of multilateralism. The second half of the nineteenth century was an era of intensive public health diplomacy marked by a series of international sanitary conferences aimed at the exchange of epidemiological information on cholera and other disease outbreaks within Europe, harmonization of quarantines, creation of an international surveillance system, and the creation of multilateral health organizations.[30] One positive result of this multilateral endeavour was the evolution of the International Health Regulations[31] as the legal framework for global surveillance of certain infectious diseases as well as the starting point for the establishment of international health organizations[32] to enforce the emergent multilateral legal strategies for disease surveillance. Applying all of these to *microbialpolitik*, Fidler's term for 'a mixture of the ordinary dynamics of international relations and the special dynamics produced by the challenges posed by pathogenic microbes,'[33] Fidler, like most lawyers, posits global infectious disease threats within international legal and treaty regimes: a combination of what he calls the 'concept of global health jurisprudence' and a proposal for a WHO Framework Convention on Infectious Disease Prevention and Control.[34]

Fidler's treatise, albeit comprehensive, does not exhaust the complexities of global health governance in an interdependent world.[35] The present study focuses on global health governance from a different perspective, viewing South-North disparities as a chief propelling factor in mutual vulnerability and the proliferation of diseases globally and examining the place of international law in this process. Despite the substantial anchorage of my study on South-North disparities, I nonetheless draw heavily from Fidler's analysis of the historical origins of public health diplomacy in the nineteenth-century international sanitary conferences.[36] In his discussion of 'globalization of public health,' Fidler observes that 'the vulnerability States sense today is analogous to the vulnerability that forced nineteenth-century European States into international health co-operation and international law on infectious disease control,'[37] while in his discussion of the history of international law in the control of infectious diseases, he argues that the nineteenth-century development of multilateral public health cooperation was motivated by fear of importation of non-European diseases (notably Asian diseases) into Europe.[38] This study thus benefits from Fidler's application of international relations theories to microbialpolitik, colonial origins, and post-colonial implications of the nineteenth-century international (Eurocentric) health order and the relevance of international law (including international human rights treaties) in the promotion and protection of global public health.

Scholars working in the fields of history,[39] international relations,[40] development,[41] and the undisputed owners of public health, epidemiologists,[42] in contrast to international lawyers, have enriched vast areas of global health scholarship with more incisive analytical seminal inquiries. From the discipline of history emerges the fact that cross-border spread of epidemics is as old as humanity. The plague of Athens, according to medical historians, resulted from cross-border movement of troops during the Pelopeonnesian War; the arrival of Columbus in the Americas marked the beginning of a process that led to the devastation of Native American populations by imported European diseases: measles, mumps, chicken pox, and scarlet fever.[43] From the perspective of international relations, commentators observe that the cross-border spread of infectious diseases constitutes a security threat deserving of urgent attention by governments,[44] while scholars of development theorize that policies of powerful multilateral financial institutions like the World Bank and the International Monetary Fund (IMF) are hostile to their host social and economic environments in the developing world, the end result being globalism-from-above, with deleterious effects on the health of populations in the recipient countries.[45] Epidemiologists, for their part, use macro-economic models to explore the unequal distribution of the burdens of disease and health risks in a world sharply divided by socio-economic inequalities.[46]

What emerges from these various perspectives is the obvious fact that a cross-border resurgence of diseases, as the WHO observes, now constitutes a global crisis requiring multilateral approaches.[47] Application of this range of perspectives makes this study multidisciplinary and enriches its analysis from both theoretical and policy angles. The history of multilateralism in the field of public health in nineteenth-century Europe allows us to understand the colonial origins of public health diplomacy and its legacy in a post-colonial world; international relations perspectives enable us to explore the politics and theoretical complexities of multilateralism and international regimes. Finally, our understanding of the dynamics of development equips international lawyers with additional skills to study and explain South-North disparities within the confines of our international legal domain.

Drawing on these interdisciplinary perspectives, the originality of this study is subject to a range of critical caveats. It would be wrong to claim originality in international legal scholarship on the vast terrain of South-North relations: the past fifty years have witnessed an accelerated momentum in the scholarly exploration of the multiple dimensions of South-North issues – development, human rights, sovereignty over natural resources, environment, culture, and imperialism. There are numerous seminal works by international jurists[48] on South-North issues, including declarations and 'soft-law' mechanisms by multilateral institutions. The intense debate by 'Southern' and 'Northern' scholars on the content of the New International Economic Order (NEIO), and the existence or otherwise of the right to development, falls within the broad construction of South-North scholarship. This study thus complements and builds on an existing body of South-North scholarship by the various ways in which it:

(a) hypothesizes mutual vulnerability and the vulnerability of multilateralism as inseparable concepts in multilateral global health cooperation marked by South-North disparities;
(b) posits nineteenth-century public health diplomacy within the colonial origins of international law;
(c) relies on mutual vulnerability and globalization of public health in an interdependent world to argue for procedural fairness in reshaping the normative boundaries of global health governance within a humane multilateral system;
(d) strives to develop cross-sectoral linkages between public health, human rights, colonial and post-colonial discourses, politics, development, and international law;
(e) strives to create a prominent role for international law in the complex dynamics of the interface between humanity and diseases through the strengthening of multilateral surveillance capacity for diseases and a global funding facility;
(f) agrees with international relations scholarship that public health is a global public good and strives to find partnership and collaboration with international law to fulfil the public goods vision of unity and harmony in the global neighbourhood;
(g) coins and uses the term communitarian globalism to argue for an inclusive multilateral health framework that involves all relevant actors and stakeholders: (multilateral institutions, state actors, non-state actors, and civil society); and
(h) explores the pros and cons of the phenomenon of globalization in multilateral-global health discourse and projects globalization as a dynamic process that paradoxically has the capacity to integrate cultures as well as the tendency to erode traditional medical therapies in the developing world.

As already stated, international lawyers have explored global health challenges in segmented ways. This study, by contrast, attempts to devise an interdisciplinary and holistic approach to health protection and promotion in a divided world, from a Third World perspective. Developing a synthesis of discourses from multiple disciplines – history, international relations, international law, and development studies – is an arduous task. Because poverty and underdevelopment affect public health in a variety of ways, and because the South-North health divide implicates the discourse of development, it is imperative to heed Ivan Head's warning that, 'No algebraic formula will solve a problem if a host of variables is found on each side of an equation. If "development" is susceptible of a range of definitions, as it is, and "international law" is so often found in the eye of the beholder – or at least the textbook author – the topic invites a display of dipsy-doodling. ... Development is a tough concept to discuss with intellectual rigour – not because it is any more complex or elusive of definition than many others, but because everyone has his or her own view of what it is.'[49] With this in mind, the interdisciplinary focus of this study is squarely on perspectives from the allied disciplines that are either humanist or fairness oriented. In the pages that follow, I strive to synthesize multidisciplinary perspectives that deconstruct the inequities of the contemporary multilateral system with emerging approaches to humane governance anchored in the transnational bonds that unite all of humanity in a shared global compact. The legal, moral, and normative components of these bonds fall within the rubric of Falk's 'the law of humanity.'[50]

III Clusters of Research Questions

This study raises the following clusters of questions:

(a) To what extent was the mutual vulnerability of populations to infectious diseases a factor in the earliest multilateral cooperation in the field of public health? What legacy did early international law bequeath to the present, and how has this legacy affected indigenous ethno-medical therapies found in the developing world? How (if at all) did politics and the strategic interests of nation states (vulnerability of multilateralism) affect early multilateral health initiatives?

(b) Has international law played any role in the dynamics of the historical interaction between humanity, nation states, and diseases? What role(s) can law and legal interventions play in contemporary public health multilateralism and scholarship?

(c) What impact(s) do South-North disparities (social and economic inequalities) within and among countries have on multilateral efforts aimed at the protection and promotion of humanity's health? In what ways do poverty or underdevelopment increase or diminish the propensity of mutual vulnerability in the global village?

(d) In view of (a), (b), and (c) above, what are the best possible interventions that would lead to a humane global health order? Is there any evidence that public health policies of multilateral institutions like the WHO's RBM campaign constitute globalism-from-above? To what extent do indigenous medical practices (such as traditional malaria therapies) of societies in developing countries form part of the core framework of multilateral policies? How can public health programs on the ground be effective, and how can international or multilateral involvement best contribute to their effectiveness? With respect to the transnationalization of disease, does mutual vulnerability currently induce sufficient self-interest to commit scarce but moderate global resources towards the protection and promotion of health of populations? Is the state-centric Westphalian system still capable of effectively responding to every emerging multilateral health issue of our time and age, or do we require a more inclusive, multistakeholder participation based on animation of transnational civil society?

In answering these questions, this study combines a number of approaches. For reasons elaborated below it is important to note here that I do not completely follow the strict rules of social science research methodology. For question (d) I rely on interviews conducted in a Nigerian rural community, as well as my observations of traditional malaria therapies of populations in the same community. For the other questions, this study adopts critical and analytical approaches in analysing the literature, mandate, and policies of multilateral institutions.

IV Expected Research Findings

The expected findings of this inquiry are set out below.

(a) Mutual vulnerability of populations to diseases and pathogenic microbes, although a persuasive factor since nineteenth-century public health diplomacy, has yet to induce enlightened self-interest in the interdependent world of the twenty-first century.[51] Support for this phenomenon is found in the widening South-North divide, as documented by multilateral institutions,[52] and in the unequal distribution of the global burdens of disease on populations in developing and developed worlds.[53] Juxtaposing the twenty-first-century infectious disease diplomacy with its nineteenth-century precursor, the fingerprints of isolationism remain conspicuous. The protectionism and economic interests of European nation states that hindered effective collaboration to find multilateral solutions to cross-border outbreaks of cholera in the nineteenth century are visible phenomena in contemporary global health governance. In many ways, the industrialized world continues to draw an isolationist distinction between the diseases of the developed and the developing worlds. It would be a fatal mistake for nation states to fall back on the illusion of protectionism within the framework of contemporary interstate relations as globalization of diseases, global travel, trade and commerce, and migration continue to erode national boundaries. Nonetheless, protectionism sounds like a vindication of the theory of realism in international relations. To a typical apostle of the realist school, if the world is yet to witness an effective multilateral cooperation in the field of public health, then why bother today? The realist school uses examples of this sort to assert that law and order is elusive in the relations between sovereign states in the absence of a multinational police force to enforce such laws in the global arena. The public health imperatives of our contemporary globalizing and interdependent world are far too complex for any one single theory or school of thought to explain satisfactorily.[54] Only a cross-fertilization of perspectives from various theories and disciplines will prove useful as a way forward. Realism, liberalism, and critical theories of international regimes must therefore inform one another.

(b) The first finding inevitably leads to the second – the necessity of reform of public health multilateralism in an interdependent world. Here, there are two identifiable interrelated issues. The first relates to the evolution of a humane multilateral health regime; the second focuses on projects, policies and programs of multilateral institutions that are often characterized as globalism-from-above.[55]

(c) International law has been at the margins of the work of multilateral health institutions, especially the WHO. Despite the ambitious definition of 'health' in its constitution[56] and the innovative legal powers[57] it possesses, the WHO has, since its inception in 1948, largely treated international law as a 'no go area.' International legal scholars Allyn Taylor,[58] Katarina Tomasevski,[59] and David P. Fidler,[60] have strongly criticized the WHO's timidity and the organization's preferred use of narrow medical-technical standards to pursue its global health mandate. As observed by Fidler, the WHO isolated itself from general international legal developments in the post-1945 period. This isolation was not accidental, but reflected a particular outlook on the formulation and implementation of international health policies. The WHO operated as if it were not subject to the normal dynamics of anarchical society; it acted as if it were at the centre of a transnational Hippocratic society of physicians, medical scientists, and public health experts.[61] Regrettably, a window of opportunity seems to have been lost in the post-1945 years, which were marked by an exciting array of international legal developments that could have been of immense assistance to the WHO's pursuance of its global health mandate. International environmental law, by contrast, has steadily developed into a mature area of inquiry that is now used to forge South-North consensus and collaboration on a range of environmental issues: ozone depletion, climate change, biodiversity, trade in endangered species, and marine pollution.[62] This study offers a brief analysis of two multilateral environmental governance mechanisms – the Montreal Protocol to the UN Convention for the Protection of the Ozone Layer, and the World

Bank's Instrument Establishing the Global Environmental Facility – and argues for the use of similar mechanisms in the domain of global public health. Recognizing the uneven landscape for present-day multilateral coop-eration, these environmental governance mechanisms, inter alia, emphasize the principle of 'common but differentiated obligation' through the transfer of resources from the industrialized to the developing world. Whatever their shortcomings these initiatives are still commendable, because environmental issues, like public health, are global issues that raise acrimonious South-North debate in multilateral fora.

(d) It follows from (c) above that if underdevelopment is responsible for either the non-existence or collapse of public health infrastructures in parts of the developing world, then resources (mainly financial) that would flow from any global sharing formula would be channelled towards the revitalization of disease surveillance capacities in the developing world based on agreed multi-lateral rules and regulations. But where will these resources come from, and which multilateral agencies will be entrusted with the task of developing the rules to be used in sharing the resources? Obviously, the WHO does not have the resources to rebuild national public health infrastructures in developing countries. In recent years, the World Bank has become a critically important player/actor in the funding of public health projects in the developing world.[63] A partnership of the World Bank, the WHO, and other relevant multilateral institutions, foundations, and leading donor countries is inevita-ble in this endeavour. Mutual vulnerability and the vulnerability of multilat-eralism would be significantly diminished by a humane multilateral Instrument Establishing a Global Public Health Fund, led by the WHO and the World Bank. This would operate in principle as a 'disease non-prolifera-tion facility.' By analogy it compares with similar funding mechanisms on international/multilateral environmental and marine pollution issues.

(e) Globalization erodes ethno-medical therapies and behavioural practices on malaria and other prevalent diseases in most of the developing world. The prohibitive cost of Western medicines and the simultaneous erosion of tradi-tional medicine by the phenomenon of globalization take their toll on the health of endangered populations. The complexity and dynamics of global patent law and the liberalization of international trade rules, in some ways, conspire to endanger public health in the developing world.

B Research Methodology

This study, albeit premised on international law, reaches out to the social sciences and other relevant disciplines, especially international relations. It combines legal research methodologies with minimal social science qualitative methods in the study of the interaction between multilateral malaria control policies and ethno-medical therapies in malaria-endemic regions of the global South. The ethno-graphic and qualitative aspects of the traditional malaria therapies described are based on the author's insights drawn from the social and economic context of rural life in eastern Nigeria. The facts and observations obtained from the inter-views should be limited to the sociocultural context of the community where the interviews were conducted. However, since there is a chance that most developing countries, especially in the malaria-endemic regions of Africa, share some cul-tural, natural, climatic, and social commonalties, findings from the rural Nige-rian community may be used to critically analyse malaria control strategies of multilateral institutions like the WHO as they relate to most of Africa. A major advantage of qualitative methodology is that it allows the researcher to gain deeper insights into the behaviour and trends of the group studied.[64]

Complementary to the qualitative ethno-medical approaches to malaria are other methodological approaches – critical analysis of literature in search of useful deductions and use of secondary data from multilateral organizations to explain South-North disparities in the context of globalized public health. This study is thus critical, analytical, and interdisciplinary. The global scope of this work makes it impossible to collect data from every country. With some caveats, I rely on the WHO's *Global Burden of Disease*,[65] which uses disability adjusted life years (DALYs) to measure disease burdens in various regions of the world based on mor-tality and morbidity. One major problem with the use of DALYs is that many developing countries do not compile official data on ailments, clinical cases, hos-pital admissions, and cause of deaths. In his foreword to the *Global Burden of Dis-ease* study, William Foege rightly observes that 'many developing countries find it difficult to acquire accurate mortality statistics, let alone morbidity and quality-of-life information ... Many countries face difficulties in accurately determining infant mortality rates, or even AIDS and tuberculosis incidence and prevalence rates, let alone acquiring a comprehensive understanding of the total burden of dis-ease ... they face.'[66] To this extent, data used in calculating DALYs in most of the developing world are, at the very best, estimates.

This study also draws from the Pan American Health Organization (PAHO)'s volumes on *Health in the Americas*.[67] PAHO membership presents a perfect set-ting for the study of South-North disparities and unequal disease burdens between developed and developing worlds in a multilateral context, as it includes Canada and the United States, two of the most developed countries in the world, and some of the world's least developed countries, such as Haiti, Honduras, Gua-temala, and El Salvador. Disparities among the countries of the Americas con-tinue to impact on health of populations in the region. As observed by the former director of PAHO, an understanding of the impact of regulations and institutions on the health sector in the Americas must necessarily be viewed in light of the problems the region faces – problems which differ in accordance of each society's level of development – and the challenge those problems pose. Because of the many differences and for the purpose of simplification, it is important to distinguish between the situation prevailing in the Hemisphere's two most developed countries: Canada and United States of America, and in the developing countries of Latin America and the Caribbean.[68]

In sum, this study combines critical, analytical, and qualitative approaches to explore global health challenges in a world sharply divided by poverty and underdevelopment. While this inquiry is critical of contemporary multilateral initiatives under the rubric of vulnerability of multilateralism, it does not adopt the approach used by critical legal scholars who admirably deconstruct mainstream legal thought but shy away from constructing viable alternatives.[69] Rather, it uses the vulnerability of multilateralism to deconstruct contemporary health globalism and communitarian globalism to reconstruct and reconfigure the contours of global health governance.

C Contributions of the Study

The globalization of public health in a paradoxically interdependent and divided world is an important global issue. Its interdisciplinary reach combines with its global scope to benefit international law, international relations, and development scholarships.

For the social sciences, the analysis of traditional medical therapies of non-Western societies vis-à-vis the WHO's RBM campaign raises a number of questions relating to the ethnographic study of medical pluralism in divergent societies, cultures, and social contexts. Following the canons of 'law and anthropology'[70] as well as 'law and development'[71] schools of thought, it is pertinent to pose the following questions: how is law related to other aspects of culture and social organization, especially sociocultural attitudes to disease and illness? Is it possible to synthesize behavioural and ethno-medical practices in radically different cultures? Applying these questions by analogy to the RBM campaign, and especially to its perceived integration or exclusion of traditional medicine in Africa, this study offers the social scientist useful tools for hypothesis generation and study of health practices in non-Western societies.

Exploring the vulnerability of multilateralism underscores the gaps and shortcomings of multilateral initiatives on globalized public health. From this perspective, this study stands to benefit policy makers in the global multilateral institutions that serve as incubators of global public health policies – the WHO, the FAO,

UNICEF, the World Bank, and the UNDP. Related to this is policy making at the regional and national levels. Although I explore public health from a predominantly global perspective, global surveillance for diseases and other urgent international health events would be futile without core capacity at national levels. It is only when humanist-oriented policy initiatives at national levels merge with global humanist-oriented initiatives that South-North health disparities, unequal distribution of disease burdens, and the global health divide will be narrowed.

The potential contributions of this study to the academic disciplines; to social science ethnographic study of medical therapies in Africa where malaria is endemic; and to policy making in multilateral institutions together may diminish the unequal distribution of the global disease burdens across the world. In very modest ways, this study uses mutual vulnerability of populations to the threats of disease pathogens in a globalizing world as the *sine qua non* for the renegotiation of global health accords.

Chapter 2

The Paradox of a Global Village in a Divided World

A Overview of the Argument

If health, as the Constitution of the World Health Organization provides, is 'a state of complete physical, mental and social well-being and not merely the absence of disease or infirmity,'[1] then the age-old health divide between the developed and developing worlds deserves pre-eminent attention from scholars and multilateral institutions. Paradoxically, global health challenges in the past decades have focused not only on the South-North divide, but also on the phenomenon of globalization as a process that integrates nation states, ideas, identities, markets, cultures, and peoples across the world. Never before in history has humanity been so bonded together, and at the same time so sharply divided by underdevelopment, poverty, and unequal distribution of the mortality and morbidity burdens of disease. This paradoxical matrix elicits various responses in the discourse of global public health. While it is uniformly agreed that poverty and underdevelopment breed disease, the impact of globalization on public health remains controversial and hotly contested. Viewed from one of its simplest positive connotations as a process towards the emergence of a 'borderless' world, globalization arguably reinforces the global neighbourhood metaphor. In this sense, the complex interaction of globalization (in some ways the precursor of the emergent global neighbourhood) and socio-economic disparities (the precursor of a divided world) provides a perfect intellectual setting to explore mutual vulnerability – the transnational threats of disease in an interdependent world.

Both ends of the paradoxical matrix spell doom for the health of humankind. Underdevelopment, the end product of poverty and socio-economic disparities between countries, fosters disease and microbial pathogens. Globalization, on the other hand, enables disease pathogens to transcend national boundaries with ease. This crisis is not limited to infectious/communicable diseases. The burden of non-communicable diseases on populations also points to poverty and under-development as leading causes, especially in the developing world. The paradox of a global village in a divided world is therefore inseparable from the challenges of global protection and promotion of public health. Both ends of the paradox affect public health in various ways and have therefore generated certain visible synergistic manifestations. Even within the related concepts of mutual vulnerability and vulnerability of multilateralism, the centrality of this paradoxical under-pinning in the relations between nation states and populations raises issues that are hardly recondite for public health. If, due to underdevelopment, surveillance capacity in a country either does not exist at all or breaks down, any disease event could easily transcend national boundaries to render populations in distant places vulnerable. It is the disparity between the developed and developing worlds that has led to intractable South-North acrimony in most multilateral institutions, including the World Health Organization. The developing world has come to characterize the international system as unfair, inequitable, and non-responsive to the developmental and public health needs of the South.

If health, as has been persuasively postulated, is a public good[2] then global health policies must confront the paradoxical variables of a global neighbourhood and a divided world, especially the various ways each extreme of the paradox impacts on health of populations. Public health, like other global public goods, must meet two conditions. First, its benefits must have strong qualities of *public-ness* as marked by non-rivalry in consumption and non-excludability. Second, its benefits must be quasi universal in terms of countries (covering more than one group of countries), people (accruing to several, preferably all, population groups), and generations (extending to both present and future generations, or at least meeting the needs of current generations without foreclosing development options for future generations).[3] Following these criteria, it is important to explore the extent to which socio-economic disparities among countries in a divided world exclude the 'underdeveloped', 'developing,' 'poor,' and 'Third World' countries from sharing in the beneficial dividends of health as a public good in the global arena. This chapter explores this exclusion from the paradoxical matrix of a global neighbourhood and a divided world, and argues that both have contributed in various ways to mutual vulnerability and the vulnerability of multilateralism.

B   A Global Neighbourhood?

The global neighbourhood metaphor describes the increasing interdependence of nation states and populations. The past fifty years have witnessed a phenomenal emergence of the reinforcing vicissitudes of a global neighbourhood: international airline networks, flows of foreign direct investment, ingenious discoveries in communication technology, ecological tourism, religious pilgrimages, international sports festivals, regionalism and free trading blocks, increased migrations, and global trade liberalization. Each of these developments erodes national boundaries and precipitates mutual spread of disease and pathogens.

Scholars, multilateral organizations, and policy makers explore the public health implications of these reinforcing phenomena of global interdependence under the rubric of globalization. Globalization is both variegated and multidimensional.[4] Its multiple dimensions conspire with the uneven multilateral landscape in which it is practised to affect public health in many complex ways. For the majority of humanity to reap the fruits of health as a public good in the global village, there must be utmost respect for neighbourhood values – peace, respect for life and other human rights, lack of institutional and structural violence in the international system, justice and equity, mutual respect and caring, economic security, sustainable development, and access to basic necessities of life by the poor.[5] These values are inexorably inter-connected, and the linkages compel a further inquiry to determine if globalization has enhanced or eroded neighbourhood values,[6] and how it has consequently impacted on public health within the boundaries of sovereign states. In pursuing this inquiry my focus is on the human right to health and the health implications of the prescriptions given to the developing world by the international financial institutions such as the World Bank's structural adjustment programs (SAPs).[7]

C A Divided World?

The dawn of the twenty-first century has witnessed an accelerated polarization of the world less by geo-political boundaries and ethno-cultural affinities and more by poverty and underdevelopment. Since the 1970s heralded economic disarray in most of the developing world, the gap between developed and developing countries has widened at an alarming speed. In 1997 the United Nations Development Program (UNDP) reported that 'the share of the poorest 20% of the world's people in global income now stands at a miserable 1.1%, down from 1.4% in 1991 and 2.3% in 1960. It continues to shrink. The ratio of the income of the top 20% to that of the poorest 20% rose from 30 to 1 in 1960, to 61 to 1 in 1991 – and to a startling new high of 78 to 1 in 1994.'[8] In 1998 the UNDP reported the widening gap and disparities not only among countries but also within them. In 1960, the 20 per cent of the world's people who live in the richest countries had thirty times the income of the poorest 20 per cent; by 1995 that figure had reached eighty-two times as much income. Income distribution even within industrialized countries shows disparities between rich and poor. In the worst case, Russia, the income share of the richest 20 per cent is eleven times that of the poorest 20 per cent. In Australia and the United Kingdom it is nearly ten times as much.[9]

In its *World Development Report, 1993*, which focused on health, the World Bank classified countries into four major categories:

(i)   Low Income Economies (including the two most populous countries on earth – India and China – as well as most of Africa) with per capita GNPs of about US $350 in 1991;
(ii) Lower Middle Income Economies with per capita GNPs up to US $2500;
(iii) Upper Middle Income Nations with per capita GNPs up to US $3500; and
(iv) High Income Nations (mostly OECD countries) with per capita GNPs on average of US $21,500.[10]

From this projection, it has been argued that about 3.1 billion, well over half of the world's population, live in countries in the poorest group. A further 1.4 billion live in the lower-middle-income nations and 630 million in the upper-middle-income nations. About 820 million live in the high-income nations, which are rich in part because of their ability to exploit the resources, such as oil, minerals, and food, of poorer nations. Over 80 per cent of the world's people live in nations that collectively have less than 20 per cent of the world's wealth and productive capacity.[11]

Whatever criteria are used to classify countries,[12] poverty and underdevelopment remain the two most important factors dividing countries and populations.[13] As observed by Arnold, 'poverty is the single most important factor dividing the North and South.'[14] The term 'South-North,' and the dividing line between the two entities, are somewhat problematic. The South is not socially, culturally, and politically homogeneous, nor is the dividing line between South and North an accurate geographical demarcation between the developing and the industrialized worlds. These difficulties notwithstanding, 'South-North' has emerged as a popular expression used in exploring a divided world. In 1990, the South Commission observed that,

Three and half billion people, three quarters of all humanity, live in the developing countries ... Together the developing countries – accounting for more than two thirds of the earth's land surface area – are often called the Third World. We refer to them as the South. Largely bypassed by the benefits of prosperity and progress, they exist on the periphery of the developed countries of the North. While most of the people of the North are affluent, most of the people of the South are poor; while the economies of the North are generally strong and resilient, those of the South are mostly weak and defenceless; while the countries in the North are, by and large, in control of their destinies, those of the South are very vulnerable to external factors and lacking in functional sovereignty.[15]

If all of humanity were to be a single nation state, the present South-North divide would have made it an ungovernable, semi-feudal entity, split by internal conflicts. A small portion would be prosperous and industrialized while most of it would be poor and underdeveloped.[16] What then are the implications of a world divided by poverty and underdevelopment for global health challenges? How do poverty and underdevelopment impact on the health conditions of the three-quarters of humanity who live in the South? The WHO's director-general put it succinctly thus, 'poverty breeds infections; and infections breed poverty.'[17] Poverty, according to the WHO, is the world's most ruthless killer and the greatest cause of ill health and suffering. It is the main reason why babies are not vaccinated, clean water and sanitation are not provided, curative drugs and other treatments are unavailable, and mothers die in childbirth. Poverty is the cause of reduced life expectancy, handicap, disability, and starvation. Poverty is a major contributor to mental illness, stress, suicide, family disintegration, and substance abuse.[18] The WHO argues further that 'poverty wields its destructive influence at every stage of human life from the moment of conception to the grave. It conspires with the most deadly and painful diseases to bring a wretched existence to all who suffer from it.'[19]

Another consequence of a divided world, global development apartheid, is the unequal distribution of the global burdens of disease on populations within the South and North.[20] As indicated in the previous chapter, the current approach of disability adjusted life years quantifies burdens of illness and health risks globally, focusing on health discrepancies in various regions of the world. What emerges from this quantification is that cumulatively the countries of the South lag behind those of the North. Risks harmful to health and the endemic nature of certain diseases that confront populations in the South abridge life expectancy, increase the burdens of disease, and significantly impact on their quality of life.[21] To give one example, a person born in Uganda, who lived and died there aged fifty and was struck by malaria and other tropical diseases many times before his[22] death, cannot be said to have lived fifty healthy years. Compare the life of this Ugandan with that of a Canadian who lived for the same fifty years in Canada without suffering from malaria and other tropical diseases – the quality of life is unlikely to be the same. The heavier disease burden in Africa may have abridged the Ugandan's healthy life-years from fifty to forty. This is not to suggest that the burden of diseases such as cancer, Alzheimer's, flu, diabetes, sexually transmitted diseases, respiratory infections, and cerebro-vascular and cardiovascular diseases, and the risks posed by tobacco use and road accidents do not impose heavy disease burdens on populations in the North. Comparatively, however, the diseases endemic in most of the global South – malaria, American trypanosomiasis (Chagas' disease), African trypanosomiasis (sleeping sickness), dengue, onchocerciasis (river blindness), lymphatic filariasis, and guinea worm, to name just a few – impose far heavier mortality and morbidity burdens on populations in the South.

The WHO has identified the health implications of living in a divided world as an inequity that should stir the conscience of the world. According to 1993 calculations, a person in one of the least developed countries has a life expectancy of forty-three years. In one of the most developed countries, it is seventy-eight years. That is a difference of more than a third of a century. As of 1995, in a space of a day, passengers flying from Japan to Uganda leave the country with the world's highest life expectancy – almost seventy-nine years – and land in the one with the world's lowest – barely forty-two years. A flight from France to Côte d'Ivoire takes only a few hours, but in terms of life expectancy, it spans almost twenty-nine years. A short air trip between Florida in the United States and Haiti represents a life expectancy gap of over nineteen years.[23] It is in the context of this South-North divide that the globalization of public health will be explored, and the interaction between globalization and the development of the South will be questioned in the context of the globalization of poverty.

D The Globalization of Poverty: Two Levels of Inquiry on Public Health and South-North Disparities[24]

Globalization means different things to different people in different places and disciplines, and its scope and historical antecedents lie in the particular eyes of the beholder. Globalization affects different people in different parts of the world differently.[25] The link between globalization and public health is even more complex. According to Yach and Bettcher, 'the link between the lives of individuals and the global context of development is evident in another face of globalization, an often forgotten one: global health futures are directly or indirectly associated with the transnational economic, social, and technological changes taking place in the world. As a result, the domestic and international spheres of public health policy are becoming more intertwined and inseparable.'[26] Similarly, Lee and Dodgson observe that 'an understanding of the linkages between globalization and health depends foremost on one's definition of globalization and precise dating of the process.'[27] There is an overwhelming literature indicating that the emergence of certain processes significantly erodes national boundaries, and as a result, the Westphalian sovereign state is incapable of controlling what occurs within its geo-political territories.[28] Thus, globalization, according to Held et al., underscores the emergence of a historical process that transforms the spatial organization of social relations and transactions, generating transcontinental or inter-regional networks of interaction and the exercise of power.[29] The historical process, which scholars explore as globalization, encompasses a range of dynamic transnational issues as well as the potential of this process to transform human lives across societies driven perplexingly by markets, trade liberalization, environment, cultures, travel and tourism, the information superhighway, and telecommunication technology.

The complexity of globalization, especially its linkage with globalism, global interdependence, internationalization, modernization, and liberalization has led to controversies. While each of these concepts may constitute an aspect of globalization, Scholte has correctly described them as 'redundant concepts of globalization.'[30] Clarifying the link and confusion between globalization, globalism, and interdependence, Keohane and Nye argue that 'Globalism is a state of the world involving networks of interdependence at multicontinental distances. These networks can be linked through flows and influences of capital and goods, information and ideas, people and force, as well as environmentally and biologically relevant substances (such as acid rain or pathogens). Globalization and deglobalization refer to the increase or decline of globalism.'[31]

Globalization de-emphasizes territorialization or nationalization. This form of globalism, which Scholte characterizes as 'the spread of supraterritoriality,'[32] according to Lee and Dodgson, 'conceives the world as a single place because of increased travel and other shared experiences that lead to more localized, nationalized and regionalized feelings of spatial identity.'[33] Contemporary globalization is characterized by what Held and McGrew identify as 'distinctive spatio-temporal and organizational attributes ..., particular patterns of extensity, intensity, velocity and impact in global relations, flows and networks, alongside different degrees of institutionalization, modes of stratification and reproduction ... unique spatio-temporal and organizational features, creating a world in which the extensive reach of global relations and networks is matched by their relative high intensity, high velocity and high impact propensity across facets of social life ...'[34]

The complexities of the definitional parameters of globalization are as formidable as the controversies of its precise dating. Here there are two competing schools – the 'recent,' and the 'ancient.' According to the recent school, globalization is a concept of the 1990s, propelled by the global nature of the activities of multinational corporations. Ray Keily observed that 'The 1990s have seen a boom in writing about globalisation. According to one sociologist, ... it is the concept of the 1990s, a key idea by which we understand the transition of human society into the third millennium ... Much of the debate surrounding globalisation has been extremely abstract. There is often a lack of clarity in definitions of the term, its novelty and how it is experienced by people throughout the world.'[35] The ancient school argues that notwithstanding the emergence of new globalizing forces in the global scene in the last one or two decades, globalization has historical roots in the fifteenth century.[36] If globalization, as I argue in this monograph, is characterized by the demise of geographical and physical geo-political boundaries, then the historical antecedents of transnational spread of disease makes the contention that globalization 'is the concept of the 1990s' less persuasive. In his account of the plague that ravaged Athens during the Peloponnesian War, Thucydides wrote that 'the plague first originated, so it is said, in Ethiopia above Egypt and then descended into Egypt and Libya and much of the Persian Empire. It fell suddenly upon Athens and attacked in the first instance the population of the Piraeus ... Later it also arrived in the upper city and by this time the number of deaths was greatly increasing. The question of the probable origin of the plague and the nature of the causes capable of creating so great an upheaval, I leave to other writers, with or without medical experience ... I caught the disease myself and observed others suffering from it.'[37] In support of the ancient origins of globalization, Keohane and Nye Jr have argued that 'One of the most important forms of globalization is biological. The first smallpox epidemic is recorded in Egypt in 1350 B.C. It reached China in 49 A.D., Europe after 700; the Americas in 1520, and Australia in 1789. The plague or Black Death originated in Asia, but its spread killed a quarter to a third of the population of Europe between 1346 and 1352. When Europeans journeyed to the New World in the fifteenth and sixteenth centuries, they carried pathogens that destroyed up to 95% of the indigenous population.'[38]

The place of globalization in contemporary South-North disparities and the socio-economic inequalities among countries are hardly supportive of the argument that globalization is a concept of the 1990s. To come to terms with the root causes of global inequalities, questions must be asked about how globalization, the shrinking of geo-political boundaries, affects the process of development and consequently impacts on human health. From its simpler meaning to the diverse theoretical and practical complexities of the 1990s, globalization is implicated in the hegemonic foundation of international law and relations, especially the differential standards among nation states: the civilized, and the barbaric, primitive, or uncivilized societies.[39] Globalization is an age-old institutionalization of polarizations, which climaxed in the 1990s through ingenious discoveries in communications and computer technology, a massive flow of capital transnationally, and the colossal influence of multinational corporations with complicated global networks, networks that globalize wealth and poverty differentially across the world. Because respect for human rights and dignity, especially the right to health, is one of the global neighbourhood values, and because underdevelopment and poverty impact on human health in a variety of ways, we must understand how these emergent global forces have continued to globalize poverty. The double-edged inquiry that follows focuses on human right to health and development prescriptions by international financial institutions, and the various ways they affect human health in a divided world.

I Globalization of Poverty and the Human Right to Health[40]

There are two main reasons why the right to health deserves scholarly attention in connection with the globalization of public health. The first relates to the obligation undertaken by state parties to the International Covenant on Economic, Social and Cultural Rights (ICESCR) 1966 to 'take steps individually and through international assistance and co-operation, especially economic and technical, to the maximum of [their] available resources,' to realize the rights enumerated in the ICESCR.[41] The second reason – which is related to the first – involves the express provisions of international conventions on the right to health that recognize the financial and economic needs of developing countries. One example is the United Nations Convention on the Rights of the Child, which provides in Article 24(4) that in striving to realize the rights of children, states shall take 'particular account ... of the needs of developing countries.'[42]

The relevance of these approaches lies in the socially and economically holistic definition of health offered by the constitution of the WHO,[43] as well as in the impact of underdevelopment on human health. Taken together, these two factors point to the importance of economic development and financial resources to the realization of the right to health. Unfortunately, the right to health, and by extension all economic, social, and cultural rights, have been treated peripherally by policy makers and multilateral institutions.[44] To many, they are not rights but lofty wishes and mere statements of idealistic social desires. To others, they exist textually as 'soft law' but are so all-encompassing, indeterminate, and vague that their actual meaning and contents are difficult to articulate. Tomaseveski argues that Article 12 of the ICESCR, which provides for the right to health, is imprecise and vague because 'guaranteed access to health care services for all people remains an issue of disagreement. There is no agreement on the specific obligations of States in providing access to health care to all of its population, let alone whether it is obliged to undertake the provision of health care services at all.'[45] It is difficult to overlook the imprecision that has characterized international normative provisions on health as a human right. A number of reasons can be advanced to explain why the human right to health (and most other economic, social, and cultural rights) has been relegated to a platform of irrelevance and impotency. The first is the subordination of economic, social, and cultural rights to civil and political rights. Civil and political rights are frequently referred to as 'first generation' human rights, while economic, social, and cultural rights, including the right to health, are 'second generation' rights. Although the first/second generation distinction does not reflect a hierarchy of importance, it means that civil and political rights come 'first in time.'

The second reason relates to the way human rights have been construed in Western liberal democracies, which unduly emphasize justiciability predicated on an individual making a claim against the state, before a court or tribunal, seeking redress for the violation of her rights. This construction raises the question whether a person can prosecute a claim in a court or tribunal against the state based on the state's failure to guarantee him access to conditions necessary for health protection and promotion.[46] Put another way, the state is incapable of guaranteeing access to good health to all of its citizens. Thus, the litmus test for any claim to qualify as a human right is 'justiciability.' A further reason relates to a glaring misunderstanding and confusion among scholars on the meaning of the concepts of health, health care, health services, and medical services.[47] In response to most of these contentions, a persuasive literature has emerged from a formidable league of scholars aimed at giving the right to health a concrete meaning in the international legal order.[48] In thinking about human rights we should de-emphasize justiciability and stress human dignity, indivisibility, and the interdependence of all human rights – civil, political, economic, social, and cultural.[49] Of what relevance is voting in an election or enjoying freedom of expression (civil and political rights) to a woman in a rural village in Mozambique, Guatemala, or Burundi who is sick but cannot afford to buy Aspirin? Does freedom of association mean anything to a man who, together with his family, is malnourished and cannot afford basic food, housing, and health care? The indivisibility and interdependence of all human rights and a strong emphasis on human dignity are the starting points for a reconceptualization of the right to health. Leary has developed seven key elements for a rights-based perspective on health:

(i)   conceptualizing something as a right emphasizes its exceptional importance as a social or public goal (rights as 'trumps');[50]
(ii) rights concepts focus on the dignity of persons;
(iii) equality or non-discrimination is a fundamental principle of human rights;
(iv) participation of individuals or groups in issues affecting them is an essential aspect of human rights;
(v)   the concept of rights implies entitlement;
(vi) rights are interdependent;
(vii) rights are almost never absolute and may be limited, but any limitations should be subject to strict scrutiny.[51]

In the same vein, Lawrence Gostin and Jonathan Mann propose a human rights impact assessment for the formulation and evaluation of public health policies.[52]

This proposal would enable public health practitioners, human rights advocates, and community workers to explore the human rights dimensions of public health policies, practices, resource allocation decisions, and programs. The process includes a clarification of the public health purpose, an evaluation of the likelihood of the effectiveness of the policy, the target of the particular public health policy (including the risks of either over- or under-inclusion), and an examination of the proposed public health policy for possible human rights burdens.[53] How then would the human rights burdens of public health policies be measured? Three important factors to be considered include the invasiveness of the intervention, the frequency and scope of the infringement, and the duration of the public health policy.[54]

Beyond the indivisibility and interdependence of all human rights, which represent the minimum core content of the right to health, governmental regulatory failures either to adequately address health hazards or to provide access to basic health services and information have been identified as 'a pattern of concentric circles' of the scope of the right to health.[55] These concentric circles encompass governmental failures to regulate adequately public and private activities that pose threats to human health,[56] failure to provide access to basic health services and information,[57] and governmental responsibility to provide access to basic factors that affect health.[58] As these emerging perspectives show, enormous efforts have been made to concretize the contents of the right to health in international law. Any inquiry aimed at unmasking the reason(s) why these efforts are still largely marginalized and peripheral in international policy making would inevitably indict the current international system, which has failed to adequately empower the United Nations Committee on Economic, Social, and Cultural Rights. Philip Alston, former chair of the committee, summarized his frustrations in a detailed commentary:

The UN Commission on Human Rights devotes about five percent of its time to economic and social rights issues: other human rights bodies usually ignore them. The only body mandated to do work in this area, the UN Committee on Economic, Social and Cultural Rights, was established in 1987 on the *implicit condition that it be ineffectual and inactive* ... As the Committee's Special Rapporteur, I am keenly aware of its problems ... We receive little institutional support from anyone. The UN secretariat provides only rudimentary clerical help; I myself typed about half of our report for lack of a secretary with word processing experience. The International Labour Organisation and the World Health Organisation observe Committee sessions from time to time, but neither group has made a single serious contribution to its work. The Committee lacks expertise. The membership consists of attorneys general and diplomats who are nominated and elected and arrive at their positions through the spoils system – the prestige of a seat on the Committee, six weeks a year in Geneva (expenses paid). Of the eighteen elected members, only some are capable of a real contribution ... [59]

If the right to health remains vague and indeterminate, it is not because it means nothing. It is rather because nation states in the contemporary international system continue to stultify its progressive development by wilfully creating enforcement mechanisms that lack the capacity to articulate a practical human right to health.[60]

The UN Committee on Economic, Social, and Cultural Rights has maintained its tradition of regular issuance of 'general comments' on state obligations under the right to health. Its most recent general comment is arguably ambitious and holistic.[61] It states that the right to health is closely related to and dependent upon the realisation of other human rights as contained in the International Bill of Rights.[62] These include the rights to food, housing, work, human dignity, life, non-discrimination, equality, prohibition against torture, privacy, access to information, and the freedoms of association, assembly, and movement.[63] General Comment No. 14 calls for coordinated efforts towards the realization of the right to health to enhance interaction among all relevant actors, including various components of civil society. Relevant international organizations – the WHO, the ILO, the UNDP, UNICEF, UNFPA, the World Bank, regional development banks, the IMF, the WTO, and other bodies within the UN System – should cooperate effectively with states parties, building on their respective expertise, in relation to the implementation of the right to health at national levels. In particular, the international financial institutions, notably the World Bank and the IMF, should pay greater attention to the protection of the right to health in their lending policies, credit agreements, and structural adjustment programs.[64] Although commendable for its vision and coverage, it is highly debatable whether General Comment No. 14 can radically change the behaviour of states with respect to their obligation under the right to health. Pessimism still looms large because many critically important issues remain unresolved, including the wealth disparity among states. Does the financial, technical, and economic handicap of most developing countries impede the progressive realization of the right to health? If this question is answered in the affirmative, as most scholars suggest, then what is the extent of an obligation (if any) owed by the rich and industrialized states under international human rights law to commit financial and economic resources towards the eradication of disease or promotion of health in a developing country? Does Article 2 of the International Covenant on Economic, Social, and Cultural Rights contemplate that countries have obligation(s) to aliens abroad? Attaran put the question thus: Are states obliged to promote health abroad?[65] International lawyers who are still trapped within the 'decaying pillars' of the Westphalian international system[66] argue that such an obligation offends state sovereignty. Henkin, a progressive international legal scholar, has indicted the Westphalian state system that continues to use 'the sword' of state sovereignty against promotion of human rights abroad: 'the failure of the international human rights movement to address the responsibility of a state for human rights of persons in other states may reflect only the realities of the state system. States are not ordinarily in a position either to violate or to support the rights of persons in other states. States are reluctant to submit their human rights behaviour to scrutiny by other states; states are reluctant to scrutinize the behaviour of other states in respect of their own inhabitants; surely states are reluctant to incur heavy costs for the sake of rights of persons in other countries ...'[67]

Although this view represents the 'realities of the state system,' it seems antithetical to Article 2 of the International Covenant on Economic, Social, and Cultural Rights. Is there an escape route from an extreme view of state sovereignty insofar as the vexed question of international assistance comes within the purview of Article 2 of ICESCR? Although this question poses a serious conundrum, it has nonetheless been answered in the affirmative by a sizeable number of commentators and multilateral institutions. In a good scenario, according to Attaran, the resources and management employed to meet international obligations could be wholly domestic and located within the donor state.[68] Henkin has argued persuasively that a rigid notion of state sovereignty can be circumvented in some ways.[69] A logical extension of this proposition is that an industrialized state is obligated to devote a certain percentage of its resources to – for instance – commission research that would target the health problems of inhabitants of another country that may be poor. While I endorse this view, I do not suggest that all is well with the language of Article 2(1) of the International Covenant on Economic, Social, and Cultural Rights. The undertaking by a state party to, 'take steps ... to the maximum of its available resources, with a view to achieving progressively the full realization of the rights recognized in the present covenant' is vague, verbose, and too encompassing. As argued by Robertson, 'maximum of its available resources,' is a difficult phrase of two warring adjectives describing an undefined noun. 'Maximum' stands for idealism and 'available' stands for reality. 'Maximum' is the sword of human rights rhetoric; 'available' is the wiggle room for the state.[70] The vagueness of this provision has offered an escape route to state parties to the ICESCR, thus leading to the unfortunate conclusion that the right to health is an illusion. Virginia Leary remains one of the few legal scholars who persistently argue that Article 2(1) of the ICESCR can be interpreted ingeniously to give some meaning to it.[71] This is without prejudice to the fact that it could be re-drafted in more practical language. All countries, Leary argues, 'have at least some "available resources" – even if severely limited in comparison with other countries. Hence, under the Covenant, all ratifying States are obligated to respect the right to health, regardless of their level of economic development. The same paragraph of the Covenant also refers to the possibility of States calling upon international assistance to achieve the respect for the right to health.'[72]

Although Robertson's argument that the noun 'resources' is undefined under the ICESCR can hardly be faulted, the pertinent question is whether the perceived vagueness of the provisions of the ICESCR can be circumvented if we shift the focus, locus, and paradigm of the right to health discourse from the ICESCR to other international normative or even soft-law mechanisms. This question stems from the perceived failure – in most of the developing world – of the 1978 WHO-UNICEF Alma-Ata Declaration on Health for All by 2000 (Alma-Ata Declaration).[73] In other words, since the provisions of the Alma-Ata Declaration are unambiguous, why did it fail to improve the health of populations in developing countries? Although the answer is complex, the failure to realize Health for All by 2000 in most of the developing world raises the vexed question of resource transfer from rich to poor countries. The failure of resource transfer frustrated the Alma-Ata Declaration, which to date remains one of the most pragmatic articulations of global health challenges, including right to health discourse. The Pan-American Health Organization observed that 'the goal of Health for All by the year 2000 is ... the most concrete and useful definition of the programmatic social right to health protection, and may more succinctly express the common view of the responsibility of the state for the health of its people.'[74]

An exploration of the right to health in global health scholarship reveals one undeniable fact: that wealth disparities among countries have stymied efforts to tackle global health challenges. The Alma-Ata Declaration captured these disparities in the following terms, 'The existing gross inequality in the health status of the people between developed and developing countries as well as within countries is politically, socially and economically unacceptable, and is therefore of common concern to all countries.' The inability of the international system to narrow the development gap between the South and the North frustrated not only the ideals of the Alma-Ata Declaration, but also the pragmatic efforts to articulate a viable human right to health. This is one way in which the international system has globalized poverty, which intentionally or accidentally exacerbates inequalities and avoidable turbulence within the global neighbourhood. The next level of inquiry focuses on yet another medium of resource transfer aimed at fostering development in the South – Structural Adjustment Programs – and its implications for the health of populations in the recipient countries.

II Globalization of Poverty, Structural Adjustment Programs and Public Health in the Global South

Structural adjustment programs (SAPs) prescribed by international financial institutions (IFIs) – the World Bank and the International Monetary Fund (IMF) – for most developing countries became intensely controversial in the 1990s.[75] SAPs involve an economic liberalization scheme founded more on market forces and

strong private sector participation, and less on government intervention in the provision of social services. In particular, SAPs involve the removal of barriers to
exports and imports as well as increased foreign investment in the economies of the
recipient countries in the developing world. As stated by Cleary, SAPs are closely
identified with the ideological belief in the superiority of the market over economic
planning.[76] They are rooted in an almost mystical faith in the private sector, which
operating under freer domestic and external market conditions is thought to provide the motivation and power for a resumption of growth and development.[77]
The ideology of SAPs is a revival of economic liberalism with market-oriented
strategies, free trade, and a minimal state intervention as its key elements.[78] The
controversy surrounding SAPs, particularly their linkage with poverty and public
health in the developing world, has polarized scholars who analyse SAPs from
diverse disciplines: political science, economics, law, and public health. A recent
study argued that there is no conclusive evidence that SAPs cause poverty.[79]

The divergence of scholarly opinion underscores the complexities of SAPs, and
makes any attempt to analyse the interaction of SAPs and public health in the
developing world a difficult task. To give a balanced view, it is important to
explore the pros and cons of SAPs, their implementation, and their perceived
impact on public health. Advocates of SAPs maintain that there is no alternative
to them and that adjustments have resulted in the stabilization of most economies so that these countries can now repay their debt to the IFIs. The recipient
countries of SAPs are now able to restore credit, attract foreign investment, and
reverse unsustainable economic policies that compelled the prescription of SAPs
in the first place. It is undeniable that SAPs have the noble objective of propping
up ailing economies through sustainable economic policies. However, the implementation of SAPs has led to difficult socio-economic problems due to cuts in
social programs: public health, education, housing, and jobs. Michel Chossudovsky calls this 'economic genocide,' by which he means 'a conscious and delib-
erate manipulation of market forces by global institutions' – the World Bank, the
IMF and the World Trade Organization (WTO).[80] SAPs affect the lives of more
than four billion people in the global South and Chossudovsky observes that 'this
new form of economic domination – a form of market colonialism – subordi-
nates people and governments through the seemingly 'neutral' interplay of market forces'.[81] The cumulative end result of the multiple dimensions of SAPs,
according to Chossudovsky, has been the collapse of internal purchasing power,
disintegration of families, closure of schools and health clinics, and the denial of
the right to primary education to millions of children. In many regions of the
developing world, World Bank reforms have precipitated the resurgence of infectious diseases, including tuberculosis, malaria, and cholera.[82] In other development prescriptions outside the boundaries of SAPs, IFIs are now confronted with
a strange paradox – the World Bank's mandate of 'combating poverty and pro-

tecting the environment' and its support for large-scale hydroelectric and agro-industrial projects. These projects speed up the process of deforestation and the destruction of natural environment, leading to the forced displacement and eviction of several million people in the developing world.[83]

From the perspective of public health, in particular the epidemiology of infectious diseases, the adverse health effects of unsustainable development are underscored by the 'balance model' used by epidemiologists to study the emergence and re-emergence of infectious diseases. The model refers to the interaction of three forces: agent (A), host (H), and environmental (E) factors. It is based on the prediction that if a disease agent's infectious ability increases, or its ability to survive becomes more efficient, epidemic outbreaks of illness will occur, even if everything else among the three factors remain unchanged. Also included in the factors that precipitate disease in the interaction of these three forces are the modification of the host's ability to resist disease (e.g., malnutrition, mass starvation, famine), and the modification of the environment (e.g., unsustainable construction of dams) to make it more conducive for infectious agents to develop and survive.[84] Using the balance model, the World Health Organization observed that the alteration of the environment through the unsustainable construction of hydro-electric dams in China, Egypt, Ghana, and Senegal has led to an increase in schistosomiasis outbreaks.[85] The public health implications of SAPs and similar development prescriptions by IFIs have become the subject of powerful critiques by leading scholars of humane world order. Richard Falk characterizes contemporary market-driven global civilization as having fallen victim to the logic of global capital; indifferent to the plight of the poor and jobless; insensitive in the face of oppression and exploitation; irresponsible with respect to the environment; and complacent about the crisis of sustainability that will be bequeathed to future generations born in the twenty-first century.[86] Thus, 'The current ideological climate, with its neo-liberal dogma of minimizing intrusions on the market and "downsizing" the role of government in relation to the provision of public goods that compose the social agenda, suggest that the sort of global civilization that is taking shape will be widely perceived, not as a fulfilment of a vision of unity and harmony, but as a dysutopian result of globalism-from-above that is mainly constituted by economistic ideas and pressures.'[87]

Acknowledging that the implementation of SAPs have not been as successful as intended, the World Bank stated that future strategies should include a 'continuous pursuit of adjustment programs, which should evolve to take fuller account of the social impact of the reforms, of investment needs to accelerate growth, and of measures to ensure sustainability.'[88] The indictment of SAPs as hurting the poor and as globalism-from-above maps the road for alternative approaches. Because most scholarly discourse on Third World development has been characterized as unnecessarily reactive in nature and deconstructive in scope,[89] I will adopt an approach that synthesizes deconstruction/reaction with reconstruction. The relevance of this approach in the global health domain stems from the need to narrow South-North disparities and reduce the persistent unequal global distribution of burdens of diseases between developed and developing worlds.

E Bridging South-North Health Divide: Law and Development

'Development' means different things to different people in different disciplines. As already stated, one of the major criticisms of SAPs is that they are hostile to their host environments. They are prescriptions from a hierarchical paradigm and therefore alien to the social, economic, and cultural context of their recipient countries. This raises a number of questions, which many disciplines – law, political science, anthropology, economics, and sociology – are bound to answer in different ways. In the global arena, the concept of development acquires more complexity and elusiveness because of the strategic interests of nation states fuelled by myopic protectionism and hard-nosed realism, as well as the acrimonious tone of the South-North debate on global issues in multilateral forums. Is the concept of development thus completely elusive? Viewed from global health challenges, it is now widely accepted that development in the global health context connotes such conditions as 'peace, shelter, education, food, income, stable eco-system, sustainable resources, justice and equity.'[90] Thus, 'development is a process intended to better socio-economic conditions and to contribute to human dignity.'[91] The goals of development – through the reduction of poverty – therefore, are to contribute to social, economic, and political enrichment within a society and so reduce the likelihood of conflict within and among societies.[92] The WHO's director-general argues that the road out of the vicious cycle of poverty, infection, and illness begins with efforts that contribute to a person's ability to meet basic needs.[93] The problem does not end with establishing a working definition or an idea of what development entails. Definition is not an end in itself. The real problem is that since the South-North health divide is intertwined with development, and development is a variegated concept from multidisciplinary perspectives, how then do we study different societies to ensure that development processes (including SAPs) are not hostile to public health? Put another way, how can development be humane within the context of global multiculturalism, diversity, and medical pluralism across societies? If market-driven global civilization, as Falk argues, is 'a dysutopian result of globalism-from-above,'[94] then the solution lies in exploring ways to adopt a bottom-up approach: globalization-from-below. This would, inter alia, involve an effective integration of sustainable indigenous practices in the development process.

Although lawyers have studied these issues peripherally, seminal works from the schools of comparative law, law and development, and law and anthropology provide some useful legal insights. As Laura Nader puts it: 'while I do not believe that we can adopt a wholesale Western jurisprudential categories of law for use in non-Western cultures, it is possible that we could explicitly state that we are using an outline of Aglo-American common law, for example, against which or from which we view exotic legal systems. At least we would be clear about what our biases were.'[95] Theorists of law and development remind us that theories of modernization and dependency appear to reflect the ideological hegemony of Western capitalism and the dominant forces of contemporary imperialism. These theories assume that the developing world must necessarily follow a path roughly similar to that of the developed capitalist countries.[96] Back in 1972, Trubek argued that the so-called core conception of modern law misdirected the study of law and development by asserting that only one type of law, that found in the West, is essential for economic, social, and political development in the Third World.[97]

These legal theoretical perspectives are in *pari-materia* with emerging views in mainstream economics. With respect to SAPs and African economies, economists have moved from scholarship of reaction and deconstruction to an elaborate articulation of 'African perspectives on adjustment.'[98] In sum, the canons of this school of thought underscore the need, among others; to (i) make policy design sensitive to each individual country's historical and initial conditions; and (ii) evolve a sound policy framework to address the fundamental crisis of poverty and underdevelopment and enable Africa to compete in a globalized world. To achieve this, however, the state cannot be reduced to a passive entity, as the World Bank insists. Rather, decisions, consultations, and debate are needed to identify sectors that could yield long-term comparative advantages for African countries.[99] It seems that the World Bank has begun to acknowledge the relevance of these emerging perspectives. In one of its numerous reports, the bank observed that 'development practitioners from the North have often prepared programs for the South without the participation of local officials ... These programs often inspire little commitment from the countries involved and as a result have often been ineffective.'[100]

Taken as whole, alternatives to contemporary global development policies, whether in law or economics, underscore the need to create policies that are sensitive to local conditions in the Third World. A humane multilateral health order holds a certain promise towards the progressive realization of public health as a global public good.

F Summary of the Arguments: Are We Still in a Global Neighbourhood?

This chapter has argued that all of humanity is bonded by values of human dignity that transcend geo-political and ethno-cultural boundaries. In our time and age, these bonds have decayed as a result of vicious forces of poverty and underdevelopment. Our contemporary international society, in which 80 per cent of the world's population is confined to the penitentiary of poverty, malnutrition, underdevelopment, food insecurity, inadequate housing, and environmental pollution, is comparable to medieval feudalism. The paradox of a global neighbourhood in a divided world is not a prophecy of doom, but a strategy to rethink ways to salvage our global health future by avoiding the errors of past decades. The beginning or end of a millennium provides an occasion for stock-taking on multiple dimensions of global relations. The transition from the dusk of the twentieth century to the dawn of the twenty-first presents humankind with a window of opportunity to rethink the complex socio-economic conditions that impact on humanity's health in a multilateral context. There are old lessons to be relearned, the most basic being that all human life is of value.[101] In subsequent chapters, I argue that all of humanity will be mutually vulnerable should we fail to re-learn these lessons. I argue as well that contemporary multilateralism that remains insensitive to humane values, if unreformed, will adversely affect human health in parts of the developing world in ways that will cause significant turbulence in the entire global neighbourhood. When one part of the human body is sick, the whole body can hardly function properly; especially, when one part of the global village is a reservoir of preventable diseases, the entire neighbourhood may be perpetually endangered. In the discourse of globalization, Held and McGrew have explored the dynamics of the global village–divided world paradox as 'Globalization/Anti-Globalization.'[102] These dynamics come within the rubric of Stiglitz's 'discontents' of globalization.[103]

Mutual Vulnerability and Globalization of Public Health in the Global Neighbourhood

A Overview of the Argument

Mutual vulnerability is the accumulation of the vicious threats posed to humans by disease and pathogenic microbes in an interdependent world, the susceptibility of humans to these threats, and the obsolescence of the traditional distinction between national and international health threats. Diseases once thought to be limited to certain regions of the world have emerged in other regions, while diseases thought to be under control have re-emerged in the same regions with renewed vigour.[1] Within the global neighbourhood, populations in both the South and North are now mutually vulnerable to the traditional and re-emerging powers of the microbial world. The globalizing forces of trade and travel combine with the imperatives of human migrations caused by political conflicts, civil wars, and environmental crises to propel both the efficacy of microbial threats and the complex dynamics of mutual vulnerability. Were disease pathogens to carry national passports or respect geo-political boundaries, the concept of mutual vulnerability would, at best, be a national security issue within the domestic jurisdiction of nation states. But the phenomenon of globalization has shattered the illusions of protectionism and isolationism. An obvious consequence of globalization is the increased vulnerability of national boundaries to transnational microbial threats. As observed by Nakajima,

> In the late twentieth century, an era characterized by the globalization of the world's political economy, the threat of infectious disease transmission across national borders and the expansion of the trade and promotion of harmful commodities, such as tobacco, represent transnational health problems ... These issues pose threats to the security and well-being of citizens in all states ... The fact that the political boundaries of sovereign states do not represent natural barriers to infectious agents or to

harmful products underscores the need for interstate co-operation to address these global health issues.[2]

Globalization is not the only factor that contributes to transboundary spread of emerging and re-emerging infectious diseases. The power of nature, complacency, the breakdown of surveillance capacities, and socio-economic and environmental degradation also play a role.[3] Together, these factors require the global society to revisit the ideals of enlightened self-interest.[4]

The concept of mutual vulnerability is not new.[5] As we have seen, the earliest historical accounts of the cross-border spread of diseases provide evidence of what one writer aptly calls 'the microbial unification of the world.'[6] The arrival of Columbus in the Americas marked the beginning of a new era in mutuality of vulnerability. According to Porter, the meeting of far-flung peoples who had never previously had contact had major consequences for epidemic infections. The vulnerability of native populations in the 'New World' meant that pandemics decimated the Caribbean Indians, and swept through urbanized societies in Mexico and Peru at a catastrophic rate.[7] The microbial unification of the world was almost concluded when the Amerindian populations began to die out as a result of 'imported' European diseases, and Europeans began to replace their lost labour power with slaves from West Africa. West African slaves brought falciparum malaria to the Americas, and the water casks on the slave ships brought the mosquito that carried yellow fever. The triangular and tripartite disease exchange between Europeans, Native Americans, and Africans propelled mutual vulnerability in ways hitherto unknown in human history.[8] Hays rightly observes that 'since the sixteenth century the world has shrunk, with greater opportunities for the rapid movement of microbes to new populations.'[9]

This chapter revisits the historical accounts of the transnationalization of diseases, explores the origins of contemporary public health diplomacy, and argues that in a globalizing world, mutual vulnerability is the single most important catalyst to re-kindle mutual self-interest between the South and the North. I use the re-emergence of tuberculosis and the cases 'airport' or 'imported' malaria in parts of the industrialized global North (especially North America and Europe) to explore mutual vulnerability in the present era of emerging and re-emerging infectious diseases.

B Retrospective Vision: Diseases, Peoples, and Nation States in Historical Perspective

In *Plagues and Peoples*, McNeill argues that infectious disease, which antedated the emergence of humankind, will last as long as humanity itself, and will surely remain as one of the fundamental parameters and determinants of human history.[10] From time immemorial, human societies across cultures have reacted to diseases in various ways. In the pre-Hippocratic[11] period the Jews, early Christians, and pagans who formed part of the ancient Greek and Roman civilizations developed a variety of beliefs, practices, and even folklore to deal with bodily disorders occasioned by disease.[12] Likewise, societies in Africa, Asia, and the Americas, prior to their contacts with European colonial powers, reacted to disease events in various natural, supernatural, and superstitious ways. Zinsser observed that before the time of the Greeks, the interpretation of infectious diseases was, in most instances, largely guesswork.[13] This 'guesswork,' due primarily to inconclusive scientific proof of the cause of certain diseases, adversely affected nineteenth-century infectious diplomacy – the efforts by European states to forge multilateral cooperation to combat mutual vulnerability. The absence of scientific proof of the cause of diseases (such as cholera) allowed some European nation states to resist early attempts at multilateral regulation of cholera through a series of international sanitary conferences and conventions; it also revived the various conceptions of disease held by populations in ancient times. In Goodman's words, 'at the time when epidemic disease was thought to be a punishment from the gods, little could be done to prevent its spread save prayer and sacrifices.'[14] It is in this context that mutual vulnerability and the evolution of nineteenth-century multilateral initiatives on public health will be explored.

C Mutual Vulnerability and the Evolution of Public Health Multilateralism

The microbial unification of the world, which was concluded by the European conquest of the Americas and the transatlantic slave trade from Africa to America, opened a new vista in microbe-human interaction. Across the world, pathogenic microbes travelled long distances with unprecedented speed, permeated national boundaries with ease, and constituted serious menaces to populations. Driven by the desire to protect their populations, most nation states introduced and enforced strict quarantine regulations.[15] Goodman has identified three reactions by nation states to the transboundary spread of disease prior to 1851. The first was the predominant view that disease was a punishment from the gods that could only be cured by prayers and sacrifices. The second was the isolation of a healthy society from an unhealthy one through the practice of *cordon sanitaire* to prevent either importation or exportation of disease. The third was the practice of quarantine, which enabled governments to isolate goods or persons coming from places suspected of suffering an outbreak of disease to protect the community from disease importation.[16] Goodman also observed that between the fourteenth and nineteenth centuries nearly all 'civilized' countries adopted some form of quarantine control. This control consisted mainly of imposing an arbitrary period of isolation on the ships, crews, passengers, and goods arriving from foreign ports believed to be reservoirs of major epidemic diseases, especially plague, yellow fever, and later cholera.[17] The inconsistency and nuisance value of national quarantine regimes, and the way in which their enforcement adversely affected movement of cargo and people, are better appreciated from a detailed account given by one scholar:

> On disembarking, the Master of an infected or suspected ship was required to stand before an iron grille, swear on oath to tell the truth, and then throw the ship's bill of health into a basin of vinegar. An official would then plunge the bill beneath the sur- face with the aid of iron tongs and, when it was judged to have been well soaked, remove it by the same means, lay it on the end of a plank, and thus present it to the 'conservateur de la santé', who would read it without touching it. Letters from the unfortunate sick or suspect passengers confined to a lazaret had to be thrown for a distance of ten paces, retrieved with long tongs, plunged into vinegar, and then passed through the flame and smoke of ignited gunpowder. The personnel of the laz- aret wore wooden clogs and oilskin jackets, trousers and gloves.[18]

The nuisance value of quarantine is also illustrated in popular art. In Shakespeare's *Romeo and Juliet*, an outbreak of an infectious pestilence and a subsequent impo- sition of quarantine led to the isolation of Friar John on his way to Mantua. As a result of his isolation, Friar John was prevented from delivering a letter from Friar Lawrence to Romeo informing him that his lover Juliet was not dead, but only asleep. Had Friar John not been isolated, the tragic deaths of Romeo and Juliet would have been averted.[19]

To what extent, if at all, were extreme national protectionist policies effective in controlling the transboundary spread of disease? Did isolationism protect popula- tions within national boundaries from microbial threats? Did extreme protection- ism diminish mutual vulnerability in any significant ways? It took only two epidemics of cholera in Europe, in 1830 and 1847, to expose the impotence of quarantine. European cholera epidemics discredited the myth that quarantine, *cordon sanitaire*, or other domestic protectionist policies of the time provided a watertight defence against, or insulation from, an infectious disease. The mid-nine- teenth-century epidemics decimated populations and opened a new vista in mutu- ality of vulnerability. For centuries, as Goodman observed, 'cholera ha[d] been considered a disease, albeit terrible in its rapidity and high mortality, largely con- fined to Central Asia and particularly to Bengal ... But between 1828 and 1831 it passed out of India and spread rapidly to the whole of Europe and to the United States ...'[20] From Punjab, Afghanistan, and Persia:

It reached Moscow in 1830 and infected the whole of Europe, including England, by the end of 1831. It reached Canada and United States of America in the Summer of 1832. Another pandemic followed in 1847 and five others in the next fifty years. This was a new and terrifying disease to the western world and quarantines, even though at once tightened up under the pressure of public opinion and hence more vexatious than ever, seemed to be impotent to stop the spread. Just as within each national boundary fear of cholera overcame local jealousies and vested interests, so the nations were more inclined to consult together and try to devise measures against the common peril.[21]

A second motivation for the evolution of multilateral cooperation in the field of public health lies in the exponential rise in international trade, travel, and maritime commerce in Europe after the Industrial Revolution. The development of the steamship (ca. 1810), the railway (ca. 1830), and the construction of the Suez Canal in 1869 boosted trade and commercial transactions in nineteenth-century Europe. With new commercial opportunities came new challenges. To facilitate transboundary movement of goods and populations, trade-hurting national quarantine regulations had to be harmonized in a multilateral forum.[22]

The mutual vulnerability occasioned by the cholera epidemics of 1830 and 1847 and the need to harmonize quarantine regulations created by the nineteenth-century imperatives of trade, travel, and maritime commerce catalysed the earliest 'multilateralization' of public health. The trade-health dynamic of the evolution of public health diplomacy meant, as Siddiqi notes, that with one eye on the common peril (cholera and other diseases), and the other on the worsening outlook for their maritime trade, governments found themselves without any other option than to attempt international collaboration.[23]

At the initiative of France, eleven European states[24] and Turkey were represented at the first International Sanitary Conference, which opened in Paris on 23 July 1851.[25] From 1851 to the end of the nineteenth century, ten international sanitary conferences[26] were convened and eight sanitary conventions were negotiated on mutual vulnerability: the spread of infectious diseases (cholera, plague, and yellow fever) across European boundaries and the harmonization of inconsistent national quarantines.

Although most of the conventions were never ratified by the countries that participated in the conferences, and thus never entered into force *stricto sensu*, the nineteenth-century public health/infectious disease diplomacy nonetheless signified the necessity of tackling the cross-border spread of epidemics multilaterally. The second half of the nineteenth century was an era of intensive infectious disease diplomacy, and one obvious consequence of this development was the frequent use of international law to strengthen multilateral public health cooperation.[27] The number of conferences convened and conventions/agreements/treaties negotiated should not, however, be confused with success or progress on the multilateral control of infectious diseases. As Fidler rightly observes, it took states a long time to arrive at a 'universal' regime on infectious disease control.[28] Forty-one years and six European-led international conferences elapsed before the first effective international convention (restricted to cholera) was adopted at the International Sanitary Conference held in Venice in 1892.[29] According to Howard-Jones, 'This convention was the first tangible fruit of seven international conferences spanning 41 years. The seventh conference, of which this convention was the outcome, was only concerned with cholera and, more specifically, with the sanitary control of westbound shipping traversing the Suez Canal, most of which was British. Continental European countries were deeply concerned that the canal might be a conduit for the importation of cholera from India to Europe. History has proved these fears to be entirely groundless ...'[30]

In 1897, the tenth International Sanitary Conference was held in Venice, with a specific mandate. As Howard-Jones notes, the 1897 conference set a precedent chiefly because it dealt exclusively with plague.[31] Most of the nine preceding conferences had wasted an enormous amount of time discussing multilateral approaches to cholera. The mode of transmission of cholera and whether it was a suitable subject for international consideration sharply divided delegates, and there was no consensus on these issues until the ninth sanitary conference in 1894.[32] The breakthrough on the etiology of cholera enabled countries to shift their attention to other diseases. At the 1897 sanitary conference Great Britain was criticized because of the spread of a serious and persistent epidemic of plague from Bombay to the north-west littoral of India – Austria-Hungary had indeed proposed the 1897 conference because it feared its Muslim subjects from the Mecca Pilgrimage might bring plague with them after being in contact with pilgrims from India.[33] The 1897 conference led to an International Sanitary Convention dealing solely and exclusively with plague and signed by all the participating twenty sovereign powers except Denmark, Sweden/Norway, and the United States.

In 1903, the 1892 and 1897 International Sanitary Conventions, dealing with cholera and plague respectively, were consolidated and replaced by a new convention. As the European states approached the end of the 'long nineteenth century' with intensive public health diplomacy, international conventions treaties alone were not capable of providing either the 'magic bullet' against mutual vulnerability or the 'end of history' of the infectious disease menace. The development of multilateral regimes to govern transboundary disease menace coincided with the need to establish multilateral institutions to enforce the emergent regimes. The dawn of the twentieth century witnessed a more global spread of multilateral initiatives outside Europe. In 1902 an International Conference of American States, held in

Washington, D.C., established the first multilateral public health institution – the International Sanitary Bureau.[34] In 1907, the bulk of the European states that negotiated the nineteenth-century international sanitary conventions met in Rome and adopted an agreement establishing the Office International d'Hygiène Publique (OHIP) (International Bureau of Public Health) with a permanent secretariat in Paris. The interwar years then witnessed institutional deficiencies and rivalries in enforcing international health regimes. The Health Organization of the League of Nations (HOLN) in Geneva, the Pan-American Sanitary Bureau in Washington, D.C., and the OHIP in Paris existed independently of each other. Each was autonomous and enforced sanitary or health conventions and treaties within its respective area of competence.[35] Siddiqi observes that between 1920 and 1936 the OIHP rejected four proposals from the League of Nations to rationalize international activities, eradicate any overlap in functions, and establish a single international health organization.[36] The HOLN died naturally with the League of Nations at the outset of the Second World War, but the remaining international health institutions continued to operate independently until the formation of the World Health Organization in 1948, when OIHP was subsumed within the WHO. Notwithstanding the setbacks suffered by the health institutions and the decades it took to conclude the earliest international sanitary conventions, these efforts established one undeniable fact: that multilateral cooperation was a useful tool against mutual vulnerability to microbial threats. As observed by Fidler,

> the creation of the Pan American Sanitary Bureau (PASB) in 1902, the Office International d'Hygiène Publique (OIHP) in 1907, the Health Organization of the League of Nations (HOLN) in 1923, and the Office International des Épizooties (OIE) in 1924, put international co-operation on public health into institutional forms that facilitated greater inter-governmental collaboration than could be achieved through ad hoc conferences. A sign of this greater potential for co-operation is the expansion of PASB, OIHP, and HOLN into areas of public health not previously a topic of inter-governmental collaboration, such as expanding the number of infectious diseases subject to international co-operation, working on chronic diseases such as cancer, or studying nutrition.[37]

Another major achievement of the multilateral approaches to preventing the cross-border spread of epidemics in this period was the use of sanitary treaties and multilateral institutional mechanisms to create an international surveillance system and share epidemiological information. For instance, the 1903 International Sanitary Convention that consolidated notification duties of the 1893 and 1897 treaties required contracting parties to notify the other parties of the appearance of authentic cases of plague and yellow fever in their territories.[38] Sharing epidemiological information and the corresponding obligation on states to report outbreaks in their territories was clearly within the scope of many of the sanitary conventions and was also evident in the mandates of the emergent multilateral health institutions. As observed by Fidler, the treaty establishing the Office International Office des Épizooties (OIE) required contracting parties to notify it of certain infectious diseases of animals either in connection with first cases or at regular intervals.[39] Because a functional international surveillance system was tied to the mandates of these international institutions, the Pan-American Sanitary Bureau was a core element of the Pan-American surveillance system. The OIHP played an important surveillance role after it was created in 1907, and surveillance was also part of the work and mandate of the HOLN.[40] The precedent set by nineteenth-century infectious disease diplomacy on mutual vulnerability can be seen in contemporary public health multilateralism with respect to the mandate of the WHO and the global surveillance of emerging and re-emerging infectious diseases.

D Mutual Vulnerability and Contemporary Public Health Multilateralism

The complexities and parameters of the multiple dimensions of mutual vulnerability in contemporary public health diplomacy are overwhelming. Any discourse of mutual vulnerability in the post-1948 decades will necessarily proceed from the present crisis of emerging and re-emerging infectious diseases.[41] Nonetheless, there is also a need to reference the re-emergence of tuberculosis and the sudden outbreaks of malaria in Europe and North America.

In 1995, the U.S. government inter-agency Working Group on Emerging and Re-emerging Infectious Diseases (known as the CISET Working Group) listed twenty-nine examples of new infectious diseases identified since 1973.[42] The second category of EIDs includes diseases that have re-emerged in the last twenty years as public health problems. The CISET Working Group categorized re-emerging infectious diseases into three groups: (i) infectious diseases that have flared up in regions in which they historically appeared; (ii) infectious diseases that have expanded into new regions; and (iii) infectious diseases that have developed resistance to anti-microbial treatments and have spread through traditional and/or new regions because of such resistance.[43] Tuberculosis falls into each of the three categories of re-emerging infectious diseases. It is an old disease that has re-emerged as a major health problem in regions where it historically occurred, it has returned as a problem in both the South and the North, and certain strains of tuberculosis have developed strong resistance to antibiotics and other pharmaceutical treatments.[44] The WHO blames the crisis of re-emerging EIDs on what it calls 'fatal complacency.'[45] The discovery of antibiotics, the worldwide eradication of smallpox, and the progress made in rolling back the morbidity and mortality of poliomyelitis, leprosy, measles, guinea worm, and neo-natal tetanus created the misleading impression that the battle between humanity and the microbial world was being won by humans. This over-optimism, argues the WHO, is costing millions of lives annually.[46] Diseases that used to be restricted geographically are now striking in regions once thought to be safe. In the contest for supremacy, observed the WHO, 'the microbes are sprinting ahead. The gap between their ability to mutate into drug-resistant strains and man's ability to counter them is widening fast.'[47] To contextualize the crisis of EIDs the discussion below focuses on tuberculosis and malaria.[48]

I   The Re-Emergence of Tuberculosis as a Threat in Europe and North America

Tuberculosis (TB) is a contagious disease that spreads through the air. There are many types of tuberculosis, but only people who have pulmonary tuberculosis are infectious. When an infected person coughs, sneezes, talks, or spits, he propels TB germs – *bacilli* – into the air. An inhalation of a small number of bacilli germs leads to an infection. The WHO estimates that tuberculosis kills 2 million people annually.[49] It is further estimated that between 2000 and 2020, nearly one billion people will be newly infected, 200 million will get sick, and 35 million people will die from TB, if control is not strengthened.[50] The WHO estimates that the majority of TB sufferers live in the developing world, particularly in Southeast Asia, the Western Pacific, and Africa.[51]

A disturbing phenomenon is the fact the TB has formed a lethal partnership with HIV/AIDS.[52] According to the WHO, the AIDS virus damages the body's natural defences, the immune system, and accelerates the speed at which TB progresses from a harmless infection to a life-threatening condition. Tuberculosis is already the opportunistic infection that most frequently kills HIV-positive people. Of an estimated one million HIV-related deaths in 1995, about a third might have been due to tuberculosis. While only 9 per cent of the total of three million tuberculosis deaths in 1995 were related to AIDS, the percentage was expected to reach 17 per cent in 2000.[53] A second disturbing phenomenon about the global TB crisis is the emergence of strains of the disease that are resistant to available drugs. The WHO defines 'drug-resistant tuberculosis' as a case of tuberculosis (usually pulmonary) excreting *bacilli* resistant to one or more anti-tuberculosis drugs.[54] If properly treated, the WHO believes that tuberculosis is curable in virtually all cases, provided it is not caused by bacteria resistant to a range of drugs[55] – but incomplete or inappropriate treatment has spawned the development of strains that *are* resistant. If untreated, the disease is fatal in half the cases. Non-vaccinated babies are most vulnerable to developing the severest forms after becoming infected.[56]

Of relevance to mutual vulnerability in the global health context is the fact that the morbidity and mortality of tuberculosis in Europe and North America from the 1950s to the 1970s were very low, as TB was almost completely eliminated as a public health threat. Today it has re-emerged with brutal force in these substantially industrialized continents. Quoting from the 104th Congressional Hearings on Emerging Infections, Fidler observes that in the 1980s and 1990s, New York City public health officials waged a battle to contain a reappearance of TB.[57] Immigration of tuberculin-infected persons from developing countries to New York City has been widely cited as a leading cause of the re-emergence of TB in that city. Tuberculosis has thus expanded from places where the disease is fairly common to an environment once relatively free from the disease.[58] The WHO has reported that TB outbreaks have been increasing in the United States from the mid-1980s: Tuberculosis had declined from 84,300 cases in 1953 to 22,200 in 1984, but between 1985 and 1993 the number of cases increased by 14 per cent. Of the 25,300 cases reported in 1993, 73 per cent were among racial and ethnic minorities. Recent outbreaks in the United States have included several of the multi-drug-resistant forms in hospitals and prisons, with mortality of up to 70 per cent.[59]

In Canada, although the overall infection ratio is low, the spread of multi-drug-resistant strains of tuberculosis is also on the rise. The threat is becoming apparent in the culturally diverse city of Toronto, where about 3 per cent of TB cases are multi-drug-resistant.[60] Richard Bedell, a Vancouver doctor, has offered persuasive reasons why the global TB threat is indeed a Canadian problem. From the perspective of mutual vulnerability, he argues thus,

> I can think of three levels on which people might take an interest in tuberculosis. The first is self-interest: Can it affect me or my loved ones? The second is obligation: What ought we do as a country? The third I call the 'will for supererogation': What is good to do even if we are not obligated to do it? I want to address the failures to interest the world (including Canadians) on these levels. Canada is a diverse society and many Canadians come from countries with a high prevalence of TB. As well, Canadians travel extensively for business and tourism, often visiting countries with high TB rates ... You have only to share the same air in a room, a bus or an aircraft with someone who has infectious TB to have some risk of infection.[61]

In Europe the morbidity and mortality rates of TB have also increased astronomically in the past two decades. In Denmark and Germany, for instance, the percentage of TB patients resistant to a single drug rose by 50 per cent in 1996.[62] New outbreaks of TB have occurred in Eastern Europe after about forty years of steady decline in TB mortality.[63]

II 'Imported' and 'Airport' Malaria in the Global North

Malaria is endemic in ninety-one countries, mainly in Africa, where it is one of the biggest contributors to the mortality and morbidity burdens of disease. The WHO estimates that annually there are 300–500 million clinical cases of malaria, and between 1.5 million and 2.7 million deaths.[64] Malaria's capacity to undermine the ability of infected people to work links it to poverty and socio-economic development.

Malaria is caused by species of parasites belonging to the genus *plasmodium*. It is transmitted by a bite of an infected female mosquito of the genus *anopheles*. Early symptoms include fever, shivering, aches and pains in the joints, and headache.[65] In falciparum malaria, infected red cells can obstruct the blood vessels of the brain, causing cerebral malaria, which is often lethal. Other vital organs can also be damaged, with fatal consequences.[66] Malaria has been eradicated in most of the industrialized world. The failure of the WHO's efforts to eradicate malaria globally in the 1970s, and the present endemicity of the disease in the global South (mainly in Africa), has given the mistaken but fatal impression that malaria is simply an African problem.

Cases of 'imported malaria' and 'airport malaria'[67] have re-emerged in Europe and North America and other regions of the world where the burden of malaria has historically been low. The differences between the South and the North on the burdens of malaria are still vast, with an overwhelming majority of malaria morbidity and mortality occurring in Africa. Nonetheless airport malaria can no longer be neglected as infectious agents ignore national borders and increasingly find their way to Europe.[68] According to the WHO, there have been reports of a surprising number of malaria deaths in northern countries following unrecognized infection through a blood transfusion or a one-off mosquito bite near an international airport. Brussels, Geneva, and Oslo have all had recent cases of airport malaria.[69] Cases of airport malaria in Europe, which mostly occur in the absence of anamnestic signs of any exposure to the malaria risk, are often difficult to diagnose.[70] From 1969 to 1999 confirmed cases of airport malaria have been reported in France, Belgium, Switzerland, the United Kingdom, Italy, the United States, Luxembourg, Germany, The Netherlands, Spain, Israel, and Australia.[71]

Cases of imported malaria have also spread from endemic areas to non-endemic regions due to the increase in global travel, tourism, and human migration. Epidemiological data in Europe suggest that 1,010 cases were imported into the countries of the European Union in 1971; 2,882 in 1981; about 9,200 cases in 1991, and 12,328 cases in 1997.[72] In 1993, some thirty years after the eradication of malaria in the former U.S.S.R., some 1,000 cases of malaria were registered in the Russian Federation and in the newly independent states of Belarus, Kazakhstan,

Ukraine, Azerbaijan, Tajikistan, Turkmenistan, and Uzbekistan.[73] In the United Kingdom, a total of 8,353 cases of imported malaria were reported between 1987 and 1992. A breakdown of this figure shows that U.K. nationals who visited their friends and relations in malaria-endemic regions accounted for 49 per cent of the cases, visitors to the U.K. accounted for 19 per cent, tourists accounted for 16 per cent, and immigrants and expatriates accounted for 11 and 5 per cent respectively.[74]

Mutual vulnerability is not limited to tuberculosis and airport malaria. Between 1994 and 1999, the WHO identified about thirty-five unexpected outbreaks of emerging and re-emerging infectious diseases.[75] Among these outbreaks is the appearance of West Nile Fever in New York City, which caught public health officials by surprise,[76] as well as the recent transboundary spread of Severe Acute Respiratory Syndrome (SARS). The cross-border spread of tuberculosis, malaria, and other emerging diseases through global travel, trade, and human migrations renders the distinction between national and international public health threats obsolete. Malaria, tuberculosis, and other emerging and re-emerging diseases may have heavier burdens in the global South, but they are no longer the exclusive problems of the South. Mutual vulnerability has transformed them into globalized challenges that immerse all of humanity in a single germ pool.

E The Obsolescence of the Distinction between National and International Health in a Globalizing World

Scholars of public health, policy makers, and multilateral institutions agree that the reasons for outbreaks of new diseases and the re-emergence of old ones thought to be under control are varied and complex. The U.S. Centers for Disease Control and Prevention (CDC) identified eight demographic and environmental conditions that favour the spread of infectious diseases:

(i)   global travel;
(ii) globalization of food supply and centralized processing of food;
(iii) population growth and increased urbanization and crowding;
(iv) population movements due to civil wars, famines, and other man-made or natural disasters;
(v)   irrigation, deforestation, and reforestation projects that alter the habitats of disease-carrying insects and animals;
(vi) human behaviours, such as intravenous drug use and risky sexual behaviour;
(vii) increased use of antimicrobial agents and pesticides, hastening the development of resistance; and
(viii) increased human contact with tropical rain forests and other wilderness

habitats that are reservoirs for insects and animals that harbour unknown infectious agents.[77]

These eight factors are similar to the ones that have featured prominently in epidemiological literature.[78] One obvious consequence of these factors, as the WHO noted, is the fact that 'national health has become an international challenge. An outbreak anywhere must now be seen as a threat to virtually all countries, especially those that serve as major hubs of international travel.'[79]

Travel is not a new factor in the transnational spread of disease. In the Middle Ages, rats infested by plagues were shipped from one continent to another on board ships. Before the discovery of aircraft, the volume of travel and migration across national boundaries increased so much that quarantine practices became ineffective.[80] However, air traffic has averted a surge in global travel with a propensity for disease spread that is unparalleled in human history. In 1993, it was estimated that 500 million persons crossed international borders on board aircraft.[81] Today, this number has soared to 1.4 billion persons. The opportunities for travel to spread disease have likewise increased. Travel has contributed to the cross-border spread of malaria, yellow fever, plague, cholera, tuberculosis, influenza, HIV/AIDS, Lassa fever, smallpox, hantaviruses, gonorrhea, syphilis, and many other diseases.[82] Fidler observes that the potential for global pandemics fuelled by the ease of travel is illustrated by the AIDS virus. The opportunities offered to a virulent airborne pathogen by air travel are perhaps even more frightening.[83]

Public health has clearly become globalized. Transboundary disease spread now constitutes a global crisis that requires the pooling of efforts and resources by nation states in a multilateral context. In no other sphere of global relations is the global village metaphor more practical than in contemporary 'public health diplomacy,' with its twin offshoots: the permeation of national boundaries by disease pathogens and the consequent vulnerability of populations within those boundaries to microbial threats. The contemporary crisis of EIDs offers incontrovertible proof that the distinction often drawn between national and international health has become anachronistic. Malaria, dengue, yellow fever, HIV/AIDS, plague, and indeed any disease in any part of the world, must now be seen as global problems.

F Summary of the Arguments: Self-Interest Revisited

This chapter argued that the interaction between humanity and disease pathogens is as ancient as human history itself. The evolution of the Westphalian nation state and the consequent institution of strict isolationist and protectionist domestic policies diminished neither the potency of microbial pathogens nor the degree of vulnerability of populations to disease. Neither diseases nor pathogenic microbes have shown any respect for political and geographical lines drawn on a map. Many diseases originally endemic in certain regions of the world have re-emerged in other regions due to a host of factors. Given that all of humanity is now mutually vulnerable to the transborder threats of disease, does it make sense to maintain a distinction between diseases of the South and those of the North? Or should powerful countries such as the United States look beyond their own narrow self-interests with regard to transnational public health policy?[84] The widely cited report of the U.S. Institute of Medicine, *America's Vital Interest in Global Health*,[85] provides answers founded precisely on self-interest: the direct interests of the American people are served when the United States promotes world health. In partnership with other countries and multilateral institutions, the United States can become a leader in global health, especially in the areas of research and development, surveillance, education, coordination, and training.[86] Placing the vision of self-interest squarely within world health, mutual vulnerability is antithetical to either isolationism or protectionism. The 'us' and 'them,' 'our disease' and 'their disease' distinctions have become anachronistic. 'Our common health future'[87] depends on 'innovative, intersectoral interventions, involving a high degree of international co-operation and political will.'[88] Neither parochial foreign policy objectives anchored in isolationism and protectionism nor empty rhetoric in the face of glaring global health dangers can protect our global neighbourhood from the 'coming plague.' The next chapter discusses the gaps in multilateral health diplomacy and cooperation, the shortcomings of multilateral health institutions, and the critical role international law must play in remoulding and reconfiguring the emergent global health architecture.

Vulnerability of Multilateralism and Globalization of Public Health in the Global Neighbourhood

A Overview of the Argument

Multilateralism is vulnerable to what nation states perceive as being consistent with their strategic interests. The broad range of issues encompassed within, and the wide terrain covered by, what constitutes strategic interests according to the subjective judgment of each nation state inevitably politicizes multilateralism. 'Politicization', in turn, produces visible gaps and adverse impacts that destabilize multilateral initiatives. Crisis in multilateralism is not a new phenomenon. Siddiqi observes that strains arise for a number of reasons, including disagreements over political issues, philosophical approaches, and more mundane issues such as proper ways to administer, staff, finance, and prioritize programs and policies within multilateral organizations.[1] Multilateral public health initiatives are no exception; they are not insulated from politicization and other age-old destabilizing vicissitudes of multilateralism. Like multilateral initiatives to forge consensus on other global issues – ozone depletion, climate change, biodiversity conservation, and food (in)security – public health diplomacy is subject to the vagaries and vulnerabilities of politics and a range of challenges in forging global health accords. Because the bulk of academic and policy discourses of global health challenges emanate largely from the disciplines of epidemiology and public health, international legal scholars are yet to explore the dimensions of these vulnerabilities exhaustively. Focusing on infectious diseases and international relations, Fidler, as we have seen, coined the term microbialpolitik to describe the international politics produced as states attempt to deal with pathogenic microbes multilaterally. Microbialpolitik points to the ordinary dynamics of international relations combined with the special dynamics produced by the nature of the microbial world.[2] Although microbialpolitik is within the parameters of what I broadly contemplate in this chapter as 'vulnerabilities of public health multilateralism' politics is nonetheless just one limb of this dynamic.

This chapter argues that since the first International Sanitary Conference in 1851, multilateral health diplomacy has grappled with complex regime deficits – confusion and ignorance of etiologies of certain diseases as well as gross underutilization of the legal, normative, and regulatory approaches to cross-border spread of disease. There is also a glaring institutional incapacity for the enforcement of the existing albeit skeletal legal/regulatory regime, and an acrimonious South-North engagement in the proceedings of multilateral health institutions. For purposes of coherence and clarity, the dynamics of these vulnerabilities are divided into two broad categories. First, I discuss the impact of 'politicization' on multilateral health initiatives from the second half of the nineteenth century until the formation of the WHO in 1948, an era marked by intensive infectious disease–public health diplomacy. Second, I discuss the shortcomings of contemporary public health diplomacy, covering the decades since the formation of the WHO.

These two epochs expose enormous but varied challenges for multilateral health initiatives. To articulate these varied challenges, this chapter focuses particularly on:

(i)   the colonial and post-colonial implications of the nineteenth-century multilateral health order,

(ii) the impact of trade and economic interests of leading European states during the evolution of public health multilateralism and how these interests affected cross-border regulation and multilateral governance of disease and related public health risks,

(iii) the relevance of international law in contemporary multilateral health governance, and

(iv) selected South-North issues at the World Health Assembly, the supreme policy-making organ of the WHO.

The assertion that, 'if in the old colonial days, it was true that trade follows the flag, it was equally true that the first faltering steps towards international health cooperation followed trade,'[3] underscores the enormous challenges that economic interests of countries continue to pose for multilateral health governance. Exploring the shortcomings of multilateral public health cooperation since 1851 paves the way for innovations to emerge. This chapter does not discuss innovations per se; nonetheless, it sets the stage for innovative approaches to global health governance explored in chapters 6 and 7.

B Nineteenth-Century Infectious Disease Diplomacy: The Politics of Law and Public Health Among Sovereign States

As argued in the previous chapter, the lack of incontrovertible scientific proof of the etiology of the diseases that were to be regulated by International Sanitary Conventions and the maritime/commercial interests of leading shipping countries at the time impeded efforts to get sovereign states to agree on the text of a treaty that was, inter alia, to regulate the cross-border spread of diseases via the harmonization of national quarantines that were hurting trade and travel across Europe. Howard-Jones observes that in convening the first International Conference in 1851, the French government was inspired by the eminently reasonable desire that international agreement should be reached on the standardization of quarantine regulations aimed at preventing the importation of cholera, plague, and yellow fever. Smallpox was then such a universal disease that it was not brought within the scope of international sanitary legislation until seventy-six years later.[4] Lofty and admirable as the French initiative may have been, it was not surprising that 'its outcome was compromised by inherent and insuperable difficulties; the delegates, whether physicians or diplomats, were equally innocent of any knowledge of the etiology or mode of transmission of the diseases under discussion.'[5] The majority view at the conference was that plague and yellow fever were in some ways communicable from the sick to the healthy, but it was otherwise with cholera. G.M. Menis, the Austrian medical delegate to the conference, declared that he was under instructions from his government to discuss only plague and yellow fever. Austria's quarantine measures against cholera, he claimed, far from preventing the ravages of the disease, only made it more frightening and fatal. According to Menis, the most eminent physicians of the Austrian Empire agreed that cholera was 'a purely epidemic disease.'[6] This view received support from J. Sutherland, the British medical delegate, who argued similarly that in England cholera was believed to be 'purely epidemic,' and therefore quarantine measures had no efficacy against it.[7] Ignorance of the etiology of cholera, which polarized delegates at the 1851 conference, breathed new life into the ancient debate between the public health theories of 'miasmism'[8] and 'contagionism'[9] as modes of transmission of disease. The divergent views expressed by delegates deeply interlocked with the overall commercial interests of participating countries. It was in the interest of Great Britain, as a leading maritime power at that time, to follow 'miasmism' school of thought and argue that quarantine or any other international regulatory regime had no effect against cholera because it was not a contagious disease. This view was supported by France, which derived enormous shipping benefits from the Suez Canal, then under its jurisdiction and control. Quarantine, whether at the national or international level, was going to hurt their shipping interests. Little wonder then that the 1851 International Sanitary Conference achieved absolutely nothing; the participating countries could not strike a balance between public health and their shipping/commercial interests. Both the draft International Sanitary Convention and the International Sanitary Regulations annexed thereto were never ratified by any of the eleven countries. As Howard-Jones observes,

From the point of view of practical results, the first International Sanitary Conference was a fiasco. Everyone went on doing in their own what they had done before. Yet there was more to it than that. The fact that the conference took place established the principle that health protection was a proper subject for international consultations even though international health co-operation was for many years to be limited to defensive quarantine measures. The French Government of the time had planted a seed that was not to germinate for some forty years and then, after a complicated cycle of development, to blossom more than a half century later into the World Health Organization.[10]

The destabilizing impact of commercial and other interests of countries on multilateral health cooperation and governance did not end with the 1851 conference. It conspicuously manifested in subsequent international sanitary conferences throughout the nineteenth century, even after substantial scientific progress had been made to prove the etiology of cholera by pioneer epidemiologists: John Snow, William Budd, Filippo Pacini, and Robert Koch. The sixth International Sanitary Conference held in Rome in 1885, and the seventh conference held in Venice in 1892, laid bare the commercial rivalry between Britain and France. France claimed that cholera was always imported to Europe from British India, especially Bombay, and therefore proposed tougher sanitary measures onboard westward-bound ships from the Red Sea traversing the French-controlled Suez Canal. Because four-fifths of all the ships passing through the canal were British, and 770 of those ships arrived at British ports from India in 1884, Britain threatened to divert all its ships away from the canal. Siddiqi observed that problems also occurred 'when Persian and Turkish sensitivities were offended by the claim that cholera was endemic within their borders. They considered any call for tougher quarantines of ships leaving Persian and Turkish ports to be an infringement of their sovereignty.'[11]

These commercial interests impeded early attempts at multilateral health governance. In the second half of the nineteenth century public health diplomacy was driven by the international sanitary conferences, but as Fidler observes 'forty-one years and six European-led international conferences elapsed from the first ... conference in 1851 until the first effective international convention saw the light of day in the 1892 International Sanitary Convention. The conventions negotiated in 1851, 1859, 1874, and 1884 never became effective.'[12] What is conspicuous in the dynamics of politics, law, and public health vis-à-vis sovereignty and multilateral regulation of disease in the nineteenth century is the slow but inevitable process of forging a multilateral agenda on the cross-border spread of disease. The nineteenth-century oscillation between commercial interests and the multilateral regulation of diseases by an international treaty can help us to comprehend the failures and gaps of contemporary multilateral health initiatives. To facilitate a good understanding of contemporary inadequacies, however, nineteenth-century public health multilateralism must necessarily be scrutinized against the backdrop of colonial legacy and post-colonial discourse in international law. The multilateral governance mechanisms (conventions, treaties, and regulations) employed to combat disease and pathogenic microbes evolved at a time when the 'law of nations' was engaged in series of complex manoeuvres with colonialism and colonized people across the world.

C Nineteenth-Century Public Health Multilateralism: Its Colonial Origins and Post-Colonial Underpinnings

Multilateral health diplomacy in the nineteenth century was founded on a state-centric model of internationalism that received its normative imprimatur from the seventeenth-century Treaty of Westphalia. The state-centric as well as the Euro-centric character of the Westphalian system has been the subject of intense scholarship. The Westphalian model notwithstanding, international legal historians trace the colonial origins of international law back to the fifteenth and sixteenth centuries, when Europe 'discovered' the 'new world of the Americas':[13] the intercourse between Spaniards and American Indians following the voyages of Columbus. Interestingly, the beginning of the Columbian era in the fifteenth century, as already argued, remains central in global health discourse because it marked the 'microbial unification of the world,' or what most medical historians call 'the Columbian exchange.'[14] In post-colonial discourse, the fifteenth and sixteenth centuries are important because the interaction between the New and Old Worlds became the driving force behind the polarization of the world between 'civilized and uncivilized,' 'primitive and modern,' standards of modernity and savagery that received tacit approval in the international legal scholarship of that historical era.[15] This questionable dichotomy was maintained in 1648, and by the dawn of the nineteenth century, the civilized-uncivilized construct was firmly entrenched in the vocabulary of international law. The law carried with it the baggage of a despicable distinction between modernity and primitivity, which it inherited from the fifteenth century, and was also confronted with the difficult questions of how to rationalize the European partition of Africa and the conquest of large parts of Asia and the Pacific. As aptly stated by one scholar, 'following the industrial revolution in Europe after the late eighteenth century, in the nineteenth century the international community to a large extent had virtually become a European one on the basis of either conquest or domination. By about 1880, Europeans had subdued most of the non-European states, which was interpreted in Europe as conclusive proof of the inherent superiority of the white man, and the international legal system became a white man's club, to which non-European states would be admitted only if they produced evidence that they were civilised.'[16]

This view accords with Bedjaoui's often-cited categorization of classic international law as a 'predatory economic order' obliged to assume the guise of oligarchic law governing the relations between civilized states, members of an exclusive club.[17] Classic international law, according to Bedjaoui, 'consisted of a set of rules with a geographical basis (it was a European law), a religious-ethical inspiration (it was a Christian law), an economic motivation (it was a mercantalist law), and political aims (it was an imperialist law).'[18] Another feature of nineteenth-century international law was the triumph of positivism as the dominant analytical tool employed by lawyers.[19] Nineteenth-century positivist international law, according to Anghie, developed an elaborate vocabulary for denigrating (non-European) 'uncivilized' peoples, presenting them as suitable subjects for conquest to further the 'civilizing mission.'[20]

The juxtaposition of this peculiar context of the nineteenth century with the desire of European states to regulate the cross-border spread of disease by a multilateral sanitary treaty (convention) raises a series of questions: how international were the nineteenth-century international sanitary conferences? How universally applicable were the international sanitary conventions that emerged from these 'Euro-centric' sanitary conferences? How inclusive or exclusive were the evolutionary processes through which the international sanitary conventions emerged? It is incontrovertible that most of the developing world, almost all of Africa and many parts of Asia and the Pacific, were under European colonial rule in the nineteenth century. The question is thus not whether the fact that the international sanitary conferences excluded a sizeable percentage of peoples then under colonial rule would constitute a vitiating element that could render those international sanitary conventions nugatory.[21] The relevant question is whether the dichotomy of 'civilized' and 'uncivilized' peoples/societies sanctioned by nineteenth-century international law, and the triumph of positivism as the dominant analytical tool for international lawyers, contributed, or continues to contribute to the present South-North heath divide in the global village. In other words, what legacy did the nineteenth century bequeath to international lawyers of today, and in what way(s) has this legacy affected multilateral health initiatives? Has the legacy of the nineteenth century exacerbated contemporary South-North disparities, and thereby propelled the emergence and cross-border spread of diseases and other public health risks? Has it impeded emerging innovations in health protection and promotion from the developing world? Has it accelerated or impeded the synthesization of developing world traditional healing and ethno-medical approaches with multilateral health policies?[22]

These questions highlight two inseparable issues in contemporary multilateral health governance: persistent/systematic exclusion, and power/hegemony in the relations between nation states and peoples. Persistent/systematic exclusion is an indicator that the global North has continued to discover the global South, and has done so many times over, even in the twentieth and twenty-first centuries.[23] This continuous discovery leads to persistent exclusion of public health therapies/practices from the South in multilateral forums. As the next chapter argues, persistent exclusion has resulted in the dismissal of indigenous biomedical, ethno-biological, and pharmacological practices in parts of the developing world as magic, sorcery, superstition. The continuous discovery of the developing world is evidenced in Edward Said's ingenious work, *Orientalism*. By orientation he meant, inter alia, a style of thought based upon ontological and epistemological distinctions made between *the Orient* and (most of the time) *the Occident*.[24] In another, related sense, it also means 'the corporate institution for dealing with the Orient – dealing with it by making statements about it, authorizing views of it, describing it by teaching it, settling it, ruling over it: in short, Orientalism as a Western style for dominating, restructuring, and having authority over the Orient.'[25]

Power/hegemony implicates nineteenth-century international law as the precursor of contemporary power relations in multilateral interdependence between nation states. The hegemonic and colonial origins of nineteenth-century international law set the stage for the institutionalization of contemporary global inequalities. One country, one vote, may be the de jure rule to be followed in the proceedings of multilateral institutions, including the WHO, but there is de facto inequality between member states. In a recent article, Fidler called this power/hegemony in the relations between states 'a kinder, gentler system of capitulations.'[26] The colonial and hegemonic legacies of nineteenth-century public health initiatives still abound. These legacies afford us a window of opportunity to study contemporary public health multilateralism: the mandate of the World Health Organization, selected South-North issues in the proceedings of the organization, and the WHO's limited use of international legal strategies in global health governance.

D Vulnerabilities of Contemporary Public Health Multilateralism: South-North Politics at the World Health Assembly

The World Health Organization was founded on 7 April 1948, when its constitution, adopted at the 1946 International Health Conference in New York, entered into force. The objective of the WHO is the 'attainment by all peoples of the highest possible level of health.'[27] In order to achieve this objective, the organization shall, inter alia;

(i) act as the directing and co-ordinating authority on international health work,
(ii) propose conventions, agreements, and regulations, and make recommendations with respect to international health matters, and perform such duties as may be assigned to it that are consistent with its objective,
(iii) promote and conduct research in the field of health,

(iv) establish and revise as necessary international nomenclatures of diseases, causes of death, and public health practices, and

(v) develop, establish, and promote international standards with respect to food, biological, pharmaceutical, and other products.[28]

In performing these global health governance functions, the WHO is often bogged down by South-North disagreements on a range of issues that traverse public health, disarmament, politics, human rights, cultural diversity, and even the admission of entities not fully recognized as states by the international community. In recent years, the vulnerabilities of public health multilateralism in the guise of South-North debate at the World Health Assembly have, inter alia, focused on the following issues:

(i) the admission of Palestine and Taiwan as members of the WHO,

(ii) the health conditions of the Arab population in the occupied Arab territories, including Palestine,

(iii) repercussions on health of economic and political sanctions between states,

(iv) an international code for the marketing of breast-milk substitutes, and

(v) the health and environmental consequences of the use of nuclear weapons by states.

Since this study cannot fully explore the dynamics and complexities of each of these non-exhaustive South-North issues vis-à-vis the mandate of the WHO, it focuses on the South-North dimensions of the nuclear weapons debate at the World Health Assembly as a microcosm of the larger politicization of public health multilateralism in the post-1948 decades.

The debate and politicization of the link between nuclear weapons and public health at the World Health Assembly dates back to the early 1970s. In May 1973, the twenty-sixth World Health Assembly, conscious of the potentially harmful consequences for the health of present and succeeding generations from any contamination of the environment resulting from nuclear weapons testing, passed Resolution WHA26.57. Recognizing that fallout from nuclear weapons tests is an uncontrolled and unjustified addition to the radiation hazards to which humanity was exposed, the Assembly expressed serious concern that nuclear weapons testing has continued in disregard of the spirit of the treaty banning nuclear weapons tests in the atmosphere, outer space, and under water. Recalling two important provisions of the WHO constitution that

(i) the enjoyment of the highest attainable standard of health is one of the fundamental rights of every human being without distinction of race, religion, political belief, economic and social conditions, and

(ii) the health of all peoples is fundamental to the attainment of peace and security and is dependent upon the fullest co-operation of individuals and states,

Resolution WHA26.57 deplored all nuclear weapons testing that results in such an increase in the level of ionizing radiation in the atmosphere and urged its immediate cessation.

In 1979, the thirty-second World Health Assembly passed Resolution WHA32.24, entitled 'The role of physicians and other health workers in the preservation and promotion of peace.'[29] Resolution WHA32.24 noted the UN General Assembly resolutions on the maintenance and strengthening of peace, the extension of détente, averting the threat of nuclear war, prohibition of the development of new types of weapons of mass destruction, the banning of aggressive military conflicts, and attaining the objectives of true disarmament. The Assembly urged the director-general of the WHO to prepare a report on the further steps which the organization as a United Nations specialized agency, would take in the interests of international socio-economic development, and also with the aim of assisting in the implementation of the UN resolutions on the strengthening of peace, détente, and disarmament.[30] Pursuant to Resolution WHA34.38 of May 1981, the director-general established an International Committee of Experts in Medical Sciences and Public Health, which in 1984 published a report on the 'effects of nuclear war on health and health services.'[31] The expert committee concluded that it is impossible to prepare health services to deal in any systematic way with any catastrophe or cataclysm resulting from nuclear warfare, and that nuclear weapons constitute the greatest immediate threat to the health and welfare of humanity.

In the early 1990s the debate on public health consequences of nuclear weapons at the World Health Assembly became a serious South-North issue.[32] Developing countries (mostly non-nuclear states) that sponsored resolutions on nuclear weapons and health at the World Health Assembly sought to move from a 'soft-law' approach (non-legally binding resolutions of the World Health Assembly) to a legally binding/obligatory norm. This move, which was to start with an advisory opinion of the International Court of Justice on the legality of the use of nuclear weapons by states,[33] was vehemently opposed by states that possessed nuclear weapons, and the politics of nuclear weapons almost tore the WHO apart. The organization suffered a credibility crisis when nuclear weapons states threatened to withhold their financial and other contributions to the WHO if it went ahead with the nuclear weapons debate. To focus discussion particularly on the vulnerabilities of multilateral public health to South-North acrimony, I outline below the way in which the forty-sixth World Health Assembly in May 1993 became entrapped in the South-North politics of the health and environmental effects of nuclear weapons, and explore whether indeed the WHO could seek an advisory opinion on nuclear weapons from the International Court of Justice.

In 1993, the forty-sixth World Health Assembly of the WHO voted to request an advisory opinion from the International Court of Justice framed thus: 'In view of the health and environmental effects, would the use of nuclear weapons by a State in war or armed conflict be a breach of its obligations under international law including the WHO Constitution?' Ms Lini, the delegate of Vanuatu, expressed a view typical of a majority of the countries of the South that voted massively in favour of the resolution. Vanuatu, she argued, 'had sponsored the draft resolution in order to be consistent with its principles and its commitment to safeguarding the future of the global environment and of the human race ... Any nuclear accident, any atmospheric testing, and any nuclear weapon deployment not only affected health and the environment but could also threaten the survival of humanity through its impact on the food chain ... Vanuatu had sponsored the draft resolution aimed at obtaining the view of the International Court of Justice on the use of nuclear weapons because it saw such use not only as a health issue but also as a threat to humanity.'[34] Mexico, a non-nuclear state, but paradoxically and geographically a developing country in the global North, voted in favour of the resolution because 'non-nuclear weapon states had a nuclear sword of Damocles hanging over them and were powerless to change the situation.'[35]

Nuclear weapon states, led by the United States, countered and argued at the World Health Assembly that the question of legality and illegality of the use of nuclear weapons is an arms control question that is beyond the public health mandate of the WHO. The draft resolution on legality of nuclear arms, the U.S. delegate argued, 'would push the WHO into debates about arms control and disarmament that are the responsibility of other organisations in the United Nations system as well as other multilateral bodies.'[36] After intense debate on South-North lines, the Assembly, by a vote of 75–33 (with five abstentions), voted in favour of requesting an advisory opinion from the International Court of Justice on the legality of the use of nuclear weapons. On 8 July 1996, the International Court of Justice declined to give the opinion requested and ruled that the legality of the use of nuclear weapons was *ultra vires* the public health mandate of the WHO as provided in its constitution.[37]

The nuclear weapons debate at the World Health Assembly presented enormous challenges for the WHO as a specialized agency of the United Nations system. Nonetheless, it paved the way to rethink the relevance of international law in global health governance: the debate raised broad questions traversing disarmament, international humanitarian law, international peace and security, use of force, public health, and protection of the global environment, all within the fuzzy confluence of law and politics. Nuclear weapons arguably may not be *stricto sensu* public health issues, but a plethora of global public health issues that are squarely within the mandate of the WHO also raise multidisciplinary concerns as nuclear weapons. What role(s) ought international law play in this emergent global health fabric vis-à-vis the mandate of a multilateral institution charged with directing and coordinating international health work? I explore this question in what follows with an inquiry into two regulatory approaches used by the WHO to pursue its multilateral public health mandate: the International Health Regulations (IHR) and the Framework Convention on Tobacco Control (FCTC).

E International Law and Governance of the Mandate of the World Health Organization: Two Levels of Inquiry

There are two major reasons why the relevance (or otherwise) of international law in global health governance deserves pre-eminent attention in academic and policy discourses. The first is what Franck identified as the *maturity* and *complexity* of contemporary international law and its simultaneous transformation from a defensive ontological[38] to a creative post-ontological[39] discipline capable of regulating and governing every conceivable global issue of our time.[40] With respect to global health governance, post-ontological international law, for instance, enables us to assess the fairness and effectiveness of the law in regulating the cross-border spread of disease and health risks in a divided world through a disease non-proliferation facility. Other transnational health problems arising from tobacco control and international trade in illicit drugs and narcotics also require multilateral regulation. L'Hirondel and Yach have identified such global health problems as tobacco use, the misuse of anti-microbial drugs, the international trade in blood and human organs, standards for biological and pharmaceutical products, and xenotransplantation as issues that require the intervention of international law in the pursuit of the WHO's mandate.[41] Coterminous with international law's post-ontological transformation is the fact that the structure and dynamics of international relations force states to use international law in transnational health cooperation.[42] Thus international law must necessarily play an active role in the distribution or redistribution of the dividends of health protection and promotion as a public good in a sharply divided world.

A second reason to explore international law's relevance in global health governance relates to the need for a critical assessment of the historical evidence of the formidable role played by international law in forging consensus on cross-border health problems at the nineteenth-century international sanitary conferences. International scholars largely agree that post-1948 international health developments have sustained a systematic marginalization of international legal mechanisms, a phenomenon that is clearly antithetical to the use of treaties and conventions in nineteenth-century public health diplomacy.[43]

Taken together, these two factors would hardly explain the WHO's present timidity, in contrast to other United Nations specialized agencies, in using international legal mechanisms (treaties) to pursue its global health mandate. In over fifty years of its history, the WHO has underutilized the enormous and innovative legal powers provided in its constitution. Article 19 gives the organization treaty-making powers very similar to those of most multilateral institutions, providing that 'the Health Assembly shall have the authority to adopt *conventions* or *agreements* with respect to any matter within the competence of the Organization. A two-thirds vote of the Health Assembly shall be required for the adoption of such conventions or agreements, which shall come into force for each Member when accepted by it in accordance with its constitutional processes.'[44] Although there is nothing expressly or radically innovative about Article 19, some scholars argue that when combined with the ambitious objective of the WHO, 'the attainment by all peoples of the highest possible level of health,' and the organization's equally ambitious definition of health as 'a state of complete physical, mental, and social well-being and not merely the absence of disease or infirmity,' Article 19 provides the WHO with virtually limitless treaty-making power that surpasses any treaty power possessed by the organization's precursors: the Pan American Sanitary Bureau, the International Office of Public Health, and the Health Organization of the League of Nations.[45]

Article 21 of the WHO's constitution provides for an innovative treaty-making and norm-creating procedure that is novel in the practice of multilateral institutions: the power of the World Health Assembly to adopt legally binding regulations concerning

(a) sanitary and quarantine requirements and other procedures designed to prevent the international spread of disease;
(b) nomenclatures with respect to diseases, cause of death and public health practices;
(c) standards with respect to diagnostic procedures for international use;
(d) standards with respect to the safety, purity and potency of biological, pharmaceutical and similar products moving in international commerce;
(e) advertising and labelling of biological, pharmaceutical and similar products moving in international commerce.

Article 21 is innovative because it dispenses with the time-wasting treaty-making procedure whereby states, like parties to a contract in domestic law, have to sign and ratify treaties before they are legally bound by such treaties. Article 21 procedure gives the World Health Assembly the power to adopt legally binding regulations without the positive act of consent by states as symbolized by the time-hallowed treaty-making practice of signature and subsequent ratification.[46] For

Regulations adopted under Article 21, an equally innovative procedure of 'contracting out' is available in Article 22: 'Such Regulations shall come into force for all Member States of the WHO after due notice has been given of their adoption by the Health Assembly except for such Members as may notify the WHO Director-General of a rejection or reservation(s) within the period specified in the notice.' Articles 21 and 22 of the WHO's constitution have been described as creating a quasi-legislative procedure that constituted a radical departure from the conventional international rule making and norm generation in the late 1940s, when the WHO was founded.[47]

Finally, Article 23 of the WHO's constitution gives the Health Assembly the authority to make recommendations with respect to any matter within the competence of the organization. The relevance of international law in global health governance can only be exhaustively explored within the scope of the legal, constitutional, and treaty-making powers of the WHO: Article 19 (conventional treaty-making power), Article 21 (innovative legislative power to adopt legally binding regulations), and Article 23 (power to make non-binding recommendations).

An intense debate has raged among scholars and policy makers on the possible reason(s) why the WHO has consistently underutilized its innovative legal powers. Put another way, should the WHO, as a specialized and technical agency within the United Nations system, adopt legally binding approaches or indeed use international law in pursuit of its global health mandate? There are two opposing schools of thought in this debate, with lawyers on one side and doctors/epidemiologists on the other. Expressing a view typical of the lawyers, Fidler argues that the 'WHO was isolated from general developments concerning international law in the post-1945 period. This isolation was not accidental but reflected a particular outlook on the formulation and implementation of international health policy. WHO operated as if it were not subject to the normal dynamics of the anarchical society; rather, it acted as if it were at the centre of a transnational Hippocratic[48] society made up of physicians, medical scientists, and public health experts. The nature of this transnational Hippocratic society led WHO to approach international public health without a legal strategy.'[49] Similarly, Taylor argues that the 'WHO's traditional reluctance to utilize law and legal institutions to facilitate its health strategies is largely attributable to the internal dynamics and politics of the organization itself. In particular, this unwillingness stems, in large part, from the organizational culture established by the conservative medical professional community that dominates the institution.'[50]

The view of the doctors/epidemiologists in the debate is understandably influenced by the giant strides made by science in proving the germ theory correct. Once epidemiologists understood how humans were infected by disease, they automatically turned to diagnosis and healing, and not to international law as a solution. International lawyers who are very critical of WHO's non-legal approaches to global health work recognize this point. As observed by Fidler, 'The common argument used to explain WHO's antipathy towards international law is that WHO is dominated almost exclusively by people trained in public health and medicine, which produces an ethos that looks at global health problems as medical-technical issues to be resolved by the application of the healing arts. The medical-technical approach does not need international law because the approach mandates application of the medical and technical resource or answer directly at the national or local level.'[51]

Science catalysed the development of international health law in the 1890s because it provided the breakthrough needed to facilitate agreement by states on common rules and values. But in the contemporary era, the antibiotic revolution impeded the development of international health law: doctors and public health officials go directly after microbes rather than seek recourse to international legal regimes on global health issues.[52] Little wonder then, that as early as 1948, Sir Wilson Jameson, president of the first World Health Assembly, showed scant respect for international law when he asserted, 'Let us face the facts and refrain from a discussion of legal technicalities into which we, as an assembly of public health experts, are perhaps hardly competent to enter.'[53]

It is by no means an easy task to synthesize the antithesis of the legal and medical/epidemiological schools of thought; the reach and grasp of each has its pros and cons. Nonetheless, a strong emphasis on medical-technical ethos with a glorified celebration of the healing art would amount to what I call *an undue medicalization of public health*. While medicine is always part of public health, public health is broader and more encompassing than medicine alone. If we recall the expansive definition of health found in the WHO's constitution as *a state of complete physical, mental and social well-being and not merely the absence of disease or infirmity*, then linkages must be created between public health and poverty, underdevelopment, human rights, food (in)security, environmental change and natural disasters, wars and weapons of mass destruction, international trade, and globalization, as each of these affects human health. On all of these transnational issues international law has played a formidable role in forging agreements between states, and these agreements must in turn feed into global health governance with respect to the mandate of the WHO.[54] The decades since the birth of the United Nations have witnessed the evolution of international legal mechanisms on human rights (including the right to health), global environmental issues, humanitarian law, food and agriculture, and trade-related health concerns, among others. The WHO seems to have missed these normative developments and regime-creating paradigms relevant to global public health. With the exceptions of the WHO-FAO Codex Alimentarius Commission on food safety and the very recent Framework

Convention on Tobacco Control (FCTC), the WHO remains overly passive in both collaborating with other international agencies and exercising its treaty-making and constitutional/legal powers towards the creation of international health conventions.

Having critiqued the WHO's limited use of international law, it is important to note the dangers and limitations inherent in advocating extreme legalistic approaches to multilateral health governance. Fidler argues that 'world health through world law, is just as fanciful a notion as the ridiculed slogan of "world peace through world law." Law is ultimately an instrument in human affairs, not an end in itself ... Neither international law nor global health jurisprudence provides a magic bullet against public health problems in the world today.'[55] In reconciling the tensions between legal and medical approaches, placing global health governance within the normative ambit of international law is extremely important, but legalism must be accompanied by incentives that would significantly induce compliance with such legal rules and norms.

Before comparing global health governance mechanisms with global environmental governance, where financial and technical assistance have been used as incentives to induce compliance, I turn briefly to the two legal/regulatory approaches used by WHO in pursuit of its mandate mentioned above: the International Health Regulations (IHR) and the recent WHO Framework Convention on Tobacco Control.

I International Health Regulations

The historical evolution of the IHR[56] dates back to the mid-nineteenth century, when epidemics of cholera swept Europe. These epidemics paved the way for public health diplomacy and multilateral initiatives. When the constitution of the World Health Organization came into force in 1948, certain multilateral sanitary conventions and sets of regulations were already in force. These conventions and regulations were within the mandates of the autonomous and independent multilateral organizations discussed in chapter 3 – the International Office of Public Health (in Paris), the Health Organization of the League of Nations (in Geneva), and the Pan American Sanitary Bureau (in Washington, D.C.). In 1951 the WHO, pursuant to its legal powers under Article 21 of its constitution, adopted the International Sanitary Regulations, the product of nineteenth-century public health diplomacy. The WHO renamed these regulations the International Health Regulations in 1969, and slightly modified them in 1973 and 1981.

The IHR, represent one of the earliest multilateral regulatory approaches to global surveillance for certain communicable diseases. As of 1997, the IHR were legally binding on all the WHO's 192 member states, except Australia. They are a regulatory surveillance mechanism for the sharing of epidemiological information on the transboundary spread of three infectious diseases – cholera, plague, and yellow fever – and their fundamental principle is to ensure 'maximum security against the international spread of diseases with a minimum interference with world traffic.' To achieve this goal, the IHR oblige WHO member states to notify the organization of any outbreaks of cholera, plague, and yellow fever in their territories.[57] Notifications sent by a member state to the WHO are transmitted to all the other member states with acceptable public health measures to respond to such outbreaks. This is part of the WHO's surveillance mandate for the global spread of infectious diseases aimed at providing maximum security against transnational proliferation of disease.

The IHR list maximum public health measures applicable during outbreaks, and provide rules applicable to international traffic and travel. These measures cover the requirements of health and vaccination certificates for travellers from areas infected by the three diseases at issue to non-infected areas and the deratting, disinfecting, and disinsecting of ships and aircraft; they also precribe detailed health measures for airports and seaports in the territories of WHO member states.[58] Measures listed in the IHR are the maximum measures allowed in outbreak situations and are designed to protect the country that suffers an outbreak against the risk of overreaction and unnecessary embargoes that could be imposed by neighbours, trading partners, and other countries. These embargoes are often damaging economically, with severe consequences on tourism, traffic, and trade. Outbreak situations therefore require multilaterally measured and evidence-based responses founded on sound public health reasoning by a neutral multilateral organization like the WHO.

Airports and seaports in the territories of WHO member states are required to have a core surveillance capacity and capabilities to detect and contain outbreaks of the diseases subject to the IHR (Articles 14–22). Every port and airport must be provided with pure drinking water and wholesome food supplied from sources approved by the health departments of member states.[59] Every port and airport must be provided with an effective system for the removal and safe disposal of excrement, refuse, waste water, condemned food, and other matter dangerous to public health.[60] There must be an organized medical and health service staff, equipment and premises, and facilities for the prompt isolation and care of infected persons in as many ports and seaports as practicable.[61] Also, as many ports and seaports as possible must have facilities for disinfection, disinsecting, deratting, bacteriological investigation, collection and examination of rodents for plague infection, and the collection of food and water samples and their despatch to a laboratory for examination.[62] Other core surveillance facilities required at ports and seaports by the IHR include adequate personnel competent to inspect ships,[63] designation of certain airports as sanitary airports for purposes of yellow fever vaccination and related health measures,[64] and measures against malaria and other diseases of international epidemiological importance.[65]

Part IV of the IHR (Articles 23–49) makes detailed provision for health measures applicable to international traffic and outlines procedure for their application. Article 25 contains precautionary provisions on the application of these measures. It provides that disinfection, disinsecting, deratting, and other sanitary operations shall be carried out so as:

(a) not to cause undue discomfort to any person, or injury to his health;
(b) not to produce any deleterious effect on the structure of a ship, an aircraft, or a vehicle, or on its operating equipment;
(c) to avoid any risk of fire.

In carrying out these operations on cargo, goods, baggage, containers, and other articles, every precaution must be taken to avoid any damage. Part V provides for detailed but specific surveillance measures on the three diseases subject to IHR. For example, Article 52 provides that every state shall employ 'all means within its power to diminish the danger from the spread of plague by rodents and their ectoparasites.' Vaccination against yellow fever may be required of any person leaving an infected area on an international voyage.[66] A person in possession of a valid certificate of vaccination against yellow fever will not be treated as a suspect, even if he has come from an infected area.[67] The IHR also mandate that a master of a sea-going vessel making an international voyage, when required by the health authority in charge of a port, must complete and deliver to the health authority of that port a Maritime Declaration of Health, countersigned by the ship's surgeon if one is carried on board.[68] The master and the ship's surgeon, if one is carried, must supply any information required by the health authority as to health conditions on board during the voyage.[69]

An assessment of the effectiveness and enforcement of the IHR by the WHO reveals that the regulations have been unsuccessful as a global health surveillance tool. Many reasons account for this failure. Chief among them is the fear of excessive measures from other countries if a country suffering an outbreak of cholera, plague, or yellow fever notifies the WHO of that outbreak. Recent examples abound. Cholera epidemics in South America, which were first reported in Peru in 1991, were estimated to have cost over $700 million in trade and other losses.[70] In 1994, a plague outbreak in India led to $1.7 billion losses in trade, tourism, and travel as a result of excessive embargoes and restrictions imposed on India by other countries.[71] Taylor stated that such excessive measures included closing of airports to aircraft that were arriving from India, barriers to importation of foodstuffs, and in many cases the return of Indian guest workers, even though many of them had not lived in India for several years.[72] Most recently, the European Community (EC) imposed a ban on the importation of fresh fish from East Africa following the outbreak of cholera in certain East African countries.[73] At the time of the EU ban in 1997, fish exports from the affected East African countries – Kenya, Mozambique, Tanzania, and Uganda – to European countries stood at $230 million. The EU was their biggest trading partner for fresh fish.[74]

The economic cost of disease outbreaks that are not subject to the IHR remains high. The continuing concern in Europe, for instance, over Bovine Spongiform Encephalopathy ('Mad Cow Disease') has, according to Price-Smith, 'resulted in the embargo of many beef-derived British products and has dictated the culling of a significant proportion of the UK's beef stocks ... In 1996 the UK's European partners summarily banned the import of British beef (in violation of EU trade law). The European Union's ban on British beef products was lifted in 2000, but France continues to defy the EU by maintaining its ban on British beef products.'[75] The recent outbreak of Severe Acute Respiratory Syndrome (SARS), which first emerged in Southern China and spread rapidly to other countries, was reported to have 'rocked Asian markets, ruined the tourist trade of an entire region, nearly bankrupted airlines and spread panic through some of the world's largest countries.'[76] In Canada, the economic cost of the SARS outbreak was estimated at $30 million daily. It is projected that China and South Korea each suffered $2 billion in SARS-related tourism and other economic losses. Visitor arrivals dropped drastically in Singapore, while Hong Kong carrier Cathay Pacific cut its weekly flights by 45 per cent.[77]

Apart from the likely economic embargoes, other reasons often cited for the ineffectiveness of the IHR include the WHO's relative inexperience in the creation and enforcement of legal regimes;[78] the IHR's inability to adapt to changing circumstances in international traffic, trade, and public health,[79] the IHR's limited coverage of only three diseases; and the breakdown, and in many cases, the glaring non-existence, of core disease surveillance capacity in many WHO member states. Senior officials of the WHO admit that the utility of the IHR as a global health regulatory tool is of doubtful validity. Fluss, a former WHO chief of health legislation argued that 'the inconsistency of the earlier regime (for the control of the international spread of diseases) under the succession of conventions and agreements was apparent: none of these sanitary agreements entirely replaced each other, *they did not take account of new methods available for the control of the diseases they covered, and they were not framed to deal adequately with the greatly increased volume and speed of international traffic.*[80] In 1968, the WHO's deputy director-general stated that the IHR's objective of avoiding excessive and unnecessary quarantine measures has failed.[81] In 1974, the chief of the WHO's Epidemiological Surveillance of Communicable Diseases stated that the value of the IHR in ensuring minimum interference with world traffic was questionable.[82]

Because the IHR have become a 'toothless sleeping treaty,' but paradoxically one that cannot easily be banished to the dust bin of public health history, the forty-eighth World Health Assembly in May 1995 passed a resolution calling on the director-general of the WHO to initiate a process of IHR revision.[83] Fidler notes that 'the decision to revise the IHR came in response to the increasing concerns about emerging and re-emerging infectious diseases and the inadequacy of the existing IHR to deal with these growing problems.'[84] Taylor comments that 'revision and expansion of the IHR to provide a basis for effective national, regional, and global action is imperative to prevent the spread of emerging infectious diseases. The regulations have not been revised in over fifteen years and do not regulate procedures for management of highly infectious new diseases and resurgence of deadly old diseases.'[85] Pursuant to the World Health Assembly resolution, in December 1995 the WHO held an informal consultation of experts on IHR revision.[86] Taylor observes that the group of experts did not include any lawyers with expertise in international legislation.[87] The expert group proposed a range of amendments to the IHR, and in February 1998, the WHO circulated to its member states a provisional draft of the revised regulations.[88] The most important of the amendments was the expansion of diseases subject to the regulations beyond plague, yellow fever, and cholera. The requirement to report these three diseases should be replaced by immediate reporting of defined disease syndromes of urgent international importance as well as epidemiological information for their emergence, prevalence, and control. These syndromes are grouped into six categories: acute haemorrhagic fever syndrome, acute respiratory syndrome, acute diarrhoeal syndrome, acute jaundice syndrome, acute neurological syndrome, and other notifiable syndromes. In the draft, all cases of acute haemorragic fevers must be reported immediately. For the other syndromes, only clusters of urgent international importance should be reported. Five factors determine if a cluster of syndromes is of urgent international importance. These include rapid transmission of the syndrome in the community, an unexpectedly high case fatality ratio, a newly recognized syndrome, a high political and media profile, and trade/travel restrictions.

Another change in the Provisional Draft of the IHR related to the power of the WHO to request information from member states based on information the WHO received from other reliable sources: WHO Collaborating Centres, nongovernmental organizations, mass media, other international organizations, and other countries. Previously, the WHO never had this power; it simply waited for a member state to notify it of an outbreak. The rationale behind this proposal is that few, if any, disease outbreaks can be hidden because of extensive global media networks. Innovations in communications technology have rendered state sovereignty irrelevant in disease outbreaks. Independent global outbreak monitoring sources now abound. One example is the Global Public Health Information Network (GPHIN), an electronic surveillance system developed by Health Canada. According to field epidemiologists at the WHO, GPHIN continuously monitors some six hundred sources, including all major news wires, newspapers, and biomedical journals. The system focuses its search on communicable diseases but will soon cover non-communicable diseases, food and water safety, environmental health risks, and the health impact of natural disasters as well.[89] WHO field epidemiologists rely on outbreak information from GPHIN, but have developed steps to verify such information before publishing it in the WHO's authoritative *Weekly Epidemiological Record*.[90] Other internet-based information providers on disease outbreaks include ProMED, a private initiative of the Federation of American Scientists' Program for Monitoring Emergent Infectious Diseases that creates a global system of early detection and response to disease outbreaks[91] and PACNET, an internet-based information provider on disease outbreaks in the Pacific region. With the advent of these innovations disease outbreaks can no longer be hidden under the veil of state sovereignty.

As a prelude to the submission of the Provisional IHR Draft to the World Health Assembly for adoption under Article 21 of the WHO constitution, the WHO conducted a pilot study in randomly selected countries to test the efficacy of syndrome reporting and other changes proposed. The pilot study exposed the gaps and highlighted the difficulties of syndrome reporting, revealing that it was highly unpopular in both developed and developing countries where it were tested. Many developing countries lacked core surveillance capacity for early detection of clusters of the categorized syndromes in the IHR draft, while for developed countries with good surveillance capacity, turning a known disease into a syndrome was highly fanciful. To paraphrase one Swedish epidemiologist, if there is an outbreak of what public health authorities know is cholera, why turn that outbreak into acute diarrhoeal syndrome or rename it something else?[92]

The IHR revision is an ongoing process at the WHO, and regular updates on the progress made have been published in the *Weekly Epidemiological Record*. While syndrome reporting has not been totally discarded, member states will continue to have the opportunity to notify the WHO of diseases specifically by name, if they so desire. Where an entirely new outbreak occurs like the first case of ebola haemorrhagic fever, a member state will have the option of notifing by syndromes of the outbreak in question. The present trend at the WHO on the IHR revision is for all 'urgent international public health events' to be reported by member states. An algorithm of what constitutes an urgent international public health event has been developed. One certain scenario is that not only will outbreaks of infectious diseases be notifiable pursuant to the new IHR, public health risks such as the emergence of clusters of anti-microbial resistance and aspects of food safety-related outbreaks will also be notifiable. In 2001, the World Health Assembly adopted Resolution WHA54.14 *Global Health Security: Epidemic Alert and Response*, which expressly linked the revision of the IHR to the WHO's activities to support its member states in identifying, verifying, and responding to health emergencies of international concern. The Assembly expressed support for two key elements of the IHR revision: development of criteria to define what constitutes a public health emergency of international concern, and identification by all WHO member states of national focal points to collaborate in the IHR revision process. The implementation of the WHO strategy on global health security (epidemic alert and response) will link the IHR with activities at the global, regional, and national levels. The WHO's strategy on global health security has three major components: specific programs for the prevention and control of known epidemic threats such as cholera and influenza, detection and response to health emergencies resulting from unexpected circumstances and unknown etiologies, and improving preparedness through the strengthening of national infrastructure for disease surveillance and control. The WHO, through the IHR revision process, is building synergy and broad consensus with other international organizations whose mandates either overlap with, or relate to, the fundamental principles and purpose of the IHR. These include the Food and Agriculture Organization of the UN, the International Maritime Organization, the World Trade Organization, and the International Civil Aviation Organization. Most of the key proposals for the new IHR are presently being evaluated by WHO member states.[93]

There are other critically important issues to be addressed to enhance the effectiveness of the IHR as a global infectious disease regulatory tool. Focusing on improving compliance with the IHR, Taylor makes a case for the use of supervisory mechanisms, arguing that

> International supervisory mechanisms are extensively used throughout the UN system and have proven to be an effective and widely accepted form of affecting compliance with international commitments ... One effective and increasingly common form of international supervision is a system of auditing or fact-finding in which state reporting is accompanied by independent fact-finding and critical review by an independent monitoring body ... To counter the recognized weaknesses of reporting systems, some international treaty regimes supplement this procedure by an auditing process in which an independent monitoring body can obtain a measure of independent verification of state reports and critically review such reports.[94]

Fidler advances a fairly similar view in his critique of the WHO's non-use of international legal strategies.[95] While these observations are ingenious, the IHR revision process has yet to address one critical issue: the non-existence or collapse of public health surveillance capacities in many countries and the enormous amount of resources urgently needed to resuscitate them.[96] Global health governance in a world sharply divided by socio-economic disparities calls for increased use of regulatory mechanisms, but these regulations must address the pernicious effects of poverty and underdevelopment that plague the collapse or non-existence of essential public health surveillance capacity in most of the developing world.[97] The World Bank has acknowledged that enormous resources are needed to improve public health in developing countries. The bank subsequently prescribed a minimum package of essential clinical services that would include sick-child care, family planning, pre-natal and delivery care, and treatment of tuberculosis and sexually transmitted diseases (STDs).[98] In several underdeveloped countries – Burundi, Chad, Haiti, Guinea-Bissau, and many others – foreign aid accounts for more than 20 per cent of health sector spending.[99] What is needed therefore is a re-focusing of legal regimes that would emerge in the global health context to emphasize incentives for compliance. As Fidler observes, 'Today, the attention being generated on emerging and re-emerging infectious diseases, comes mainly from the developed world, which fears the spread of infectious diseases from the developing world ... Developing states need *massive financial and technical assistance* to deal with endemic diseases more than *rules* to prevent their diseases from travelling to the developed world.'[100]

The inseparable linkage between the IHR, the collapse of national public health infrastructure, and trade and other economic embargoes during outbreaks problematizes what I call *incentive-induced compliance with global health accords*. To paraphrase Thomas Franck, why do powerful nations obey powerless rules?[101] Incentives[102] remain one of the key factors that induce compliance with international norms. Leading international lawyers have explored the jurisprudential dimensions of obligation in the international system and the erudition of Oscar Schachter, Louis Henkin, and Thomas Franck in this aspect of international scholarship is remarkable. Back in 1968, Schachter enumerated thirteen theories often used by international lawyers as the basis of international obligation, and suggested that 'in all these cases the traditional sign-posts of legal obligation have limited utility, at the very least they call for further analysis.'[103] Henkin argues that the threat of sanctions is not always the primary reason why states observe or disobey international rules. States will comply with international law if it is in their best interest to do so; equally, they will disregard law or obligation if the advantages of violation, on a scale of balance, outweigh the advantages of observance.[104] Franck's fairness discourse synthesizes the imperatives of determinate/unambiguous rules with distributive justice; international law's fairness in the distribution of global resources anchored on the Rawlsian scheme of 'moderate scarcity.'[105]

Applying these perspectives to the IHR, what incentives would induce WHO member states, especially developing countries, to comply with the regulations. This question is complex because no single factor on its own can radically change the behaviour of WHO member states with respect to the IHR. While the WHO needs to step up its present ineffective enforcement strategy of the IHR, it must also strive to develop sufficient incentives to induce compliance. The present negative rewards of notification – trade, travel, and economic embargoes – must give way to positive rewards – human, financial, and technical assistance to WHO member states that lack the public health capacity to deal with outbreaks of disease. During outbreaks, the WHO must rigorously defend its global health mandate where member states impose unnecessary trade and travel embargoes beyond WHO measures. Regrettably, the WHO has shied away from this type of advocacy and proactive strategy. Its condemnation of the EU ban of fresh fish from East Africa following a cholera outbreak in certain East African countries is a rare exception,[106] as well as its issuance of travel advisories during the SARS outbreak. A combination of this type of robust advocacy and the assured promise of incentives may significantly improve the 'compliance pull' of the new IHR.

II Framework Convention on Tobacco Control

Negotiations by WHO member states for a Framework Convention on Tobacco Control directly implicate the relevance of international law in global health governance. In May 1999, the World Health Assembly, the governing body of the WHO, adopted (by consensus) Resolution WHA52.18 urging the director-general of the WHO to start a process of multilateral negotiations on the convention.[107] In the fifty-plus years of the WHO's history, the FCTC process is the first time that the organization has exercised its treaty-making powers under Article 19 of its constitution.

Tobacco use is one of the leading causes of preventable deaths, and a leading contributor to burdens of disease globally.[108] There are over 1.25 billion smokers in the world, and it is estimated that about four million people die yearly from tobacco-related diseases. Although tobacco use is a leading cause of premature death in industrialized countries, the epidemic of tobacco addiction, disease, and death is continuing to shift rapidly to developing countries.[109] Leading tobacco multinationals targeted growing markets in Latin America in the 1960s, the newly industrialized economies of Asia (Japan, The Republic of Korea, Taiwan and Thailand) in the 1980s, and increasingly targeted women and young persons in Africa in the 1990s.[110] As succinctly put by Fidler, 'Western tobacco companies succeeded in riding the waves of international trade law, liberal triumphalism and globalizing Western culture in penetrating the markets and lungs of millions of people in the developing world.'[111] It is now increasingly evident that a 'double jeopardy' looms large for developing countries: the burden of a tobacco epidemic will be added to their already heavy morbidity and mortality burdens from communicable diseases like malaria, tuberculosis, and HIV/AIDS. Today, a majority of smokers live in developing countries (800 million); most are men (700 million) and 300 million are Chinese. At current levels of consumption, the tobacco epidemic is expected to kill up to 8.4 million people per year by 2020, with 70 per cent of these deaths occurring in developing nations. If current consumption patterns remain unchecked, within the next thirty years tobacco use will be the leading cause of premature deaths worldwide.[112]

Tobacco use is medically associated with a range of diseases and fatal health conditions, including lung and bladder cancers, heart disease, bronchitis and emphysema, and increased antenatal and prenatal mortality.[113] The WHO states that the nature of the smoking epidemic varies from country to country. In developed countries, cardiovascular disease, particularly ischaemic heart disease, is the most common smoking-related cause of death. In populations where cigarette smoking has been common for several decades, about 90 per cent of lung cancer, 15–20 per cent of other cancers, 75 per cent of chronic bronchitis and emphysema, and 25 per cent of cardiovascular disease at ages 35–69 years are attributable to tobacco. Tobacco-related cancer constitutes 16 per cent of the total incidence of cancer cases – and 30 per cent of cancer deaths – in developing countries, while the corresponding figure in developed countries is 10 per cent.[114] Smoking is also associated with about 12 per cent of all tuberculosis deaths. The WHO suggests that this could be because a lung damaged by tobacco may offer a supportive environment for the infectious tuberculosis bacillus.[115] For non-smokers, inhalation of tobacco smoke – passive or second-hand smoking – poses serious health risks. Exposure to other people's smoking is associated with a risk of lung cancer and several other health ailments in children – sudden infant death syndrome, low birth weight, intrauterine growth retardation, and children's respiratory disease.[116]

The political economy of tobacco and its regulation poses difficult challenges not because a tobacco epidemic is more complex than the series of similar transnational problems that have been effectively regulated in the past decades, but because the WHO-FCTC confronts very difficult questions on a number of issues: liberalization of international trade rules; the powerful influence and enormous wealth of tobacco multinationals, as evidenced by their aggressive marketing strategies worldwide; the dependence of some developing world economies on tobacco farming as foreign exchange earner;[117] and the complexity of harmonizing cigarette taxes, policies, and advertisements nationally and multilaterally. A global tobacco treaty could therefore easily bump into the global trade arena where the WTO now holds sway as a strict enforcer of age-old trade rules such as 'national treatment' and 'most favoured nation' principles.[118] Article XX(b) of the General

Agreement on Tariffs and Trade (GATT) 1947 provides that trade-restricting measures necessary to protect human health are justifiable if those measures do not constitute arbitrary or unjustifiable discrimination between countries. In practice, striking the required delicate balance between trade and public health, especially with tobacco, has proved challenging. In the Thai Cigarettes Case (*United States v. Thailand*),[119] the United States challenged, before a GATT panel, the prohibition of importation of foreign cigarettes by Thailand as an unjustifiable and discriminatory trade restriction that violated (national treatment principle) Article XI of the GATT. The United States argued that the real objective of the Thai tobacco ban was not the protection of public health in Thailand but creating a monopoly for Thai tobacco and protecting Thai-made cigarettes from foreign competition. Thailand relied on Article XX(b) of the GATT and argued that the import ban was designed to protect public health in Thailand. Smoking was harmful to health, and opening the Thai market to imported cigarettes would lead to more smoking, deaths, and increased medical costs. Rejecting the argument of Thailand, the trade panel ruled that Thailand's practice of permitting the sale of domestic cigarettes while not permitting the importation of foreign cigarettes was an inconsistency with the General Agreement that does not come within the ambit of the public health exception in Article XX(b).

The WHO Tobacco Free Initiative, the unit responsible for the FCTC, is versed in the complexities in the relationship among tobacco, public health, and international law with respect to the WHO's tobacco treaty. As argued Taylor and Bettcher,

> trade liberalization and market penetration have been linked to a greater risk of increased tobacco consumption, particularly in low- and middle-income countries ... The tobacco industry has also taken advantage of direct forms of market penetration in cash-hungry governments of poor countries via direct foreign investment, by either licensing with a domestic monopoly in joint ventures, or other strategic partnering with domestic companies ... As the vector of the tobacco epidemic, the tobacco industry is well aware of the characteristics of globalization and is attempting to manipulate globalization trends in its favour.[120]

Notwithstanding the oscillation of tobacco control between the imperatives of trade liberalization and public health protection/promotion, negotiations for the WHO's Tobacco treaty started in 2000. In May 1999, the World Health Assembly established a working group to analyse potential elements to be included in the tobacco treaty, and an inter-governmental negotiating body (open to the WHO's 192 member states) to negotiate and draft the proposed WHO FCTC and related protocols.[121] The Tobacco Free Initiative of the WHO prepared background documents[122] for the working group enumerating possible elements to be covered by the convention[123] and other elements of subsequent protocols.[124] Component parts of the Framework Convention include preamble, principles and objectives, obligations, institutions, implementation mechanisms, law-making processes, and final clauses (signatories, reservations, ratification and withdrawal). Potential elements for subsequent related protocols include: cigarette prices and harmonization of taxes, measures against smuggling, duty-free tobacco products, tobacco advertising and sponsorship, reporting of toxic constituents of tobacco products, packaging and labelling, tobacco and agricultural policy, sharing of information. Negotiations on these issues by the inter-governmental negotiating body of over 135 WHO member states were concluded in 2003. On 21 May 2003, the World Health Assembly, comprised of the 192 member states of the WHO unanimously adopted the FCTC.[125] Under the terms of the convention, forty signatories are required before it comes into force. Although it may be too early in the day to assess the effectiveness of the FCTC as a global health promotion tool, two very important facts emerged from the three-year negotiation process. First, the FCTC is based on incontrovertible epidemiological evidence that tobacco is harmful to health,[126] and needs to be globally regulated because of the global networks of tobacco conglomerates. According to WHO Director-General Gro Harlem Brundtland, 'we need an international response to an international problem.'[127] Second, the FCTC represents a radical change of approach by the WHO in pursuing its global public health mandate. After decades of relegating international law to the margins of global health promotion, the WHO has finally decided to exercise its constitutional treaty-making power to negotiate a legally binding multilateral treaty. The WHO FCTC and related protocols are not just another international treaty but, as the WHO director-general stated, 'a product and a process and a public health movement ... a pathfinder in public health.'[128]

The WHO has now stepped into a terrain in which the organization historically has no experience: the use of international treaties in global/multilateral health governance. It is therefore useful to conduct a comparative assessment of treaties used to forge global/multilateral environmental cooperation. The FCTC is patterned after a similar framework convention process on global environmental governance: climate change and ozone depletion. Also, as argued above, the disparities between the developed and developing worlds compel a refocusing of emergent global health regimes to resuscitate collapsing or non-existent public health infrastructure across the developing world. Both the IHR and the FCTC, the WHO's only two governance mechanisms, must grapple with and confront the chronic need for financial and technical assistance to developing countries. Global environmental treaties, though hardly infallible, have addressed this question more elaborately, and the WHO, in its enforcement of a revised IHR and FCTC, will have to learn from the resource-sharing dynamics of global environmental regimes enforced by other multilateral organizations. The UN Convention for the Protection of the Ozone Layer and the World Bank's Global Environmental Facility (GEF) provide two examples.

F A Comparative Overview of Global Health Governance and Global Environmental Governance: Lessons from the Ozone Layer Convention and the Global Environmental Facility

I United Nations Convention for the Protection of the Ozone Layer, 1985[129]

In the late 1970s and early 1980s, it became obvious that ozone depletion[130] was a serious global issue that neither unilateral nor regional approaches could solve.[131] After years of intensive diplomacy under the auspices of the United Nations Environment Programme (UNEP),[132] the Vienna Convention for the Protection of the Ozone Layer was adopted on 22 March 1985.[133]

The Ozone Convention is basically a framework. It contains no legally binding commitments for countries to cut the levels of their CFC emissions because, as Birnie and Boyle point out, it was difficult for states to agree in 1985 on proposals for more specific measures to control ozone depletion.[134] The convention noted that ozone depletion was a global problem that required international cooperation because of the serious risks it posed to human health and the environment. It contains general obligations for cooperation between states for further research, systematic observation, and exchange of information.[135] Like most framework conventions, the Ozone Convention established basic principles and a permanent organ for further negotiation of related legally binding protocols. In 1987, the Montreal Protocol on Substances That Deplete the Ozone Layer was adopted.[136] The Montreal Protocol and its subsequent London Amendments[137] set an important precedent in the governance of global issues because of the special treatment given to developing countries.[138] The London Amendments endorsed a multilateral fund regime consisting of voluntary contributions from industrialized to developing countries.[139] Because of the enormous costs involved in phasing out certain CFCs and other substances by 2040, the multilateral fund covers incremental costs incurred by developing countries that switch to ozone-friendly technologies. The multilateral fund regime was instrumental in creating a functional system. Since the fund became operational in 1991, it has financed the development of thirty-nine country programs. Nine of these programs represent approximately 20 per cent of controlled substances by developing countries – including China, Mexico, Brazil, Malaysia, Egypt, and Jordan.[140] The main organ of the fund is an Executive Committee of fourteen members, seven of whom are selected by developing country states parties to the Montreal Protocol, and the other seven by industrialized states parties. The committee monitors the implementation of operational policies and guidelines and the disbursement of resources, and develops the budget of the fund and eligibility criteria for funding. Decisions are taken by consensus, or if no consensus is reached, by a two-thirds majority of the parties present and voting.[141] Despite the limits of the obligation to report information pursuant to Article 7 of the Protocol, the Ozone Convention and the Montreal Protocol have contributed positively to the governance of a global environmental problem. The view has been expressed that both the Ozone Convention and the Montreal Protocol 'have created one of the most elaborate and sophisticated models of international control and supervision for environmental purposes.'[142]

II The World Bank: Instrument Establishing the Global Environmental Facility[143]

The Global Environmental Facility was originally set up in 1990 as a three-year pilot study between the World Bank, the United Nations Environment Programme (UNEP), and the United Nations Development Programme (UNDP), with an initial sum of $1.2 billion. Its objective was grant financing of global environmental projects. Some scholars assert that the multilateral fund regime of the Montreal Protocol on Substances That Deplete the Ozone Layer influenced the GEF.[144] After the United Nations Commission on Environment and Development (UNCED) process, the Rio Conference on Environment and Development 1992 adopted a range of global environmental treaties and soft-law declarations.[145] At Rio, treaties on climate change[146] and biodiversity[147] were opened for signature; a non-binding statement of principles on global forests was declared;[148] and Agenda 21, a program of action by the international community addressing major environmental and development priorities leading into the twenty-first century, was adopted.[149] The implementation of these treaties and the soft-law declarations posed enormous financial and technical challenges in most developing countries. As a result, a decision was taken at the Rio Conference on Environment and Development to restructure the existing GEF in accordance with the principles of universality, transparency, and democracy. A new Instrument was adopted in March 1994. Birnie and Boyd observe that 'its general function is to provide funding to help developing countries meet agreed incremental costs of measures taken pursuant to UNCED Agenda 21 to achieve agreed global environmental benefits with regard to climate change, biological diversity, international waters, and ozone layer depletion. It is also specifically designated for these purposes in the Ozone Layer, Climate Change and Biological Diversity Conventions.'[150] The GEF secretariat is located at the World Bank, and the bank uses the facility to assist countries whose annual per capita income is below $4,000. The UNDP and UNEP are involved with training, technical assistance, research, and maintenance of consistency with international environmental treaties and norms. The GEF has funded many environmental projects in developing countries and has been hailed by scholars for its equitable treatment of developing countries based on the concept of 'common but differentiated responsibility.'[151] The governing body of GEF is a council composed of thirty-two members with a balance of developed and developing countries. Decisions require a double majority of 60 per cent of all members plus a majority of 60 per cent (by contribution) of all donors. Notwithstanding its imperfections, the GEF has emerged as a major funder of global environmental issues that threaten all of humanity.

Global environmental governance, through the GEF and Montreal Protocol, has used international treaties to foster cooperation and consensus in a divided world. Environmental problems such as climate change and ozone depletion are similar to public health problems such as infectious diseases and the tobacco epidemic. They are all global issues that threaten populations irrespective of national boundaries. It is therefore imperative to explore the adaptation of governance mechanisms like the GEF and Montreal Protocol in the global health context.

G Summary of the Arguments

This chapter argued that the multilateralization/globalization of public health in a world order composed of sovereign nation states is prone to the complexities of politicization based on strategic and other interests of countries. The politics are fuelled in part by South-North disparities, as illustrated by the nuclear weapons debate at the World Health Assembly, but a plethora of other political issues inhibits contemporary multilateral health accords. Emerging global health governance perspectives have failed to explore the role(s) that international law has begun to play in forging consensus on multilateral environmental issues and to seek ways to create a similar role for international law in the global health context. With its revision of the IHR and adoption of a global tobacco treaty, the WHO seems to be waking up after decades of neglect of international law. The success of the emerging legal strategies, the IHR and FCTC, requires the application of enormous human, technical, and financial resources within countries as well as sustained advocacy and political will on the part of the WHO. The principle of 'common but differentiated responsibility' on which both the GEF and Montreal Protocol are based recalls the often-ridiculed maxim of 'in terms of contribution; from each according to his wealth, and in terms of distribution; to each according to his need.' Poverty, underdevelopment, and a rigid interpretation of state sovereignty cannot impede multilateral solutions to global problems; the GEF and Montreal Protocol have instead shown that poverty and socio-economic disparities between countries can be used as a 'sword' with which to attack transnational/global threats. Both instruments emerged through international law, which must play a formidable role in the dynamics of microbe-humanity interaction. Politicization has been a dominant phenomenon of multilateralism from the earliest historical accounts, and will remain an important factor in the coming decades. Nonetheless, within the global social milieu of public health, poverty, and underdevelopment, international law emerges as an important post-ontological tool to strategize and reconfigure the boundaries of the contemporary turbulent multilateral health order based on mutual vulnerability and the canons of enlightened self-interest.

Case Study: Global Malaria Policy and Ethno-Pharmacological/Traditional Medical Therapies for Malaria in Africa

A Overview of the Argument

This chapter explores multilateral malaria control policy and its relationship with 'ethno-medicine,'[1] 'traditional medicine,'[2] or 'ethnopharmacology'[3] in Africa. The relevance of ethno-medical or ethnopharmacological approaches to a tropical disease like malaria remains controversial despite volumes of seminal works, a series of international conferences, and the elaborate multilateral eradication/control strategies the disease has generated in the past decades. One source of this controversy is science. Western scientific discourse often dismisses African traditional medicine, including ethno-medical malaria therapies, as unscientific. Staugard argues that throughout history, an ambitious search for physical, social, and mental well-being has preoccupied the minds of humankind in all cultures. As a result, two systematic responses to ill-health and disease have emerged. One is the modern system of medicine founded by Hippocrates and his pupils on the Greek Island of Kos, the other is traditional medicine, which is as old as humankind.[4] From ancient times, the two systems have co-existed, albeit with hostility. Staugard states that modern medicine has often demonstrated its hostility towards traditional health care by categorizing it as 'quackery' or 'witchcraft.'[5] This categorization arises from the often mistaken Western conception of the herbalist, diviner, magician, and faith healer as belonging to a single and indivisible health delivery compartment that lacked methodological or analytical Western scientific investigation. Before the 1970s, as Sindiga observes, most studies concerned with African traditional medicine linked it with beliefs, religion, and rituals. Such studies, pioneered by the structural functional school of British anthropology, concluded uncritically that African disease aetiologies were basically moral, social, and devoid of any scientific insights and assessment.[6] According to De Smet, 'many Western doctors and pharmacologists believe that ethnopharmacology yields nothing but armchair amusement.'[7] Since 1972, the World Health Organization has consistently called for the integration of traditional medical therapies into the corpus of national health care systems of member states.[8] Notwithstanding the WHO resolutions, however, multilateral health policy still grapples with an appalling 'regime deficit' on the integration of traditional ethnopharmacological practices as part of its core framework.[9]

There are two persuasive and related reasons why ethno-medicine is relevant in global malaria policy. The first is global multiculturalism and its implications for the health of populations across radically divergent cultures; the second reason relates to the cost and affordability of health care in Africa, where ethno-medical therapies for malaria may be readily available at a price the community can afford, while orthodox (Western) malaria medicines are not.[10] Every society, in the developing world and elsewhere, deals with illness and disease in a variety of ways. Ethno-medicine has no unifying theme across societies; thus the therapies it provides vary from one society or culture to another. Traditional medicine, according to Akerele, comprises practices based on beliefs established years before the development and spread of modern medicine.[11] Ethno-medical knowledge of plants by indigenous people across societies and cultures, for instance has 'long served as a crucial source of medicines either directly as therapeutic agents, as starting points for the elaboration of more complex semi-synthetic compounds or as synthetic compounds.'[12]

In most African societies, multiculturalism has given rise to what some scholars call 'medical pluralism,' the existence in a single society of differently designed and conceived medical systems.[13] Such systems may either compete with or complement one another.[14] Populations in the developing world resort to both traditional medicine and Western medicine simultaneously for the same illness, or at different times for different illnesses. It has been observed, for example, that 'African peoples believe in traditional medicine and it is not uncommon to see patients in hospitals permitting themselves to be treated by modern medicine during the day and having recourse to the recipes of traditional medicine at night.'[15] The holistic approach of traditional medicine to the art of healing has continued to endear it to many of its adherents: a sizeable 80 per cent of the population in most African rural areas. As persuasively argued by one scholar of ethno-medicine in Africa: 'The holistic concept in traditional medicine is commendable, in that the patient's mind and soul as well as body are considered together during treatment ... One increasingly important aspect of the African worldview is the belief that human beings cannot be separated from nature. There is therefore no overwhelming desire to conquer the natural world or dominate it ... [The] African worldview is eco-centric ... It binds humans and the rest of nature together with the same umbilical cord.'[16]

Mbiti, a renowned scholar of African Religions and Philosophy, argues that diseases and misfortunes are regarded as having social and religious origins. The treatment process must therefore go beyond merely addressing their symptoms to consider their social implications as well as strategies to prevent their reoccurrence.[17] Some scholars, however, dismiss the holistic nature of traditional medicine as falsehood. As observed by Phillips, 'stereotypes suggest, for example, that traditional medicine is holistic, whilst modern medicine sees only the disease. This might be true in relatively isolated, small-scale societies, but in large Asian and African villages and towns, there is probably almost as much impersonal treatment by traditional healers as there is by practitioners of modern medicine. The holistic appeal of traditional medicine – that it considers the patient as a whole person, in his or her domestic and social setting – may in fact be perpetuating a false image.'[18]

The holistic appeal of traditional medicine is a culture-relative phenomenon, just as ethno-medical therapies differ across societies and cultures. There may be instances in which the relationship between the traditional healer and patient is impersonal. Nonetheless, in Africa, the dominant world-views and the concept of personhood as proffered by scholars like Mbiti[19] and Kalu[20] both assert the holistic character of traditional medicine. The prohibitive cost of orthodox Western malaria medicines, the emergence of strains of malaria that resist available (Western) drugs, and the disinterestedness of leading transnational pharmaceutical companies in researching affordable malaria drugs because of the poor return on investment also help to sustain the population of traditional medicine for malaria treatment in African rural communities. Traditional medical therapies are relatively cheap, and the traditional healers who apply them are accessible. Using social science qualitative interviews, this chapter hypothesizes these facts squarely from the views and behavioural practices of populations in an Eastern Nigerian rural community. I use the emergent perspectives from these interviews to argue for an integration of traditional malaria therapies into the core multilateral initiatives on malaria control.

At present, there is a sizeable volume of literature on ethno-biological/medical knowledge of indigenous populations[21] across the world from an intellectual property perspective.[22] The concern of this chapter is quite different; I am largely concerned with fashioning an inclusive and holistic malaria globalism founded on Richard Falk's concept of globalism-from-below to counter the contemporary exclusive and peripheral malaria globalism founded on globalism-from-above.[23] The urgency of this endeavour stems from the present conundrum facing populations in the developing world, whereby globalization will likely erode traditional medical therapies while doing nothing to place Western medicines within their reach, or to synthesize their traditional therapies with Western medical therapies.[24]

B The WHO's Roll Back Malaria Campaign: Its Mission and Vision

The WHO launched a global campaign to eradicate malaria in 1955. By 1969, when it abandoned the campaign, malaria had been completely eradicated from the industrialized countries where it was hitherto endemic, while parts of Asia and Latin

America had witnessed significant reduction in its morbidity. In Africa, the WHO's eradication campaign had been focused on only three countries – Ethiopia, South Africa, and Zimbabwe – because 'eradication was considered not yet feasible in other countries.'[25] Globally, Africa continues to bear the heaviest burden of malaria mortality and morbidity. Malaria is most serious in the poorest countries and among populations living under impoverished conditions. It undermines the health and welfare of families, endangers the survival of children, debilitates the active populations and impoverishes individuals and countries.[26] Malaria is thus linked with the social and economic development of African societies. According to the WHO, 'malaria and underdevelopment are closely intertwined ... The disease causes widespread premature death and suffering, imposes financial hardship on poor households, and holds back economic growth and improvements in living standards.'[27]

In the early 1990s the WHO changed its malaria policy from eradication to control. The first Global Malaria Control Strategy was endorsed at a Ministerial Conference on Malaria Control convened by the WHO in Amsterdam in 1992. The United Nations General Assembly endorsed it in 1994, and the United Nations Economic and Social Council adopted its action plan in 1995. The four basic elements of the global malaria control strategy include:

(i) provision of early diagnosis and prompt treatment;
(ii) planning and implementation of selective and sustainable preventive measures, including vector control;
(iii) early detection, containment, and prevention of outbreaks;
(iv) strengthening of local capacities in basic and applied research to promote the regular assessment of each country's malaria situation, particularly the ecological, social, and economic determinants of the disease.

The WHO's global malaria control strategy since 1992 was presumably subsumed into the Roll Back Malaria campaign launched by WHO Director-General Gro-Harlem Brundtland in 1998. Roll Back Malaria consolidates the experience of the past twenty years, and is committed to cutting the burden of malaria in endemic areas by half by 2010. The campaign is a partnership of agencies: the World Health Organization, the World Bank, the United Nations Children's Fund, and the United Nations Development Programme. Major development agencies from the United States, Canada, Sweden, the European Union, The Netherlands, France, Germany, Belgium, and Italy, as well as foundations and research institutes, maintain close links with the campaign.

Roll Back Malaria has six basic elements:

(i) evidence-based decisions using surveillance, appropriate responses and building of community awareness;

  (ii) rapid diagnosis and treatment;

 (iii) multiple prevention: better multi-pronged protection using insecticide-
       treated mosquito nets, environmental management to control mosquitoes,
       and making pregnancy safer;

 (iv) focused research to develop new medicines, vaccines and insecticides and to
       help epidemiological and operational activities;

  (v) co-ordinated action for strengthening existing health services, policies and
       providing technical support; and

 (vi) harmonized actions to build a dynamic global movement.[28]

One of the often-cited reasons for the resurgence of malaria in Africa and other malaria endemic regions is drug resistance. The WHO argues that 'the potentially lethal malaria parasite *plasmodium falciparum*, has shown itself capable of developing resistance to nearly all available anti-malarial drugs. Chloroquine, perhaps the best ever anti-malarial drug, and certainly the most widely used, is now failing against *falciparum* malaria in most areas of the tropical world.'[29] As a result, investment in the production of effective and affordable malaria drugs is an integral part of the Roll Back Malaria project. Prior to Roll Back Malaria, the Multilateral Initiative on Malaria (MIM) in Africa was launched in Dakar, Senegal, in January 1997 as a coalition of the public and private sectors to promote malaria research in Africa. As part of the initiative, a Task Force on Malaria Research Capability and Strengthening in Africa focusing on the needs of malaria endemic countries is being coordinated by the UNDP, the World Bank, and the WHO's Department of Tropical Diseases Research. With an annual budget of about $3 billion, the main research areas to be funded are antimalarial drug policy and chemotherapy, epidemiology, pathogenesis, vectors, health systems, and social science.[30]

In November 1999, another public-private partnership for the discovery of new anti-malarial drugs, Medicines for Malaria Venture (MMV), was launched in Geneva as a new but autonomous partner to Roll Back Malaria. Initial co-sponsors of the MMV are the WHO, the International Federation of Pharmaceutical Manufacturers Associations (IFPMA), the World Bank, the U.K. Department for International Development (DFID), the Swiss Agency for Development and Co-operation, the Global Forum for Health Research, The Rockefeller Foundation, Global Roll Back Malaria Partnership, and The Netherlands Ministry of Development Co-operation. The goal of the MMV is to secure, on average, the registration of one new anti-malarial drug every five years. This will require raising US$15 million annually by 2001 and US$30 million annually thereafter. According to WHO former Director-General Brundtland, 'MMV has been created because the increased costs of developing and registering pharmaceutical products, coupled with the prospects of inadequate commercial returns, have resulted in the withdrawal of the majority of research-based pharmaceutical companies from R&D investment in tropical diseases and especially from discovery research activities.'[31]

MMV is an entrepreneurial non-profit venture legally incorporated as a foundation under Swiss law. It will negotiate licensing agreements with its partners that recognize intellectual property rights. The major goal of these agreements will be the commercialization of products/medicines for low-income populations at affordable prices. A royalty income may accrue to MMV on products that earn significant returns for MMV's commercial partners. These returns will feed back into MMV's fund to offset the need for future donations.[32]

MMV offers a new approach. It is a partnership that brings together the pharmaceutical industry, with its knowledge and expertise in drug discovery and development, and the public sector, with its expertise in basic biology and field studies. It is also argued that MMV is the response of the private and public sectors to the growing crisis of malaria and the high priority given to rolling back malaria by the WHO and other partners. Through MMV, the private and public sectors are able to bring together the best of each other's strengths, and contribute to the Roll Back Malaria goal of halving the global malaria burden by the year 2010 and sustaining this effort in the future.[33]

Roll Back Malaria and MMV are important and innovative milestones in multilateral public health. They represent a collaborative public-private partnership to tackle a disease that arguably attacks the poor, with its heaviest health and economic burden endemic within Africa.[34] Nevertheless, both Roll Back Malaria and MMV, as multilateral policies, must be analysed against the perceptions of local populations in Africa, whose disease the Roll Back Malaria public-private partnership strives to tackle. If the multilateral policy and the behavioural practices of populations in malaria-endemic societies are antithetical, then an effective synthesis must be canvassed to close the emergent regime deficit. In pursuing this goal I examine the perceptions of interviewed populations in Southeastern Nigeria on the traditional medical approaches to malaria.

C Traditional Medicine and Malaria in Southeastern Nigeria: Voices at the Margins[35]

In December 2000, I conducted semi-structured (depth/focused) interviews on traditional malaria therapies in a sample rural population: a small group of unevenly divided men and women.[36] The interviews focused substantially on behavioural practices, beliefs, and attitudes of the interviewed group with respect to malaria. The interviews were supplemented by detailed conversations I had with two traditional healers (experts on ethno-medical diagnosis and therapies for malaria) and a Western-trained physician, all of whom reside within the same community as health care providers.[37] These conversations were aimed primarily at gaining deeper insights into the traditional malaria therapies as well as the attitudes and beliefs of the interviewed population with respect to these therapies. This study investigates the importance of these traditional therapies to local communities and argues for their integration within multilateral malaria policies.

The interviews were based on the use of an interview guide: a written list of non-exhaustive questions to be covered during the interviews.[38] As observed by the WHO, depth/focused interviews assume enough prior exploration of the topic to enable the researcher to formulate the relevant questions that relate to the topic to be investigated.[39] The present investigation therefore builds on previous studies on similar issues in Southeastern Nigeria. In a study conducted in 1999, Okafor identified fifty-five plants used in traditional medicine by 75 per cent of rural populations that inhabit the low-lying *Ibo* heartland in Eastern Nigeria.[40] Local people use these plants as therapies for diseases and health conditions including malaria fever and its symptoms.

In the present study, every interviewee admitted to having had an attack of malaria many times in the past, incontrovertible proof that malaria was a common ailment that attacked local populations where ever it is endemic. An overwhelming 90 per cent of interviewees stated that they knew they had malaria if they start having such symptoms as pain, severe fever, aches (joint aches and headaches), loss of appetite, vomiting, dizziness, and fatigue.[41] Although their responses are diverse and varied, the popularity of traditional medicine is conspicuous when interviewees described the actions they take to obtain diagnosis and therapies when they suspect they have malaria. About 65 per cent consult traditional healers who predominantly use natural herbs and roots as curative therapies. About 25 per cent rely on immediate self-help by seeking to buy Western drugs from vendors popularly called 'patent medicine dealers.' The remaining 10 per cent consult medical doctors in clinics and hospitals located in the community. The two groups that either rely on self-help or consult medical doctors in clinics/hospitals admitted to having also consulted traditional healers in the past for treatment.[42] Reasons for resorting to traditional medicine, according to the interviewees, ranged from its relative cheapness to the ready availability and accessibility of traditional healers in the community. Consistent with the views of the interviewees, Salako has observed that 'in many parts of Africa, unofficial health care systems and operators exist side by side with the official system and include herbal healers, medicine vendors and spiritual healers. These alternative systems are usually more readily accessible and cheaper than the formal system, and many patients seek treatment from these groups first, turning to the formal system only when they fail. There is a clear need to improve the formal system so that it becomes more accessible, acceptable and affordable to ordinary people and thus becomes their first choice.'[43]

Contrary to the dominant school of thought that traditional healers are secretive and often unwilling to divulge their therapies, the two I interviewed were open and went as far as to show me a collection of herbs and roots which they use in a wide variety of malaria therapies. The healers had a local name for every herb, bark, or root. Some of the herbs and roots are boiled or cooked and the patient bathes in the hot water residue. Other substances (mainly roots and barks of trees) are recommended to be taken with a moderate amount of alcohol, mainly local gin. The healers recommend that most other herbs be boiled with food and taken with lunch or supper. The difficult question was how the healers knew that those herbs and roots had medicinal value. They reiterated the view that traditional medicine had been handed down from generation to generation through lineage, family, or even oral tradition, and that before Western medicine arrived in Africa with colonialism, the use of herbs for therapies was already established and widespread. Championing this school of thought, Dr Raymond Arazu, a Catholic priest and a leading traditional healer who uses indigenous herbs for multi-disease curative therapies in Eastern Nigeria, observed that 'the plants which God created are there for our needs – their roots, the leaves and so on. From time immemorial, everywhere, people have used these means to cure sick people. There are about five different kinds of plants whose leaves when used in the proper way cure ulcer ... I am only following what my people ... were doing before this modern craze for petrochemical drugs which have seemingly replaced the herbs.'[44]

Observations and responses from healers and interviewees who adhere to traditional medicines revealed two sets of related facts. First, malaria is a very common, endemic but life-threatening ailment of the populace. Almost everybody knows what it is, or at least could correctly guess its symptoms, and they called it *iba* in their mother tongue, Igbo. Second, traditional herbs are readily available within the community's forest and biodiversity resources for its treatment. These facts are consistent with the predominant world-view of the Ibo ethnic group in Eastern Nigeria as mirrored by the acclaimed novelist Chinua Achebe in his famous literary work, *Things Fall Apart*.[45] To illustrate how this world-view relates to traditional and contemporary malaria therapies, Achebe's depiction of Okonkwo, the hero and lead character, a repository of this ethno-medical knowledge on malaria, is reproduced below. Achebe wrote

Okonkwo turned on his side and went back to sleep. He was roused in the morning by someone banging on his door. 'Who is that?' he growled. He knew it must be Ekwefi. Of his three wives Ekwefi was the only one who would have the audacity to bang on his door. 'Ezinma is dying,' came her voice, and all the tragedy and sorrow of her life were packed in those words. Okonkwo sprang from his bed, pushed back the bolt on his door and ran into Ekwefi's hut. Ezinma lay shivering on a mat beside a huge fire that her mother had kept burning all night. 'It is *iba*,' said Okonkwo as he took his machete and went into the bush to collect the leaves and grasses and barks of trees that went into the making of medicine for iba. Ekwefi knelt beside the sick child, occasionally feeling with her palm the wet, burning forehead. Ezinma was an only child and the center of her mother's world ... Okonkwo returned from the bush carrying on his left shoulder a large bundle of *grasses and leaves, roots and barks of medicinal trees and shrubs*. He went into Ekwefi's hut, put down his load and sat down. 'Get me a pot,' he said, 'and leave the child alone.' Ekwefi went to bring the pot and Okonkwo selected the best from his bundle, in their due proportions, and cut them up. He put them in the pot and Ekwefi poured in some water. 'Is that enough?' she asked when she had had poured in about half of the water in the bowl. 'A little more ... I said a little. Are you deaf?' Okonkwo roared at her. She set the pot on the fire and Okonkwo took up his machete to return to his obi. 'You must watch the pot carefully,' he said as he went, 'and don't allow it to boil over. If it does its power will be gone.' He went away to his hut and Ekwefi began to tend the medicine pot almost as if it was itself a sick child. Her eyes went constantly from Ezinma to the boiling pot and back to Ezinma. Okonkwo returned when he felt the medicine had cooked long enough. He looked it over and said it was done. 'Bring me a low stool for Ezinma,' he said, 'and a thick mat.' He took down the pot from the fire and placed it in front of the stool. He then roused Ezinma and placed her on the stool, astride the steaming pot. The thick mat was thrown over both. Ezinma struggled to escape from the choking and overpowering steam, but she was held down. She started to cry. When the mat was at last removed she was drenched in perspiration. Ekwefi mopped her with a piece of cloth and she lay down on a dry mat and was soon asleep.[46]

The type of ethno-medical therapy described by Achebe abounds in every society and culture across the malaria-endemic parts of the world. It has existed for ages and is still alive in our own time. Such theropies have many adherents and many men and women, like Okonkwo in *Things Fall Apart*, are the repositories of such knowledge. Traditional therapies interact with modern medicine in an environment of medical pluralism, and thus the interaction between traditional malaria therapies and global malaria control policy warrants our attention. My evaluation of this interaction will be conducted within the paradigmatic discourse of globalization-from-above and globalization-from-below, two contrasting concepts on global governance.

D Global Malaria Control Strategies: Globalization-from-Above or Globalization-from-Below?

As we have seen, Richard Falk coined the terms globalization-from-above and globalization-from-below as operational paradigms to explore the dimensions of emergent global governance in a world order marked by the Westphalian system.[47] Contemporary global governance has witnessed tensions between states on the one hand and a coalition of transnational civil society on the other. Global policies incubated at multilateral forums by states acting as harbingers and repositories of political power within geopolitical boundaries often run counter to civil-society-oriented ideals. Falk proposes a framework aimed at the animation of civil society in relation to a transnational agenda involving human rights, environmental protection, public health, social and economic justice, disarmament, and other substantive areas in which global market forces and states are perceived to be endangering human well-being. These civic-society pressures constitute a formidable challenge to governments to be more protective of global public goods. The multiple dimensions of this civic-society challenge come within the rubric of globalization-from-below.[48] In a sharp contrast, the contemporary global social and environmental agendas are often detrimental to a range of public goods. This latter phenomenon, driven by market forces in coalition with most governments, is attributed to globalization-from-above.[49]

Globalization-from-below, in the sense that Falk uses the term, does not constitute teleological cosmopolitanism. In essence, its agenda does not foresee the extinction of the Westphalian state, nor does it postulate that the nation state is, or will become, completely moribund and irrelevant in global governance dynamics. Rather, it projects a proposal for an urgent symbiotic framework based on dialogue between emergent transnational civic society pressures/forces and states as repositories of political leadership and power. Relying on political/legal theorists like Koskenniemi and Habermas, Falk argues that,

> Dialogue is not just words, but the foundation of communicative action that is the essence of democratic practice[50] ... Given the structure of international society, and its continuing adherence to a strong doctrinal view supportive of sovereign rights, the most appropriate role for the jurist is to avoid the temptations of apologetics or of utopianism, neither relinquishing juridical autonomy to the political domain nor setting forth legalistic positions that are dismissed as pathetic fantasy by those entrusted with the responsibilities of political leadership[51] ... International law and lawyers can best contribute to the prospects of fashioning a more humane type of global civilization by self-confidently entering the dialogic space between entrenched power and transnational social forces, acknowledging the relevance of both, but subordinating their autonomy to neither.[52]

Applied analogously to the interaction between people-or civil-society-oriented traditional malaria therapies (globalization-from-below) and malaria control policies of multilateral agencies like the WHO (globalization-from-above), the pertinent question is whether the dialogue between the two, as argued by Falk and theorized by Habermas, has occurred, is occurring now, or will likely occur in the future. It is beyond doubt that traditional medicine is generally endorsed by the WHO, and that the organization has called on countries to integrate it within their national health care systems.[53] In its World Health Report 2000, which focused on improving the performance of health systems, the WHO defined a health system to include 'all the activities, whose primary purpose is to promote, restore or maintain health.'[54] Formal health services, including the professional delivery of personal health attention and actions by traditional healers, according to the WHO, are clearly within the boundaries of this definition.[55] In a seminal article, Nabarro, former project director of Roll Back Malaria at WHO stated that 'within developing countries, the private sector (whether in the form of a licensed medical practitioner, private pharmacy, or traditional healer) is very often the main source of advice and treatment for all people, including the poor. Government health services will need to acknowledge this and develop better ways of working with and regulating the different types of practitioners to provide essential public health services.'[56]

Given this tacit recognition of traditional medicine, it is curious that nothing in either the WHO's Roll Back Malaria Campaign or its partner Medicines for Malaria Venture expressly mentions the integration of traditional malaria therapies as part of their operational frameworks. The vision of the RBM and the MMV is commendable for its collaborative public-private sector partnership in global health governance aimed at a disease that has not only long been neglected, but which substantially attacks poor people in underdeveloped parts of the world. Nevertheless, this vision remains flawed so long as its reach and grasp systematically relegates traditional medical therapies to the peripheries. The prevailing emphasis on insecticide-treated bed nets (in the case of Roll Back Malaria) and the production of malaria drugs every five years (in the case of Medicines for Malaria Venture) has forced the WHO to pursue a corporate agenda by entering into agreements and joint ventures with corporate entities. These agreements cloak the corporate entities involved with a sacrosanct juristic and corporate veil marked by absolute and limitless autonomy that can be challenged neither by WHO member states nor transnational civil society organizations. Yamey observes that one problem with huge global partnerships like Roll Back Malaria is that they end up being accountable to nobody. One function of reporting their meetings and activities is to expose them to some sort of scrutiny and help them become accountable to those they serve.[57] In this sense, the RBM and MMV are both guilty of globalization-from-above.

As a way forward, I propose an immediate, urgent dialogue between civil-society-oriented traditional approaches to malaria, and governments within national jurisdictions in malaria-endemic countries. The dialogue within countries would aim at what I call 'the scientification of traditional malaria therapies.'[58] What emerges from the dialogue within countries will transcend national jurisdictions to forge further transnational dialogues to evolve an inclusive malaria globalism based on multi-stakeholder participation. My proposition for 'scientification' of traditional malaria therapies does not necessarily mean that scientification will follow the analytical methodology of Western medical science. I argue that science is, in some sense, multicultural. Multiculturalism of science, for instance, applies to traditional herbal medicine in most parts of the developing world. Most of the herbs used by populations for ages in Africa, Asia, and Latin America as therapies for ailments have now been universally acclaimed as medicinally valid and scientifically effective. As Roht-Arriaza rightly observed, 'Indigenous and local communities have a long history of using plants for almost all needs, including food, shelter, clothing, and medicine. Common remedies used today were often first developed by healers prior to contact with industrial societies. Yet, although many of today's drugs and cosmetics originated from the stewardship and knowledge of indigenous and local communities, that knowledge remains unrecognized and unvalued until appropriated from those communities by Western corporations or institutions.'[59]

Roht-Arriaza cites many examples of appropriation of indigenous scientific knowledge including quinine, a well-known and universally acclaimed cure for malaria, which comes from the bark of the Peruvian cinchona tree.[60] Andean indigenous populations used quinine as a cure for fevers, supposedly learning of its medical efficacy by observing feverish jaguars eating it.[61] Other notorious examples include the rosy periwinkle plant, unique to Madagascar, which contains properties that combat certain cancers. The anti-cancer drugs vincristine and vinblastine have been developed from the periwinkle, resulting in over $100 million in annual sales for Eli Lilly and virtually nothing for Madagascar.[62] In the same fashion, a barley gene that resists the yellow-dwarf virus has been the product of breeding and cultivation by Ethiopian farmers for centuries. Scientists and farmers in the United States patented the barley variety and now receive enormous profits from its current cultivation in the states, while the Ethiopian farming communities that originally developed the variety receive nothing.[63]

In other areas of traditional medicine where the multiculturalism of science cannot easily be established and extrapolated across diverse cultures, there is a need for further and continuous dialogue between civil society networks and national governmental authorities to forge a synthesis. In other words transgovernmental and transcivil society cross-fertilization of ideas is urgently required. This may be the only viable path to humane global health governance founded on an activation of people-oriented medical therapies that conforms to the canons of globalization-from-below.[64] An entente between civil society networks and nation states mandates further cross-fertilization of relevant legal and political theories of global health governance.

E Symbiotic Approaches: The Wealth and Poverty of Theory in Multilateral Health Governance

Multilateral health governance is inherently multidisciplinary and intensely trans-theoretical. Since I have briefly discussed aspects of these theoretical approaches in the preceding chapters,[65] I shall explore a symbiotic framework that offers a holistic, multidisciplinary, and trans-theoretical template of the entire study. Multidisciplinary and trans-theoretical grounding of multilateral health governance is important because it facilitates a cross-fertilization of ideas among various schools. No one political or legal theory, on its own, provides a comprehensive, satisfactory, or exhaustive analysis of the deluge of transnational health threats confronting the world today. From the perspective of jurisprudence/legal theory, Bodenheimer reminds us that 'the subject of jurisprudence is a very broad one, encompassing the philosophical, sociological, historical, as well as analytical components of legal theory.'[66] In a multilateral context, Bodenheimer's analytical components of legal theory implicate what scholars of international relations (political scientists) study under the rubric of theories of international regimes. Can law and order be maintained and enforced in the interaction between sovereign states? What factors (if any) motivate states to find multilateral solutions to multilateral problems like the menace of pathogenic microbes and infectious diseases? I discuss the dominant theories of international regimes, apply them to questions of fairness in the international system, and assess their relevance or otherwise in global health governance. Realism, liberalism, and Marxism are often presented as the three dominant theories of international regimes. Scholars of international relations concede that these schools are not rigidly compartmentalized because 'each of these traditions includes many variants, which frequently overlap in complicated ways such that identifying their key features is a difficult and controversial task.'[67]

Realism postulates an international system composed of political entities (i.e., nation states) that are primarily driven by pursuit of selfish interests, survival, and/ or maximization of power. Hedley Bull's classical description of the realist view of international relations based on the Hobbesian tradition characterizes 'international relations as a state of war of all against all, an arena of struggle in which each state is pitted against every other. International relations, on the Hobbesian view, represent pure conflict between states and resemble a game that is wholly distributive or zero-sum: the interests of each state exclude the interests of any other.'[68] Advocates of realism do not deny the existence of multilateral regimes, but they see in those regimes vicissitudes of hegemony and anarchy that propel states to pursue their selfish interests and maximize power instead of common interests and values. Juxtaposing this canonical exposition of realism with global health governance, especially the leading roles played by the European powers in nineteenth-century public health diplomacy, Fidler observes that realists will likely argue that in nineteenth-century public health diplomacy, 'the great powers' interests converged to produce co-operation and international law, but raw fear and concern for trade stimulated these developments, not altruism. When the developed countries managed to get infectious diseases under control within their territories, international health co-operation and law deteriorated. The IHR's history can be read as a classic story of realism: States have ignored international law to protect their national interests.'[69]

In present-day multilateral initiatives on public health, realist scholars would still argue that the rising global concern about infectious disease threats emanates from the fear of great powers that these threats will adversely affect populations within their borders and their economic opportunities abroad.[70]

Liberalism, although multifaceted, has its roots in the writings of seventeenth-century political philosophers and economists. The canons of liberalism are founded on the promotion of human freedom and dignity based on the establishment of conditions for peace, justice, and prosperity. These liberal ideals are not teleological; there is no foreseen 'end of history' in which humanity attains perfect freedom.[71] Liberalism concedes that discord and coercion are characteristics of multilateral interaction between states, but states are able to strike an accord because of 'mutualities of interests and non-coercive bargaining.' Mutual cooperation is the key to the maximization of possible benefits and the minimization of possible dangers of interactions and interdependencies between states.[72] Thus the liberal tradition is committed to political and economic strategies founded on democratization, free trade, and market capitalism. In the late eighteenth century, Immanuel Kant, one of the influential liberals at the time, argued that the essential nature of international politics lies in transnational social bonds that link individual human beings who are citizens of republican states. The dominant theme of international relations as a relationship of states is only apparent; the real relationship is the relationship of all human beings in the community of humankind, which will erode and sweep away the system of states. The growth of cosmopolitan law would subsequently enhance international peace and cooperation.[73] The classic Kantian model of international liberalism has been critiqued. Hedley Bull wrote that 'In Kant's own doctrine there is of course ambivalence as between the universalism of *The Idea of Universal History from a Cosmopolitical Point of View* (1784) and the position taken up in *Perpetual Peace* (1795), in which Kant accepts the substitute goal of a league of "republican" states.'[74]

Liberalism's anchorage in mutualities of interests and non-coercive bargaining offers a better explanation for a multilateral regulation of cross-border spread of diseases and health risks by states. Mutual vulnerability, the obsolescence of state sovereignty/national boundaries to threats of diseases and pathogens in an emergent global village, liberals argue, is a multilateral problem that requires a multilateral approach by states rooted in mutual and enlightened self-interests. Liberals admit that international law and multilateral institutions, two important mechanisms required to forge multilateral consensus, have not been profoundly effective. Nonetheless, as stated by Fidler, 'in the case of infectious diseases, States have learned that international co-operation and international law best serve national interests because the nature of the challenge from the microbial world demands such a strategy given the structure of the international system. The convergence of national interests, is not, thus, grounded only in hegemonic desires; it is based on a scientific and political foundation that involves powerful and weak States alike – both of which face the threat of infectious diseases.'[75]

Even when international regulatory approaches to diseases like the WHO's International Health Regulations have not functioned effectively, the principles behind such norms and regimes still receive tacit recognition by states. One critique of liberalism with respect to multilateral health regimes focuses on its endorsement of democratization, international trade liberalization, market capitalism, and the role of non-state corporate actors in global governance. These phenomena have astronomically increased the global influence and networks of multinational corporations, the operations of which globalize environmental, health, and food insecurity, which in turn defy orthodox multilateral governance approaches. Multinational corporations, like those found in the tobacco industry, deploy their sophisticated global networks and enormous resources to create an anarchical global society by undermining multilateral efforts aimed at regulating the public health harm of their products and activities.[76] Thus liberalism, in a well-intended effort to generate and distribute wealth via trade liberalization, sometimes suffers a derailment that ends up equipping the private sector (transnational corporations) with enormous powers and influence that may adversely impact on the health of populations within and among nations.

Critical theorists explore the international system from the perspective of socio-economic injustices and inequalities in the relations among sovereign states. Although arguably there is no articulate Marxist approach to international law,[77] critical theory is nonetheless substantially founded on the Marxist claim that the 'mode of production determines the nature of social and economic relations within political entities and among them. Domestic and international politics are fundamentally about the struggle for wealth among economic classes.'[78] As a variant of Marxism, critical theorists use the struggle among the economic classes in society to explore the disparities and inequalities among nations in the international system. Factors that propel the spread of diseases and microbes globally are rooted in poverty, underdevelopment, and other facets of social and economic inequalities.[79] Critical scholars thus argue that the contemporary international system is fundamentally predatory and coercive. Globalization, an emergent phenomenon in globalism, is essentially an engine of injustice, poverty, and underdevelopment, an enterprise aimed at the continued entrenchment of hegemony in the relations between rich and poor states, and a framework that is non-responsive to the status quo of global development apartheid among nations. As argued by Chimni, 'Since the early 1980s, the advanced capitalist world has, under the guidance of the hegemonic transnationalised fractions of its bourgeoisies, and with the assistance of the transnationalised fractions of national capital in the third world, pushed through a series of changes in international economic law which lay the legal foundation for capital accumulation in the era of globalisation. These changes appear to have two principal objectives: (i) to extend and deepen world-wide the rule of capital through the removal of local impediments; and (ii) to dismantle international laws of distribution which are based on the principle of market intervention.'[80]

Because the sovereign state is viewed as coercive, critical scholars foresee an ultimate overcoming of states and an eventual triumph of qualified cosmopolitanism. In his 'discourse ethics,' for instance, Devetak proposes a global framework in which principles of political action can be universally and democratically arrived at through cosmopolitan political and moral discourse.[81] While critical theory's linkage of emerging transnational infectious disease threats with inequalities in the international system has some merit, its proposal of a modified version of cosmopolitanism remains largely utopian. Cosmopolitanism raises a host of complex questions for the present world order composed of sovereign states. Complete erosion of sovereign states and enthronement of the cosmopolitan world order model is definitely no solution to global infectious disease threats.

The dominant theories of international regimes, as explored here, point to an irresistible conclusion. No single theoretical framework comprehensively explains all the ramifications of multilateral regulation of the cross-border spread of disease and health risks. The present South-North divide, with its implications for the health of populations within the emergent global village, implicates the reach and grasp of liberalism, realism, and critical theories of regimes. Neither exclusively power/strategic interests (as argued by realists), common interests/values (as argued by liberals and neo-liberals), nor cosmopolitanism (as proposed by critical theorists) would lead to a humane global health governance. Each theory is both rich and poor. As Fidler argues, 'in their respective interpretations of *microbialpolitik*, both realism and liberalism have strengths and weaknesses; and it is ill-advised to proclaim a victor.'[82] I refer to these strengths and weaknesses as 'the wealth and poverty of theory in global health governance.' Wealth and poverty of theory is not a demurrer for a wholesale dismissal of the relevance of theory in forging a multi-lateral consensus on infectious disease and other health threats, it is rather an incentive that propels a compelling need for a symbiosis and cross-pollination of ideas across the boundaries of the dominant schools of international regimes. Has liberalism/neo-liberalism anything to learn from, or teach, realism, and vice versa? Can the critical school inform realism? To many hard-nosed realists, liberals, or critical scholars, this is an invitation to anarchy. Its impracticality is comparable to teaching English grammar with German words.

To attempt a synthesis of the antithesis of international regime theories I apply the canons of these theories to contemporary governance discourses in an interdependent world. In no other area is this theoretical symbiosis more necessary than in the vexed question of *fairness* in the distribution of the dividends that accrue from health protection/promotion as a global public good. In other words, how does each of these theories play into the fairness question in global health challenges? Can any one of the dominant theories, on its own, lead to humane global redistribution and reallocation strategies for health protection and promotion that satisfy the preconditions of fairness?[83] On fairness in international law and international institutions, Franck wrote, 'the fairness of international law, as any other legal system, will be judged, first by the degree to which the rules satisfy the participants' expectations of justifiable distribution of costs and benefits, and secondly by the extent to which the rules are made and applied in accordance with what the participants perceive as right process.'[84] This dual-dimensional aspect of fairness discourse Franck categorizes as 'the substantive' (distributive justice) and 'the procedural' (right process).[85] Following Rawls's *Theory of Justice*, Franck identifies 'moderate scarcity' and 'community' as the two structural preconditions of a fairness discourse.[86] Applied to global health challenges, social contract philosophy embedded in liberalism explains aspects of multilateral interaction between states. However, a further enquiry is needed to explain the present South-North divide, persistent poverty and underdevelopment in the global South (which impact on health of populations), unequal global distribution of disease burdens among populations in the developed and developing worlds, and the near collapse or non-existence of core public health surveillance capacity in many developing countries. Thus Franck's version of social contractarian internationalism (neo-liberalism) comes within what I explore under the rubric of communitarian globalism in the next chapter. However, as a constitutive framework, my proposal cannot rest on neo-liberal ideals alone. It therefore makes overtures to the realist school that explains the hegemony, politics, and power relations between weak and powerful, poor and wealthy in the evolution of communitarian globalism, especially in my proposal for a disease non-proliferation facility through a multilateral health fund. Communitarian globalism also makes further overtures to the critical school that best explains South-North disparities and global socio-economic inequalities. Applying this symbiotic transtheoretical discourse to a scheme of global health governance is both timely and relevant because politics and governance along the domestic-foreign frontier have rendered the distinction between domestic and foreign affairs obsolete in our interdependent world.[87] The domestic-foreign frontier is dynamic, complex, and rugged, and the complexities of the new conditions that have shaped the frontier cannot be explained by a single source. To assess global governance, according to Rosenau, is 'to trace the various ways in which the processes of governance are aggregated.'[88] The wealth and poverty of theory I suggest is therefore a window of opportunity that symbiotically traces the linkages of the rigidly compartmentalized boundaries of the dominant international regime theories. Through communitarian globalism, it explores global health governance holistically as opposed to relying on segmented theoretical approaches to international regimes prevalent in contemporary international law and international relations scholarship. Wealth and poverty of theory, as I use it in this context, is not teleological; it does not foresee an ultimate and perfect harmony between the dominant schools of international regimes. It merely offers a holistic framework for the study and better understanding of global health governance in the face of advancing globalized health threats in a divided world.

F Summary of the Arguments

One of the formidable challenges of multiculturalism is to reconcile the vicious tensions between the core and the peripheries of global health architecture. Using multilateral malaria control policy as the subject of analysis and enquiry, this chapter explored the relevance of indigenous malaria therapies in a medically pluralistic world, a global policy universe, in which public health presents varied and complex governance challenges that continue to require multilateral and multicultural approaches. What emerges from this analysis is a largely irreconcilable tension between the core – global malaria control policy – and the peripheries – indigenous malaria therapies widely used by populations in malaria-endemic regions of the developing world. Because the core and the peripheries are bound together, any degree of tension in their coexistence inevitably leads to turbulence in global health governance. In an attempt to strike a harmony between malaria control practices at the core and peripheries, this chapter identified three useful approaches: the scientification of traditional medical therapies in the developing world, global governance mechanisms that respect globalization-from-below, and the cross-fertilization of ideas among the dominant theoretical schools of international regimes.

At the heart of these approaches is the activation of people- or civil-society-oriented approaches to multilateral health governance. Ethno-medicine is not magic, superstition, or witchcraft but an age-old health delivery system widely used by a sizeable percentage of populations in the developing world. Because alternative medical therapies are either unaffordable or unpopular among these populations, continued relegation of African ethno-medicine to the peripheries of global malaria regime is intensely discriminatory and counter productive. The vision of contemporary multilateral malaria control strategies – the Roll Back Malaria campaign and Medicines for Malaria venture – commendable as the are, ought to be accountable and responsive to the constituencies they serve: indigenous communities in malaria-endemic societies, especially in Africa where the burden of the disease is heaviest. How best can this regime deficit be closed? We need a more inclusive and multistakeholder approach to multilateral malaria control policy. My interviews with local populations have shown the existence of affordable therapies that have long been neglected by multilateral institutions. To ensure stability and peace in the global neighbourhood, innovative approaches to global health governance must harmonize the tensions between the core global malaria regime and traditional therapies at the peripheries in a way that projects globalization of public health not as a predatory, but as a humane, fair, and equitable enterprise.

Chapter 6

In Search of Prophylaxis: Communitarian Globalism and Multilateral Disease Non-Proliferation Facility

A Overview of the Arguments and a Summary of Recommendations

In the preceding chapter, I adopted Franck's two structural preconditions of fairness discourse: *moderate scarcity* and *community*. Moderate scarcity postulates that while global resources are never in short supply, only a fair, equitable, and distributive multilateral governance facility stands to protect and promote the health of populations in the emergent global village. Community underpins a conglomeration of perplexingly diverse political entities, players, and actors in the global arena: a *sine qua non* for the evolution of a fair regime for the distribution of global resources aimed at public health promotion and protection. Thus, moderate scarcity and a community of political entities are inseparable in fairness discourse. As Franck observed,

> Between the polarities of plenitude and deprivation is a vast spectrum of conditions in which everyone cannot have everything they want, but where there is enough to meet 'reasonable' expectations if the goods are allocated by an agreed rule which is perceived to be fair ... Moderate scarcity is a necessary, but not a sufficient, precondition for fruitful fairness discourse. There must also be a shared sense of the identity of those entitled to a fair share; there must be an ascertainable community of persons self-consciously engaged in a common moral enterprise. The members of such a community participate not only in the sense of receiving a share of each allocated good or obligation, but they also participate in determining the rules by which the shares are allocated. There must, in other words, be a moral community engaged in formulating itself as a 'rule community.'[1]

Building on Franck's discourse, I use the term communitarian globalism to explore the multiple dimensions and dynamic complexities of sharing scarce but moderate global resources based on consensus and agreed rules in a multilateral forum. In the face of advancing microbial threats, communitarian globalism represents a pool of efforts and resources by states, non-state actors, and multilateral agencies directed towards the protection of public health and the prevention of cross-border spread of diseases. It is communitarian because of the risk of mutual vulnerability of populations within geo-political boundaries of nation states if these states fail to negotiate effective global health accords. Conversely, communitarian globalism recognizes the dividends that could potentially accrue to populations from humane global cooperative accords based on the ideals of fairness, justice, and health security. Its globalism stems from the complex nature of contemporary international health, where the phenomenon of globalization has significantly altered the traditional distinction between national and international health threats. Communitarian globalism, as I use it in this context, does not postulate the emergence of a magic bullet against every conceivable globalized health challenge. It merely holds the potential to facilitate multilateral consensus on the governance of transnational microbial threats.

One of the numerous complexities of communitarian globalism is the conundrum of pooling resources on an unequal basis and formulating rules for the allocation of these resources based on equality of all participants, including states and non-state actors. How best do we resolve the tension of pooling resources 'from each state according to its wealth' and formulate the rules, in a multilateral forum, for allocating the pooled resources based on the equality of all the actors often embodied in the 'one state one vote' rule? Treating 'unequal actors equally' could smack of injustice in international and multilateral relations between state and non-state actors. This apprehension notwithstanding, the concept of mutual vulnerability explored in this study illuminates the tenets of enlightened self-interest to catalyse a reconceptualization of global health governance, including mutual vulnerability to traditional and re-emerging pathogenic microbes. Stark disparities in the levels of wealth, health, and development among populations is supportive of a modified version of the often-discredited maxim 'in terms of contribution, from each according to its wealth, and in terms of distribution, to each according to its need' in global health discourse.

As a way forward, I configure the parameters of communitarian globalism and identify the relevant actors within its boundaries: the World Health Organization, the World Bank, other multilateral institutions, nation states, civil society, the private sector and foundations. The sense of community starts with civil society networks within nation states. However, because disease pathogens and other microbial threats have become globalized challenges, the sense of community necessarily transcends national geo-political boundaries to include powerful multilateral institutions like the World Health Organization and the World Bank, which wield enormous influence on countries. Communitarian globalism provides some answers to the ultimate question posed in this study: what ought we to do in order to protect and promote human health and well-being in a world polarized by inequalities and differential levels of development? International law, its lawyers and multilateral institutions, in the present post-ontological era of the discipline, must strive to create a fair and humane multilateral health regime. Utmost fidelity to humanity's health compels this study to make modest proposals: a disease nonproliferation facility though a mechanism of Global Fund, future WHO–World Bank collaboration, health care reform in countries, and the envisaged role of nation states and global civil society in communitarian globalism.

B Communitarian Globalism: A Proposal for WHO–World Bank Collaboration

Since the early 1990s, the World Bank has emerged as the leading funder of public health projects in the developing world. With its World Development Report 1993, *Investing in Health*,[2] the bank has emerged as an indispensable player in global health governance. Last observed that 'the World Bank's recognition of the relationship between economic development and health is an important contribution if it leads to greater investment in material and human resources to improve health.'[3] The World Health Organization and the other institutions within the UN system – the United Nations Children's Fund (UNICEF), the United Nations Development Programme (UNDP), the Food and Agriculture Organization of the United Nations (FAO), the United Nations Fund for Population Activities (UNFPA), the United Nations Fund for Drug Abuse Control (UNFDAC), the Joint United Nations Programme on HIV/AIDS (UNAIDS), and the United Nations High Commissioner for Refugees (UNHCR) – must now pursue transparent partnerships with the World Bank.[4] The bank's relevance in these partnerships is anchored on two advantages it presently enjoys: the enormity of the financial resources it is able to muster, and the colossal influence it wields in most developing countries. In a sense, these types of partnerships are not entirely new in global health governance. They already exist on a limited basis on segmented global health issues as manifested, for instance, in the Joint United Nations Programme on HIV/AIDS (UNAIDS), and the WHO's Roll Back Malaria campaign.[5] What is needed, however, is an inclusive multi-stakeholder participation, transparency, and accountability of these partnerships to the constituencies they serve.[6] With the involvement of the World Bank in these partnerships, the need for transparency and accountability will top the agenda. This is because the bank has been criticized for its wholesale endorsement of an undiluted liberal and neo-liberal capitalistic agenda: limited state intervention, strong private sector participation, the logic of capital, and unqualified triumph of market forces. As Larkin observed,

> What we are now seeing is the growing influence of the World Bank as a major funder for health in the poorer countries and one which already eclipses that of the WHO and UNICEF. Its influence has grown steadily throughout the 1980s and 1990s as bank loans for health quadrupled. Its activities now reach into health service financing and delivery, and the prioritisation of programmes along cost-effective lines ... Given its policies of a diminished role for the state and the privatisation and marketisation of health services as well as the leverage it can exert through its support for structural adjustment, the possibilities for equity-based health services are certainly in doubt. A major cause for concern must be its lack of accountability and the disproportionate weight accorded to the richer countries in the exercise of voting rights, as well as its current commitment to neo-liberal-type policies.[7]

I endorsed similar criticisms with respect to the bank's structural adjustment policies in chapter 2, and the bank must modify its obsession with an extreme neo-liberal agenda. As a potential partner in communitarian globalism, the World Bank must shift from a neo-liberal marketization of health care to the Primary Health Care approach endorsed by the WHO if the dividends of health as a public good are to be within the reach and grasp of the world's endangered populations. In fact, the World Bank's neo-liberal approach to health promotion and health care delivery is antithetical to the World Health Organization's Primary Health Care approach. In *Investing in Health*, the bank recognized the necessity of a paradigm shift, one that recognizes the effects of social inequalities, poverty, and underdevelopment on the health of populations within and among nations. It thus departed from its insistence on a diminished role for the state by identifying three rationales for a major government role in the health sector:

(i) the need for governments to encourage behaviours that carry positive externalities and to discourage those with negative externalities so as to facilitate the enjoyment of health-related services such as control of contagious diseases as public goods,

(ii) provision of cost-effective health services to the poor in an effective and socially acceptable approach to poverty reduction as endorsed by the WHO/ UNICEF Alma-Ata Declaration on Primary Health Care 1978, and

(iii) the need for government action to compensate problems of uncertainty and insurance market failure. Governments have an important role to play in regulating private health insurance, or mandating alternatives in order to ensure widespread coverage at affordable costs.[8]

Other common grounds between the World Bank's and the WHO's approach to multilateral health promotion/protection include the recognition of HIV/AIDS as a threat to development; reducing the abuse of tobacco, alcohol, and drugs; environmental influences on health; and health system reform in developing countries based on medical pluralism and the promotion of diversity and competition.[9] With respect to the provision of health care services to the poor in a social context where a multiplicity of health systems interlock, the bank noted that in countries like Bangladesh, Kenya, Thailand, and many others, governments are supporting the work of traditional birth attendants in safe pregnancies and of traditional healers in controlling infectious diseases like malaria, diarrhoea, and AIDS.[10] In line with the tenets of mutual vulnerability, and with emphasis on the global threat of HIV/AIDS, the bank warned that 'the world can do more to deal with the global challenge of AIDS. No country is immune from a future HIV epidemic, and the costs of delay are high. A global coalition is needed that will encourage and assist governments to take bold action before it is too late.'[11]

Although local conditions vary from one social context to another, the overall public health vision of the bank is nonetheless articulated in what it calls 'the essential public health package,'[12] the highlights of which include,

(i)   an expanded program on immunization, including micronutrient supplementation,

(ii) school health programs to treat worm infections and micronutrient deficiencies and to provide health education,

(iii) programs to increase public knowledge about family planning and nutrition, self-cure or indications for seeking care, and about vector control and disease surveillance activities,

(iv) programs to reduce consumption of tobacco, alcohol, and other drugs, and

(v)   AIDS prevention programs with a strong component on other sexually transmitted diseases (STDs).[13]

Identifying the commonalties between the health vision of the World Bank and the mandate of the WHO (including the other relevant agencies within the UN system) is extremely important, as these commonalties are the determinants and decisive criteria for the success or failure of future partnerships between the bank and multilateral health institutions. Despite these commonalties, questions still abound about the World Bank's transparency, as well as the overpowering influence of its chief donor countries. The possible effects of the bank's non-transparency on its involvement in a multilateral health funding facility, especially my proposal on evolving the rules for the fund based on the juridical equality of all relevant actors, are discussed below.

C Towards a Disease Non-Proliferation Facility: An Argument for a Global Health Fund

Because poverty and underdevelopment are the root causes of disease and illness, I propose a global health fund, a disease non-proliferation multilateral facility that, inter alia, targets the improvement of prevention strategies as well as a core capacity for multi-disease surveillance and accessibility of curative therapies to vulnerable populations across the world.[14] Since the 1990s, proposals for a multilateral health funding facility have gained significant support and accelerated momentum within the UN system, other multilateral agencies, regional groupings, and civil society organizations. Propelled by the limited successes recorded by the World Bank's Global Environmental Facility (GEF), the Montreal Protocol on Substances That Deplete the Ozone Layer, and the recent Global Alliance for Vaccines and Immunization (GAVI), advocates of a global health funding facility categorize microbial threats as global issues. In an era of mutual vulnerability occasioned by the globalization of disease and health hazards, the propensity for the spread of microbial agents via the global viral superhighway underscores the need for a focused and coordinated funding mechanism. Ironically, the past ten years have instead witnessed a steady decline in health funding, especially on health issues affecting the developing world. In 1990, a study by the Commission on Health Research for Development stated that 'an estimated 93 percent of the world's burden of preventable mortality (measured as years of potential life lost) occurs in the developing world. Yet, of the $30 billion global investment in health research in 1986, only 5 percent or 1.6 billion was devoted to the health problems of developing countries. For each year of potential life lost in the industrialized world, more than 200 times as much is spent on health research as is spent for each year lost in the developing world.'[15]

Although the World Bank quadrupled its lending for health in the late 1980s and early 1990s, it nonetheless observed that such aid to middle-income countries, as well as similar aid from the other development banks, is non-concessional lending and that a considerable increase would inevitably involve a hardening of terms and conditions.[16] Against the backdrop of crisis in multilateral funding for health, in 1998 the United Nations Development Programme queried why so few financial resources are dedicated to advancing human development in countries where the need is greatest. Donor countries allocate a mere $55 billion to development cooperation – only 0.25 per cent of their GNP of $22 trillion. Official development aid is now at its lowest level since statistics began to be compiled. The share to the least developed countries continues to decline.[17] Linking disease burdens to socio-economic development, Sachs, one of the foremost advocates of a global health funding facility, argues that 'global donor support of $10–20 billion per

year, much less than 0.1 per cent of the combined $25 trillion gross national prod-
uct (GNP) of rich nations, would save millions of lives each year and would enable
Africa to escape from a downward spiral of disease and economic collapse.'[18] Poverty and underdevelopment affect health by limiting access to health services, sanitation, adequate nutrition and housing, while poor health adversely impacts
economic growth through a multiplicity of channels.[19] If epidemics of global proportions (like SARS) could take countries with good surveillance capacity (like
Canada) by surprise, the magnitude of similar outbreaks in countries like Chad,
Guinea Bissau, Burkina Faso, Haiti, Honduras, Guatemala, and Tanzania, with
more than half of their entire health expenditures dependent on foreign aid, can
only be imagined. It is not too late in the day for 'the global donor community –
governments, multilateral agencies, foundations and individual philanthropists –
to support a concerted attack on killer infectious diseases ... including HIV/AIDS,
tuberculosis and malaria.'[20] To make a difference, the emerging coalition must
make a coordinated global effort, as opposed to the disparate and segmented funding strategies employed in the past.[21]

The crisis in multilateral funding to curb the global proliferation of disease, and
calls for the establishment of a global health fund were boosted by the G8 Summit
in July 2000. The Okinawa Summit of G8 countries pledged a fund regime with
a focus on HIV/AIDS, tuberculosis, and malaria. The G8 pledge was to boost and
sustain political engagement and financial commitment, ease the procurement of
commodities, and commit new partners to the battle against microbes. At Okinawa, the G8 leaders set a goal to reduce the number of HIV and AIDS cases in
the fifteen–twenty-four-age bracket by 25 per cent in 2010. They also set 2010 target goals for malaria and tuberculosis. In April 2001, at the Organization of African Unity summit on HIV/AIDS, tuberculosis, and other related infectious
diseases, held in Abuja, Nigeria, UN Secretary-General Kofi Annan called for the
establishment of a global fund on AIDS and Health.[22] Annan argued that the best
cure for all diseases is economic growth and broad-based development. Disease,
like war, is one of the biggest obstacles preventing the development of societies in
Africa.[23] He identified five broad objectives in the global battle against HIV/AIDS
and other related infectious diseases as:

(i) Prevention aimed at halting and reversing the spread of the virus to safe-
guard the present and future generations,
(ii) Prevention of the cruellest, most unjust infections – those from mother to
child,
(iii) Putting care and treatment within everyone's reach,
(iv) Effective delivery of any future scientific breakthroughs across societies,
and

(v) Protection of those made most vulnerable to the epidemics especially orphans.[24]

As a means of achieving these objectives, Annan proposed, inter alia, the creation of a Global Fund dedicated to the battle against HIV/AIDS and other infectious diseases. The fund must be structured in a way to ensure that it responds to the needs of the affected countries and people. The fund regime must draw from the advice of the best experts in the world – whether they are found in the United Nations system, in governments, in civil society organizations, or among those who live with HIV/AIDS or are directly affected by it.[25] The African Summit led to the Abuja Declaration and Plan of Action to curb the spread of HIV/AIDS and other related infectious diseases in Africa. The declaration called on donor countries to complement Africa's resource mobilization efforts to fight the scourge of HIV/AIDS, TB, and other related infectious diseases.[26] It urged donor countries to, inter alia, fulfil the unrealized target of committing 0.7 per cent of their GNP as Official Development Assistance (ODA) to developing countries.[27] The declaration also made a commitment to explore and develop potential traditional medicine and traditional health practices in the prevention, care, and management of these diseases. Further, it endorsed the creation of a Global AIDS Fund capitalized by the donor community with a sum of $10 billion, accessible to all affected countries, to enhance the implementation of action plans, including accessing anti-retroviral programs in favour of African populations.[28]

At the fifty-fourth World Health Assembly held in Geneva in May 2001, UN Secretary-General Kofi Annan reiterated his call for the establishment of a Global AIDS and Health Fund with a focus on the five key objectives he articulated at the African summit.[29] WHO former Director-General Dr Gro Harlem Brundtland also outlined a number of emerging principles that have guided proposals for a global health fund:

(i) Additionality: the fund should not replace existing funding mechanisms, but add value in terms of resources and outcomes to what is already happening.
(ii) It must support national-level decisions and leadership and simultaneously ensure transparency and accountability.
(iii) The fund must support ongoing national development processes such as national HIV/AIDS strategies.
(iv) It should promote voluntary and private sector participation, including full involvement of civil society in the preparation of submissions and implementation of programs.
(v) Multisectoral action drawing on high-level national political support is required.

(vi) The fund should contribute to increasing the coherence and effectiveness of development assistance through the strengthening of existing government-donor coordination mechanisms.

(vii) It has to be innovative in encouraging new ways of working and ensuring that funds are disbursed both rapidly and wisely.

(viii) Streamlined management is required; applications for funding should not necessitate new and elaborate planning processes.

(ix) The fund must recognize the differences of divergent national contexts.

(x) Successive tranches of funding reward good performance.

(xi) The fund should operate in the context of international agreements, including trade related intellectual property rights (TRIPS) and the safeguards included in them, and finally,

(xii) If the fund is to help in delivering equitable health outcomes, it must operate with equity in mind: equity in process and equity in allocation of resources.[30]

The proposed Global Health Fund received its highest multilateral imprimatur at the United Nations General Assembly Special Session held in New York, 25–7 June 2001. In a declaration of commitment to fighting HIV/AIDS entitled 'Global Crisis-Global Action,' the General Assembly of the UN categorized the devastating scale and impact of the global HIV/AIDS epidemic as 'a global emergency' constituting a formidable challenge to human life, dignity, and the effective enjoyment of human rights.[31] The declaration noted that the threat of HIV/AIDS undermines social and economic development across the world and affects all levels of society – national, community, family, and individual. The General Assembly Declaration affirmed a commitment by governments to address the HIV/AIDS crisis by recognizing that:

(i) Leadership by governments in combating HIV/AIDS is essential and their efforts should be complemented by the full and active participation of civil society, the business community, and the private sector at the national, regional/sub-regional, and global levels.

(ii) Effective prevention strategies need to be strengthened to achieve internationally agreed global prevention and reduction of HIV/AIDS prevalence among vulnerable groups.

(iii) Care, support, and treatment are fundamental elements of an effective response to the global HIV/AIDS epidemic.

(iv) The realization of human rights and fundamental freedoms for all of humanity is essential to reduce vulnerability to HIV/AIDS, and respect for the rights of people living with HIV/AIDS drives an effective response.

(v) Vulnerable groups must be given priority in response, especially through the empowerment of women.

 (vi) Children orphaned and made vulnerable by HIV/AIDS need special assistance.

 (vii) The social and economic impact of HIV/AIDS should be alleviated, thus to address HIV/AIDS is to invest in sustainable development.

 (viii) There is at present no known cure for AIDS, therefore further research and development is crucial.

 (ix) Conflicts and disasters contribute to the spread of HIV/AIDS. Countries should develop and begin to implement national strategies that incorporate HIV/AIDS awareness, prevention, care, and treatment elements into programs that respond to emergency situations, recognizing that populations destabilized by armed conflict, humanitarian crises, or natural disasters, including refugees and internally displaced persons – particularly women and children – are at increased risk of exposure to HIV infection.

 (x) Resources provided for the global response to address HIV/AIDS must be substantial, sustained, and geared towards achieving results. Establishment of a global HIV/AIDS and Health Fund is a matter of urgency, in order to finance an urgent and expanded response to the epidemic based on an integrated approach to prevention, care, support, and treatment, and to assist governments in their efforts to combat HIV/AIDS. Mobilization of contributions to the fund should target private and public sources with a special appeal to donor countries, foundations, and the business community, including pharmaceutical companies, the private sector, philanthropists, and wealthy individuals.

 (xi) It is essential to monitor progress made towards realizing the objectives of the declaration at the national, regional, and global levels.[32]

At their 2001 summit held in Genoa, Italy, the G8 countries reaffirmed their commitment to a Global Health Fund to combat HIV/AIDS, malaria, tuberculosis, and other related infectious diseases. In their final declaration in Genoa, the G8 countries, in response to the United Nations General Assembly appeal for resources, pledged to commit $1.3 billion to the Global Fund to Fight AIDS, Tuberculosis and Malaria. According to the G8, the fund will be a public-private partnership based on contributions from countries, the private sector, and foundations. The fund will promote an integrated approach, emphasizing prevention in a continuum of treatment and care, and its operation will be based on the principles of proven scientific and medical effectiveness, rapid resource transfer, low transaction costs, and light governance with a strong focus on outcomes.[33]

That the proposed Global Health Fund was endorsed by agencies of the United Nations system, a special session of the UN General Assembly, the G8 Summit, civil society and non-governmental organizations, and leading scholars offers proof that it is an initiative whose time has come. Nonetheless, difficult challenges still confront the modus operandi of the fund. What is the relation- ship, if any, between the Global Health Fund and the United Nations agencies? Which entities – nation states, civil society, the private sector – have voting rights on the fund's board of directors, and how were they selected? Is it fair for the unequal donors/contributors to have equal votes on the fund's board? How best can the fund draw on the expertise of multilateral agencies, research institutions, countries, and civil society? How can the fund represent societies and cultures across the world fairly and equitably? Will the scope of the fund's operations expand in the future to cover global health threats outside HIV/AIDS, malaria, and tuberculosis? Multilateral fund regimes and partnerships on a range of other global health issues inevitably confront similar challenges.[34] In exploring these questions I highlight what I see as the basic tenets (by no means exhaustive) of a Global Health Fund regime, as well as the foreseeable objections to these tenets.

D Governance of the Global Fund to Fight Aids, Tuberculosis, and Malaria

In the deluge of proposals advanced for the establishment of the Global Health Fund, there was unanimity on two important governance issues. First, the fund should be managed independently as a public-private partnership outside the framework and structures of the United Nations agencies and other multilateral institutions.[35] In essence, it must enjoy a considerable degree of independence and autonomy outside the bureaucracy of existing multilateral institutions. Second, because the fund is an innovative partnership between developing and donor coun- tries, the private sector, civil society, and multilateral agencies within and outside the UN system, its management and operations must be transparent and account- able to its global, regional, national, and local constituencies. The fund must be based on a broad, multistakeholder inclusiveness involving all the relevant actors in both the donor and recipient countries. The fund regime, like multilateral health treaties, must serve as an intermediate public good for the delivery of good health, as the ultimate public goods, to the poor and vulnerable populations across the world.

In establishing the principles and criteria for project/program funding, the fund should draw from relevant expertise within multilateral institutions, research insti- tutions, national disease surveillance centres like the U.S. Centers for Disease Control (CDC), and civil society organizations working in the areas of public health, development, and poverty alleviation. Because the global burden of disease and health risks are unevenly distributed across the world, project/program fund- ing guidelines should reflect the peculiar needs of societies within the regions that have the heaviest mortality and morbidity burdens of particular diseases.[36] To ensure transparency and accountability to its constituents, the executive board of the fund should publish periodic reports accessible to any interested person, government, or organization, and organize public hearings open to delegates from countries and civil society organizations. The election of the fund's executive board must broadly represent the geo-political regions across the donor and recipient countries. It is important that non-state actors – civil society and non-governmental organizations – are empowered to participate in the governance of the fund through participation in selection of board members and vetting of country proposals and standard setting. The fund should be sensitive to the public opinion of the global health and development communities and divergent cultural and behavioural perceptions of health across societies, and it must maintain the highest attainable standard of financial and managerial probity.[37] In the wake of the Global Health Fund's midwifery, two leading global health experts – Gro Harlem Brundtland, former director-general of the World Health Organization,[38] and Jeffrey Sachs, chair of the WHO Commission on Macroeconomics and Health and the UN Secretary General's Special Envoy on Poverty[39] – proposed a range of governance principles on the fund's modus operandi. Brundtland proposed a small executive board, representing all constituencies (developing country governments, donor governments, foundations, corporate and other private sector donors, civil society and NGOs, UN agencies and the Bretton Woods institutions), to determine strategic priorities and criteria for decision making.[40] Recommendations on which the board acts should be based on broad-based consultations with the governments and civil societies of those countries that will use the fund, the governments and civil societies of those countries that will contribute to the fund, the private sector and foundations who are encouraged to contribute, and international agencies.[41] Sachs proposed that the fund be managed under the leadership of the WHO, with a strong backing by the leading biomedical and public health institutions such as the National Institutes of Health (NIH) and Centres for Disease Control in the United States and comparable bodies in other countries.[42] The fund should build in scientific review as a central mechanism, including operational monitoring, evaluation, and audits.[43] Governments of developing countries would submit plans for disease control to be vetted by independent expert scientific review committees. Based on the recommendations of the expert review committees, a plan would either trigger financing from the fund or be returned to the country for further work and possible funding at a later stage.[44] Part of the operational guidelines of the fund or terms of reference should focus on encouraging governments to draw upon their own national experts in the design and implementation of programs.[45]

In accord with the canons and fundamentals of communitarian globalism, these proposals emphasize broad-based multistakeholder consultations founded on a South-North entente, multicultural approaches to health, and an inclusive civil society participation both in the selection of, and representation on, the executive board of the fund. In considering projects and programs for funding, broad-based consultations as proposed by publicists like Annan, Brundtland, and Sachs would recognize each individual country's peculiar social, political, and economic contexts as animated by civil society networks in order to guard against globalization-from-above.

The Global Fund to Fight AIDS, Tuberculosis and Malaria (GFATM) has been operational since January 2002.[46] The GFATM is an independent public-private partnership designed to attract, manage, and disburse new resources to fight the global crises of AIDS, tuberculosis, and malaria. The fund's objectives are to (i) finance effective programs, balancing the needs for prevention, treatment, care, and support, in order to alleviate suffering, save lives, and help end these diseases, and (ii) dramatically increase the global resources dedicated to fighting these diseases.[47] According to the GFATM, 'the need for more rapid, sustained and concerted action on AIDS, TB, and malaria is overwhelming. Together, these diseases have a devastating global impact, killing nearly 6 million each year and causing major social and economic upheaval. While effective interventions now exist to help prevent and prevent these diseases, they remain out of reach for most people in the developing world. A dramatic increase in resources to fight HIV, TB, and malaria is urgently needed to help reduce suffering and death caused by these diseases.'[48]

Based in Geneva, Switzerland, the GFATM was incorporated as an independent private foundation under Swiss law. The World Bank serves as the fund's fiduciary trustee, charged with the responsibility of collecting, investing, and disbursing its funds as well as financial reporting of its operations. The World Bank disburses funds on the instruction of the GFATM's board of directors. Although the GFATM has no formal relationship with the United Nations agencies, it coordinates informally with them, especially the World Health Organization, and the Joint United Nations Programme on HIV/AIDS (UNAIDS).[49] The GFATM is governed by an international board of directors appointed for two years, with equal representation – seven seats each – from donor and developing countries. Donor countries currently represented on the fund's board are France, Japan, Sweden, the United Kingdom, the United States, and the European Commission. The seven developing countries on the Board are Brazil (representing Latin America and the Caribbean), China (Western Pacific), Nigeria (Western and Central Africa), Pakistan (Eastern Mediterranean), Thailand (Southeast Asia), Uganda (Eastern and Southern Africa), and Ukraine (CIS/Eastern European Region).[50] The World Health Organization, the Joint United Nations Programme on HIV/AIDS and the World Bank hold ex-officio non-voting seats on the board. A unique feature of the

GFATM, in addition to country representatives, is the inclusion of non-governmental organizations (NGOs) and the private sector with four full voting rights on the fund's board. Two NGO seats are selected from a developing country and an industrialized country NGO; the two private sector representatives are elected from a foundation and a business.[51] The board seeks to reach consensus on all matters. If consensus is not possible, the board requires double two-thirds majorities; the first from the representatives of donor countries, private sector, and foundations, and the second from the group representing developing countries and NGOs.

In two rounds of funding, the GFATM approved grants to ninety-three countries, including those with the greatest disease burden and those at risk of future disaster. Two years of initial financing, according to the GFATM, totalling US$1.5 billion has been committed to over 150 programs. Sixty per cent of this total is for Africa; 60 per cent is for AIDS. Half of the disbursements will be used by governments; the other half by NGOs. Half is for the purchase of drugs and commodities, and half is for infrastructure and training.[52] Sustaining the GFATM in the years ahead raises critical questions on the commitment of international donors. Between 2002 and 2004, contributions to the fund total US$2.6 billion, with an additional US$2.0 billion pledged for 2005 to 2008. While significant, the GFATM states that

> pledges through 2004 are not enough to finance Rounds 3, 4 and 5, which are scheduled to occur between October 2003 and October 2004. Given an expected increase in the number of applications in future rounds, as well as an anticipated approval rate of 50%, the projected needs of the Fund are US$ 3.0 billion by the end of 2004. With approximately US$ 700 million in pledges confirmed in 2004, the near-term resource shortfall is US$ 2.3 billion. In 2005, the expected need is US$ 4.5 billion based on a sixth and seventh round of new proposals and the renewal of programs approved in Rounds 1 and 2. Confirmed pledges for 2005 currently total just over US$ 600 million.[53]

Funding commitments by governments (including the G8) have decreased drastically. In a recent report, two civil society organizations, Health and Development networks and Aidspan, have critiqued emerging the donor fatigue with respect to the GFATM.[54] Expressing the view that voluntary contribution to the GFATM has failed, France et al. proposed an 'Equitable Contributions Framework,'[55] which based on $10 billion annually,

> suggests that $1 billion a year should come from the private sector, as a minimum to justify the label 'public-private partnership' and the two seats it has out of the 18 vot-

ing seats on the Fund Board. The remaining $9 billion a year should come, in pro-portion to Gross Domestic Product (GDP), from the 48 countries that have 'high' Human Development Index, or HDI. (The UN's HDI measures the overall quality of life based on standard of living, life expectancy, and literacy plus school-enrol-ment). The proposed contribution comes to 0.035% of GDP for each country. Not one country has yet given at this level. Assuming, in the absence of better data, that every contribution made thus far is entirely for use this year, the Netherlands, (con-tributing at 97% of its proposed level), Sweden (73%), and Italy (57%) have done reasonably well. Seventeen countries have given between 1% and 50% of the pro-posed level, with Japan and the USA at a very disappointing 12% and 13% respec-tively. And 28 'high development' countries have given nothing at all.[56]

Because industrialized countries and influential groups like the G8 Summit pledge the bulk of the contribution to the GFATM, the desired South-North inclusiveness of the fund faces formidable legal and political challenges: donor ambivalence and donor fatigue,[57] and a possible *nemo dat quod non habet*[58] objec-tion. There is also some concern that granting full voting rights to the profit-ori-ented private sector in partnerships like the GFATM aimed at global health governance could potentially undermine multilateral diplomacy founded on the goodwill of intergovernmental organizations like the United Nations and its spe-cialized agencies.[59] While these challenges are well founded, we must rethink the ideals of enlightened self-interest and explore possible ways to engrave mutual vulnerability and globalization of disease within emerging global partnerships like the GFATM.

E Rethinking the Concepts of Mutual Vulnerability, Globalization of Disease, and Enlightened Self-Interest

As already argued in chapter 3, mutual vulnerability, the globalization of disease and enlightened self-interest, are powerful catalysts that animate new thinking on global health governance. To bridge the contemporary South-North health divide and the uneven distribution of the burdens of disease within and among nations in the global village, these catalysts must influence the outcome of the emergent global health funding facility. Cumulatively, the dynamics of the three factors – microbial permeation of, and pathogenic disrespect for, national boundaries – provide an opportunity to tackle the transnationalization of disease multilaterally. On a balance of scale, protectionist public health agendas ideally should not blur visionary, broad-based multilateral approaches. In respect of the GFATM, donor countries and agencies must work together with the developing world on a syner-gistic basis to avoid the errors of past decades, when aid was frequently tied to conditions alien and hostile to the environment in recipient countries. Synergy, in this context, rests on enlightened self-interest because the tolerance of disease in even the remotest part of the world constitutes a threat to populations everywhere. As Brundtland rightly observes, 'enlightened self-interest compels industrialised country governments and private corporations to do what it takes to drastically reduce the current burden of disease in the developing world. To do so will be good for economic growth, be good for health and be good for the environment. Not only for the three billion people who have yet to benefit from the technological and economic revolution of the past fifty years – but for us all.'[60]

In the long term, if self-interest, is 'narrowly defined,' as opposed to 'enlightened,' the GFATM will ultimately be another haphazard policy that leaves humanity multilaterally defenceless against formidable threats of transnational pathogenic forces. Given that I have argued for disease non-proliferation and global health funding facility with multistakeholder governance structures, we must further explore the respective roles that countries and non-state actors, especially civil society, should play in communitarian globalism.

F   Communitarian Globalism and Nation States

That the phenomenon of globalization has rendered the distinction between national and international health anachronistic does not mean that the nation state has or will ultimately become completely irrelevant in global health governance, nor does it diminish the important role that countries are envisaged to play in communitarian globalism. Globalization of public health discourses simply elevates transnational health threats to a level so high on the agenda of multilateralism that state-actors will feel compelled to explore their complexities. Our contemporary world order is still predominantly structured on a coalition of nation states. In the discourse of communitarian globalism, therefore, the onus of basic curative, protective, preventive, and promotional health care services falls substantially on governments within national jurisdictions. The dimensions of these services are multiple: resource-allocation decisions, basic sanitation and environmental hygiene, food security, poverty alleviation, the regulation of medical insurance, and health care delivery. Other factors include equity and ethical issues, the assessment and reform of health systems, sustainable development, legislative interventions in health care delivery, public health education, the maintenance of core capacity for disease surveillance, and a range of other social and economic decisions. In all of these areas, governments within national jurisdictions are the predominant, if not the sole actors in making critical choices and decisions. The World Bank has articulated these various challenges to governments in three broad categories:

(i) Since overall economic growth, particularly poverty-reducing growth, and education are central to good health, governments need to pursue sound macroeconomic policies that emphasize the reduction of poverty. They also need to expand basic schooling, especially for girls, because the way in which households, particularly mothers, use information and financial resources to shape their dietary, fertility, health care, and other lifestyle choices has a powerful influence on the health of household members.

(ii) Governments in developing countries should spend far less – on average, about 50 per cent less – than they now do on less cost-effective interventions and instead double or triple spending on basic public health programs such as immunizations and AIDS prevention, and on essential clinical services. A minimum package of essential clinical services would include sick-child care, family planning, prenatal and delivery care, and treatment of tuberculosis and STDs. Low-income countries should redirect current public spending for health and increase expenditures (by government, donors, and patients) to meet needs for public health and the minimum package of essential clinical services for their populations; less reallocation would be needed in middle-income countries.

(iii) Because competition can improve quality and drive down costs, governments should foster competition and diversity in the supply of health services and inputs. This includes, where feasible, private supply of health care services paid for by governments or social insurance. There is scope for improving the quality and efficiency of government health services through a combination of decentralization, performance-based incentives for managers and clinicians, and related training and development of management systems. Strong government regulation is crucial, including regulation of privately delivered health services to ensure safety and quality and the regulation of private insurance to encourage universal access to coverage.[61]

This broad tripartite categorization of the role of governments in health care delivery shares some synergy with the canons of health promotion,[62] the WHO's Primary Health Care,[63] and what has emerged in public health literature as 'health determinants.'[64] Each of these approaches requires critical legislative, policy, regulatory, and other interventions by governments. Keeping faith with these interventions and challenges adds value to communitarian globalism. Garrett was obviously correct when she observed that,

> Health, broadly defined, may not qualify as a right of every human being. But the essentials of public health most assuredly were human rights. Every government in the world knew by 2000 – irrefutably – that an unfiltered, unclean drinking water

system could kill children. Every government knew that black market sales of antibiotics fuelled emergence of deadly drug-resistant microbes. No political leader could believably deny knowledge that allowing unfettered tobacco advertising and sales in his or her country would destroy the lungs, hearts and other vital organs of the smoking citizenry. Leaders could no longer deny that an HIV-loaded syringe, passed from one person to another, was every bit as dangerous as a loaded gun. Ignorance might have protected world leaders in the mid-twentieth century, but after the millennium it would be difficult to dodge a charge of negligent homicide against a national leader who deliberately shunned provision of safe drinking water in favor of military or grandiose development expenditures. Trust and accountability: above all else, these were the pillars of public health.[65]

It is only when national health systems begin to show effective capacities for health promotion and disease surveillance, through sound governmental interventions, that multilateralism can dismantle the microbial arsenals and reservoirs for disease proliferation within the global village. Therefore, 'an early role of government should be that of setting unequivocal, uncontestable health objectives and launching massive campaigns to make them understood.'[66]

G Communitarian Globalism, Non-State Actors, and Global Civil Society

The Westphalian system of multilateralism faces formidable challenges and a foreseeable assault from a coalition of non-state actors and global civil society. This fact notwithstanding, some scholars dismiss the idea of a 'global civil society' as an amorphous concept.[67] This school, as Wapner observed, argues that global civil society 'is not the embodiment of humane governance ... It is populated by forces that have less benign intentions. Indeed, it is a complicated arena marked by competition among various groups that uphold conflicting interests and work to advance them ... It is comprised of many who believe that they have humanity's well-being in mind when, in fact, they are operating from a purely private, self-interested perspective.'[68] Worse still, few studies explain the mechanics by which activities in global civil society engage the structures that govern global collective life; few present a theoretical understanding of power in global civil society and analyse it in a way that clarifies its ability to shape widespread thought and behaviour.[69] Notwithstanding the pessimism that surrounds the global civil society as an innovative partner and actor in global governance, it is now widely accepted that multilateral governance of global issues can no longer rest exclusively on a world order composed of a coalition of sovereign states. Ferguson and Mansbach observe that 'various factors account for the upsurge in non-state identities, not least of which is the declining importance of territory as a source of power and prosperity.

The proliferation of transnational and global networks of de-territorialized communities has further reduced the relevance of territory in global politics.'[70] An obvious aim of the coagulation and conglomeration of these transnational global networks remains the ultimate realization of what Falk calls 'the law of humanity.'[71] According to Falk, 'the character of the law of humanity is not self-evident. It could mean law that is enacted by and for the peoples of the world, as distinct from the elites who act in law-making settings on behalf of states ... In this sense, then, states are not regarded as appropriate agents for the development of the law of humanity, it depends on civil society to establish new forms of law-creation and law-application.'[72]

Because the limits of the Westphalian system compel a reassessment of contemporary global governance structures, my proposal of communitarian globalism foresees an inclusive framework that actively involves non-state actors in multilateral health policy making. From this perspective, the effect of intercultural and theoretical dialogues that I proposed in the preceding chapter is dual-dimensional. First, such cross-theoretical/cultural dialogues explore the shortcomings of globalism anchored on the Westphalian system. Second, the dialogues support an innovative agenda that strengthens the haphazard *locus standi* of non-state actors in the governance of multilateral health issues.[73] In this sense, I agree with Wapner that 'The promise of global civil society rests on the normative commitment toward humane governance. At bottom, humane governance is about managing the affairs of public life in a democratic fashion by which energies of people are co-ordinated to solve certain dilemmas and realise the many virtues that are possible in a collective setting.'[74] The promise of civil society in humane governance is further boosted by the perceived exclusion, by the nation state, of a sizeable part of humanity from its protective structures during most of the period of the ascendancy of the state from the Treaty of Westphalia, 1648, to the present day.[75]

In recent years, multilateral governance of the environment, nuclear weapons, landmines and small arms, the recently created International Criminal Court, biological/chemical weapons, and many other regimes, all bear witness to the participation of civil society and non-state actors. On some of these multilateral/global issues, non-state actors have demonstrated commendable leadership potential as well as the capacity to influence global public opinion.[76] In the public health context, global civil society should be obliged to play the multiple roles of critic, watchdog, and collaborator in multilateral health policy making, application, enforcement, advocacy, and monitoring. International non-governmental organizations like the International Committee of the Red Cross, Oxfam International, Greenpeace, Médecins Sans Frontières – to name a few – can play more active roles in global health governance than they do now. Short of having an equal vote with states in multilateral health forums, multilateral institutions should tap their expertise and use their critical perspectives to reconstruct the contours and parameters of global health governance paradigms. This way, the web of transnational bonds across cultures and societies on a plethora of common health problems already emerging will be strengthened. As Falk puts it, 'transnational social forces provide the only vehicle for the promotion of the law of humanity, a normative focus that is animated by humane sustainable development for all peoples – North and South – and seeks to structure such commitments by way of humane geogovernance (that is, governance protective of the earth and its peoples that is democratically constituted, both in relation to participation and accountability, and that is responsive to the needs of the poorest twenty percent and of those most vulnerable) ...'[77] The domain of communitarian globalism therefore traverses a wide terrain involving a multiplicity of actors – multilateral institutions, states, civil society/non-states actors – all independent entities, yet each symbiotically united with the others to ward off traditional and re-emerging microbial threats in the global village.

H Fidelity to Humanity: Bridging the South-North Health Divide – Prophylaxis for Better Health

It is now universally accepted that the resurgence and transnational spread of deadly infectious diseases and other related health hazards constitutes one of the most vicious threats to humanity at the dawn of the twenty-first century. Global/ multilateral health governance requires multiple actors – nation states, multilateral institutions, private and corporate sectors, foundations, and civil society. These actors must make critical choices within the transient window of opportunity that mutual vulnerability has offered humanity. Despite infallible epidemiological evidence that 'in the modern world, bacteria and viruses travel almost as fast as money. With globalization, a single microbial sea washes all of humankind,'[78] apostles of isolationism and protectionism continue to dismiss discourses of transnational microbial threats as either false alarms or a frivolous prophecy of doom that must be taken with a pinch of salt. A disease-free world is utopian and unachievable. But a disease non-proliferation global village is achievable and within the reach of humankind if critical choices and sacrifices along the lines suggested by this study are made. The dawn of the twenty-first century marks an important beginning: a massive search for the needed 'prophylaxis' to prevent a reoccurrence of the mistakes of the past decades, and to reconfigure the contours and boundaries of global health governance in the years ahead. As explored in this study, globalization, socio-economic inequalities within and among nations; respect for human rights, especially dignity of the person; and intercultural and theoretical dialogues are all subsumed within the complexities of this endeavour.

Without the slightest pretence that this task will be easy, global interdependence as well as the corresponding interconnection of humanity's health across societies teaches many lessons, the most important being that the world desperately needs to rebuild damaged trust. In a world that presently exhibits essential features of medieval feudalism – in which 80 per cent of the world population has access to less than 15 per cent of global resources – reconstruction of social trust to promote human health faces formidable challenges. As Garret observes,

> To build trust, there must be a sense of community. And the community must collectively believe in its own future. At the millennium much of humanity hungered for connectedness and community *but lived isolated, even hostile, existences.* Trust evaporated when Tutsis met Hutus, Serbs confronted Kosovars, African-Americans worked with white Americans or Estonians argued with Russians. The new globalization pushed communities against one another, opening old wounds and historic hatreds, often with genocidal results. It would be up to public health to find ways to bridge the hatreds, *bringing the world toward a sense of singular community in which the health of each one member rises or falls with the health of all others.*[79]

Garret's sense of a singular but isolated community of humanity comes within what I explored as the paradox of a global village in a divided world. Difficult as the task of rebuilding multilateral trust may be, it remains the critical first step towards a humane global health order. In the absence of such trust – trust that mandates every human being and every country to see the damage of another person's health as his own or another country's disease as its own – the modest policy recommendations of this study would be futile. Because all of humanity is now implicated in a global compact, the recommendations of this study are only achievable in a multilateral setting of a modified social contractual trust. In his book, *World Citizenship: Allegiance to Humanity,*[80] Nobel Laureate Joseph Rotblat reminds us that, 'The most important problems facing the human race today are global problems. This is what is meant by global interdependence ... A parochial attitude to world affairs, insensitivity to the destruction of the environment, a lack of compassion for fellow human beings, insufficient imagination to see the dangers that lie ahead: all will condemn the human race to a chaotic and violent future.'[81]

Without an iota of doubt, transnational public health threats are within the contemplation of Rotblat's 'global problems.' What then is the most effective prophylaxis, a preventive multilateral therapy for the South-North health divide in a turbulent world devoid of mutual trust and respect for endangered human lives? We ought to do that which seems to be fair. Call it obligation, moral or legal, owed by wealthy countries to the poor; equity, fairness, or justice in multilateralism; or humane governance that aims to narrow South-North disparities – at the dawn of the twenty-first century, the prophylaxis that best stands to protect and promote our endangered 'common health future' as well as to guarantee our collective health security is enlightened self-interest. Its visible imprimatur abounds in almost every society, culture, and religion, and in every social milieu where human beings interact with one another, including the multilateral public health arena.

Post-ontological international law, with its bold claims to universal protection of human rights and the enhancement of human dignity, is indispensable in reconstructing the damaged public health trust in the relations of nations and peoples. In this endeavour, the fairness of the law should no longer be assumed. Its interventions should effectively deliver the dividends of good health to the poor and vulnerable across the world. Today, a range of millennial challenges confronts humanity's health. These challenges compel us to comprehensively reassess the mechanisms with which international law responds to multilateral health promotion and governance. Will twenty-first century international law opt to remain passive in the face of advancing transnational microbial threats? One certain fact, however, is that multilateral health governance falls within the boundaries of contemporary international law. Therefore, international law's perceived passivity in global health discourse in the past years must now be reconciled and aligned with the need for a paradigm shift: one that recognizes the synergy that law and public health disciplines have long shared on the promotion and enhancement of human life and dignity. The reach and grasp of the law in this endeavour must match the expectations of the vulnerable constituents of the global village: those that live their daily lives with the heaviest burdens of infectious and non-communicable diseases, especially women and children in the developing world.

Notes

Introduction

1 D.R. Phillips, *Health and Health Care in the Third World* (New York: Longman, 1990) at 41 states that epidemiological transition assumes or implies a range of changes: in attitudes, education, diet, aspirations, urbanization, public health, and health care and its technology. Basically, it is proposed that societies during modernization will move from a period of high birth and death rates and low life expectancy (perhaps forty years of life expectancy at birth or even lower) to a stable period when life expectancy will have increased to around seventy years or longer, and death rates and birth rates will have become much lower, often approximately balancing each other numerically.

2 See 'Global Health Challenges,' Report of a Symposium Organized by Liu Center for the Study of Global Issues, Vancouver, Canada, 5 March 1999, at 2.

3 'Come, let us go down and confuse their language so they will not understand each other ... That is why it was called Babel – because there the Lord confused the language of the whole world.' See Genesis 11:7–9.

4 I.L. Head, 'The Contribution of International Law to Development' (1987) 25 Canadian Yearbook of International Law 29 at 31 (describing similar confusion surrounding the definition and meaning of 'development' as well as the role of international law in that dynamic).

5 H.L. Fuenzalida-Puelma and S.S. Connor, eds. (Washington, DC: Pan-American Health Organization, 1989).

6 R. Roemer,, 'The Right to Health Care,' in ibid. at 17.

7 Ibid.

8 V. Leary, 'The Right to Health in International Human Rights Law' (1994) 1 Health & Human Rights 25 at 31.

9 *The Right to Health in the Americas*, at 600.

10 The positive school of thought defines health ambitiously as 'a state of complete physical, mental and social well-being, and not merely the absence of disease or infirmity.'
See for instance, Constitution of the World Health Organization, opened for signature
22 July 1946 (Preamble) (defining health ambitiously in those terms).

11 The negative school of thought defines health as 'the absence of disease, impairment or
infirmity.' For a detailed analysis of the substantive and structural complexities of Public Health Law in the legal contexts of the United States and South Africa, see L.O.
Gostin, *Public Health Law: Power, Duty, Restraint* (Berkeley: University of California
Press, 2001); S. Nadasen, *Public Health Law in South Africa* (Durban: Butterworths,
2000) 2.

12 The Ottawa Charter for Health Promotion defines health promotion as 'the process of
enabling people to increase control over, and to improve their health. To reach a state
of complete physical, mental and social well being, an individual or group must be
able to identify and realize aspirations, to satisfy needs, and to change or cope with the
environment. Health is ... a resource for everyday life ... Health is a positive concept
emphasizing social and personal resources, as well as physical capacities. Health promotion is not just the responsibility of the health sector, but goes beyond health lifestyles to well-being.' See Ottawa Charter for Health Promotion, 21 November 1986,
adopted at the first International Conference on Health Promotion, held in Ottawa,
Canada, in November 1986, available at http://www.who.dk/policy/ottawa.htm
(accessed 8 April 2001).

13 The Alma-Ata Declaration on Primary Health Care 1978 defines primary health care
as the 'essential health care based on practical, scientifically sound and socially acceptable methods and technology made accessible to individuals and families in the community through their full participation and at a cost that the community and country
can afford to maintain at every stage of their development in the spirit of self reliance
and self determination. It forms an integral part both of the country's health system, of
which it is the central function and main focus, and of the overall social and economic
development of the community. It is the first level of contact of individuals, the family
and community with the health system bringing health care as close as possible to
where people live and work, and constitutes the first element of a continuing health
care process.' See Alma-Ata Declaration on Primary Health Care, 12 September 1978,
adopted at the joint World Health Organization and United Nations Children's Fund
(WHO/UNICEF) sponsored international conference held in Alma-Ata, former
USSR, 6–12 September 1978, 'Health for All' Series No. 1 (Geneva: WHO, 1978),
available at http://www.who.int/hpr/docs/almaata.html (accessed 8 April 2001).

14 The determinants of health include biological, behavioural, environmental, health system, socio-economic, and sociocultural factors, aging of the population, science and
technology, information and communication, gender, equity, and social justice. See G.
Pinet, 'Health Challenges of the 21st Century: A Legislative Approach to Health

Determinants' (1998) 49 International Digest of Health Legislation 131 at 123–4, J.M. Last, *Public Health and Human Ecology,* 2nd ed. (Stamford, CT: Appleton & Lange, 1998) at 7. For a discussion of determinants of health from the perspective of development, see Phillips, *Health and Health Care in the Third World* at 11–19.

15 Throughout this study, I will be using the term 'South-North,' as suggested by I.L. Head, *On a Hinge of History: The Mutual Vulnerability of South and North* (Toronto: University of Toronto Press, in association with the International Development Research Centre, 1991) 14. Head prefers 'South-North' as a more accurate reflection of the current international system and argues that the popular usage of 'North-South' is misleading because 'it lends weight to the impression that the South is the diminutive.'

16 See generally 'Global Health Challenges,' Report of a Symposium by the Liu Center, stating that modern transportation mechanisms have facilitated the rapid movement of peoples and goods. If the economic influence is global, so can be the patterns of disease transmission. A global economy demands extensive travel by business persons, and permits extensive travel by tourists, in both instances in congested long-range passenger confinement on aircraft with closed atmospheres: germ incubators.

17 In the field of global governance and regime discourse, Rosenau has developed the concept of the 'Frontier' to explore the obsolescence of the distinction between 'domestic' and 'foreign' affairs in an interdependent world. See J.N. Rosenau, *Along the Domestic-Foreign Frontier: Exploring Governance in a Turbulent World* (Cambridge: Cambridge University Press, 1997).

18 Ibid. at 5.

19 Ibid. at 20.

20 For a pioneer intellectual account of the global village concept, see M. MacLuhan and B.R. Powers, *The Global Village: Transformations in World Life and Media in the 21st Century* (New York: Oxford University Press, 1992).

21 I do not claim originality in the usage of 'mutual vulnerability'; the application of the concept in the multilateral relations of nation states is not new. What is new about mutual vulnerability, as employed in this study, is its relevance in, and application to, the complexities of transnationalization of disease and health hazards in a globalizing world. For earlier uses of the concept to explore the international political economy of South-North relations, development and underdevelopment, see I.L. Head, *On a Hinge of History: The Mutual Vulnerability of South and North* (Toronto: University of Toronto Press, in association with the International Development Research Centre, 1991); J. Nef, *Human Security and Mutual Vulnerability: The Global Political Economy of Development and Underdevelopment,* 2nd ed. (Ottawa: IDRC, 1999). I have benefited from the insightful analysis of both scholars.

22 R. Falk, *Law in an Emerging Global Village: A Post-Westphalian Perspective* (New York: Transnational Publishers, 1998); *Predatory Globalization: A Critique* (Oxford: Blackwell, 1999).

23 L. Nader, 'The Anthropological Study of Law' (1965) 65 American Anthropologist at 25.

24 D. Trubek, 'Towards a Social Theory of Law: An Essay on the Study of Law and Development' (1972) 82 Yale Law Journal 1.

25 F.G. Snyder, 'Law and Development in the Light of Dependency Theory' (1980) 14 Law & Society Rev. 723.

26 For a study of the gender dimensions of public health polices, see Ford Foundation, *Globalization, Health Sector Reform, Gender and Reproductive Health* (New York: Ford Foundation, 2001); R.J. Cook, B.M. Dickens, and M.F. Fathalla, *Reproductive Health and Human Rights* (Oxford: Oxford University Press, 2003).

27 See Falk, *Law in an Emerging Global Village* at 35. The *Treaty of Westphalia 1648*, which ended thirty years of wars in Europe, reversed the subordination of European civil authorities to the Holy See and led to the emergence of nation states, is often cited by international scholars as the normative foundation of the modern international system.

Chapter 1: Conceptual Framework and Methodology

1 For the global village metaphor see Introduction, note 20, above.

2 See *Our Global Neighborhood: The Report of the Commission on Global Governance*, co-chaired by I. Carlsson and S. Ramphal (New York: Oxford University Press, 1995).

3 L. Sohn and T. Buergenthal, eds., *The Movement of Persons across Borders* (Washington, DC: American Society of International Law; Studies in Transnational Legal Policy No. 23, 1992).

4 D.P. Fidler, 'The Globalization of Public Health: Emerging Infectious Diseases and International Relations' (1997) 5 (1) Indiana J. of Global Legal Studies 1. See also D. Yach and D. Bettcher, 'The Globalization of Public Health I: Threats and Opportunities' (1998) 88 Am. J. of Pub. Health 735; G. Walt, 'Globalization of International Health' (1998) 351 The Lancet 434; D. Woodward et al., 'Globalization and Health: A Framework for Analysis and Action' (2001) 79 (9) Bulletin of the World Health Organization 875.

5 World Health Organization, *World Health Report 1996: Fighting Disease, Fostering Development* (Geneva: WHO, 1996) 1.

6 P.F. Basch, *A Textbook of International Health* (Oxford: Oxford University Press, 1990); L. Garret, *The Coming Plague: Newly Emerging Diseases in a World Out of Balance* (New York: Farrar, Straus & Giroux, 1994).

7 J.M. Last, *Public Health and Human Ecology*, 2nd ed. (Stamford, CT: Appleton & Lang, 1998) 337.

8 I do not argue that every single health problem in the Third World constitutes a global problem that should be placed on the agenda of multilateralism. Nutrition, basic sani-

tation, housing, civil wars and political conflicts, environmental disasters – each affects human health in significant ways. It is the primary responsibility of the government in every country, especially in the developing world, to respond to these health-related social problems. This study focuses on health problems that are far beyond the surveillance capacity and developmental capability of individual nation states: those health concerns that are being propelled by underdevelopment and globalization in ways that threaten all populations within the global village, irrespective of the geographical origin of the pathogen in question.

9 The rhetorical juxtaposition of microbe-humanity interaction in an interdependent world as 'mutuality of vulnerability and vulnerability of multilateralism' is inspired by a similar rhetorical exploration of the inequities of the international system by Mohammed Bedjaoui. See the 'international order of poverty and poverty of the international order' in Mohammed Bedjaoui, *Towards a New International Economic Order* (Paris: UNESCO, 1979).

10 Thucydides, *History of the Peloponnesian War*, trans. R. Warner (Harmondsworth: Penguin Books, 1954).

11 The term 'vulnerability of multilateralism' is similar, but not in *pari materia*, with 'Microbialpolitik,' a term coined by D.P. Fidler, which he uses to describe the 'international politics produced as states attempt to deal with pathogenic microbes.' See Fidler, 'Microbialpolitik: Infectious Diseases and International Relations' (1998) 14 Am. Uni. Int'l Law Rev. 1. My use of the term 'vulnerability of multilateralism' embraces other variables outside politics – the gaps, failures, shortcomings, frustrations, and bureaucracy of multilateral public health initiatives.

12 For a discussion and chronology of the nineteenth-century international sanitary conferences, see N. Horward-Jones, *The Scientific Background of the International Sanitary Conferences, 1851–1938* (Geneva: WHO, 1975).

13 See Constitution of the World Health Organization, *World Health Organization: Basic Documents*, 43rd ed. (Geneva: WHO, 2001) 2.

14 R. Falk, 'The Coming Global Civilization: Neo-Liberal or Humanist,' in *Legal Visions of the 21st Century: Essays in Honour of Judge Christopher Weeramantry*, ed. Anghie and G. Sturgess, 15 (The Hague: Kluwer Law International, 1998. See also R. Falk, *Law in an Emerging Global Village: A Post-Westphalian Perspective* (New York: Transnational Publishers, 1998) 189. See generally Falk, *Predatory Globalization: A Critique* (Oxford: Blackwell Publishers, 1999).

15 'The Coming Global Civilization,' 15.

16 A *quia timet* action is 'an action based on fear or apprehension of some future injury.' See H.C Black, *Black's Law Dictionary*, 6th ed., (St Paul, MN: West Publishing Co., 1990) 1247. This expression is used in a policy context to catalyse enlightened self-interest in multilateral-global health cooperation between countries, as opposed to a legal context.

17 T.M. Franck, *Fairness in International Law and Institutions* (Oxford: Clarendon Press, 1995).
18 R.A. Falk, *On Humane Governance: Towards a New World Politics* (College Park: Pennsylvania State University Press, 1995).
19 J. Rawls, *A Theory of Justice*, rev. ed. (Cambridge: Harvard University Press, 1999).
20 Although the liberal scholarship of Franck and Rawls is persuasive, I am not completely convinced that their views are infallible pathways to humane, equitable, and fair public health multilateralism. Thus, I use the more critical approach of Falk to explore an inclusive theoretical and policy approach to health promotion in a divided world.
21 The Roll-Back Malaria Project is a global public-private partnership by the WHO, UNICEF, the UNDP, the World Bank, leading global pharmaceutical corporations, and private foundations.
22 Epidemiology is defined as 'the study of the distribution and determinants of health-related states or events in specified populations, and the application of this study to control of health problems.' See J.M. Last, *A Dictionary of Epidemiology*, 3rd ed. (New York: Oxford University Press, 1995) 54.
23 As employed here, 'mainstream multilateral health policy making' refers to multilateral approaches to, and normative governance of, cross-border health challenges that are beyond the capacity of one individual country or a group countries, including the effects of social and economic disparities within and among countries on multilateral health initiatives. These approaches and governance mechanisms involve a symbiosis of legal and non-legal interventions.
24 A.L Taylor, 'Making the World Health Organization Work: A Legal Framework for Universal Access to the Conditions for Health' (1992) 18 American Journal of Law & Medicine 301; 'Controlling the Global Spread of Infectious Diseases: Towards a Reinforced Role for the International Health Regulations' (1997) 33 Houston Law Rev. 1326.
25 *Ibid.*
26 D.P. Fidler, 'Return of the Fourth Horseman: Emerging Infectious Diseases and International Law' (1997) 81 Minnesota Law Rev. 771; 'The Future of the World Health Organization: What Role for International Law' (1998) 31 Vanderbilt J. of Transnational Law 1079; and 'International Law and Global Public Health' (1999) 48 University of Kansas Law Rev. 1. For similar arguments for increased use of legal strategies in multilateral health initiatives, see B.J. Plotkin and A.M. Kimball, 'Designing the International Policy and Legal Framework for the Control of Infectious Diseases: First Steps' (1997) 3 Emerging Infectious Diseases 1.
27 D.P. Fidler, *International Law and Infectious Diseases* (Oxford: Clarendon Press, 1999).
28 Ibid 'editor's preface.'
29 Ibid. at 5–19.

30 Ibid. at 21–52.
31 World Health Organization, *International Health Regulations*, 3rd annotated ed. (Geneva: WHO, 1983).
32 Fidler mentions the establishment of the Pan-American Sanitary Bureau in 1902, the International Office of Public Health in 1907, and the Health Organization of the League of Nations in 1923, before the World Health Organization was founded in 1948. See *International Law and Infectious Diseases*, 47–52.
33 Ibid. at 19.
34 Ibid. at 303.
35 Fidler recognized this fact when he wrote, 'although the monograph provides a comprehensive international legal analysis of infectious diseases, it does not exhaust this topic. Each area of international law analyzed is in flux, making it impossible to provide a definitive analysis. Another challenge was writing for not only international legal specialists but also public health experts who are generally unfamiliar with international law. Despite these problems, this monograph contributes to a neglected area of international legal, public health, and international relations scholarship and encourages others to explore this increasingly critical global issue.' Ibid. at 4.
36 For a recent treatment of this theme, see D.P. Fidler, 'The Globalization of Public Health: The First 100 Years of International Health Diplomacy' (2001) 79 (9) Bulletin of the World Health Organization 842.
37 *International Law and Infectious Diseases* at 7.
38 Ibid. at 28–35. South-North disparities and global health challenges received more detailed attention from Fidler in an earlier article, albeit from a strictly international relations perspective. See D.P. Fidler, 'Microbialpolitik: Infectious Diseases and International Relations' (1998) 14 Am. Univ. Int'l Law Rev. 1.
39 For some relevant works on global public health from a historical perspective see D. Porter, *Health, Civilization and the State: A History of Public Health from Ancient to Modern Times* (London and New York: Routledge, 1999); J.N. Hayes, *The Burdens of Disease: Epidemics and Human Response in Western History* (New Brunswick, NJ: Rutgers University Press, 1998); W.H. McNeill, *Plagues and Peoples* (New York: Doubleday, 1976); Howard-Jones, *The Scientific Background of the International Sanitary Conferences*; N.M. Goodman, *International Health Organizations and Their Work*, 2nd ed. (London: Churchill Livingstone, 1977); H. Zinsser, *Rats, Lice and History: A Chronicle of Pestilence and Plagues* (New York: Black Dog and Leventhal, 1963).
40 Fidler, 'The Globalization of Public Health'; M. Zacher, 'Global Epidemiological Surveillance: International Co-operation to Monitor Infectious Diseases,' in *Global Public Goods: International Co-Operation in the 21st Century*, ed. I. Kaul et al. (New York: UNDP and Oxford University Press, 1999) 266.
41 For perspectives on global underdevelopment, poverty, and public health, see R. Keily and P. Marfleet, eds., *Globalisation and the Third World* (London: Routledge, 1998);

M. Chossudovsky, *The Globalisation of Poverty: Impacts of IMF and World Bank Reforms* (Penang, Malaysia: Third World Network, 1997); K. Watkins, *Oxfam Poverty Report* (Oxford: Oxfam, 1995).

42 D. Yach and D. Bettcher, 'The Globalization of Public Health II: The Convergence of Self-Interest and Altruism' (1998) 88 American J. of Public Health 738; H. Nakajima, 'Global Disease Threats and Foreign Policy' (1997) Brown J. of World Affairs 319; Last, *Public Health and Human Ecology*; Basch, *Text Book of International Health* 6.

43 Porter, *Health, Civilization and the State* at 46; S. Watts, *Epidemics and History: Disease, Power and Imperialism* (New Haven, CT: Yale University Press, 1997) 89–121.

44 Nakajima, 'Global Disease Threats' Fidler, 'The Globalization of Public Health.'

45 Chossudovsky, *Globalization of Poverty.*

46 C.J.L. Murray and A. Lopez, *Global Burden of Disease* (Cambridge: Harvard University Press, 1996).

47 WHO, *World Health Report 1996.*

48 See for instance, Bedjaoui, *Toward a New International Economic Order*; Falk, *Law in an Emerging Global Village*; The South Commission, *The Challenge of the South* (Oxford: Oxford University Press, 1990); R.P. Anand, *New States and International Law* (Delhi: Vikas Ltd., 1972); R.P. Anand, 'Development and Environment: The Case of Developing Countries' (1980) 24 Indian J. of Int'l Law 1; T.O. Elias, *Africa and the Development of International Law*, 2nd rev. ed. (The Hague: Martinus Nijhoff, 1988). Quite recently, a formidable intellectual movement – Third World Approaches to International Law (TWAIL) – that articulates South-North disparities from the international legal perspective has emerged. See generally M. Mutua, 'What Is TWAIL,' Lecture given at the 94th Annual Meeting of the American Society of International Law, Washington, DC, 6 April 2000, *Proceedings of the 94th Annual Meeting of American Society of International Law* (Washington, DC: ASIL, 2000). For some important works by the leading scholars of South-North disparities from the developing world, see K. Mickelson, 'Rhetoric or Rage: Third World Voices in International Legal Discourse' (1998) 16 Wisconsin International Law J. 353.

49 I.L. Head, 'The Contribution of International Law to Development' (1987) 25 *Canadian Yearbook of International Law* 29 at 31.

50 Falk, *Law in an Emerging Global Village* at 33.

51 I concur with David Fidler's persuasive submission that 'globalization provides diseases with opportunities to infect human populations across the planet almost as easily as infecting the family next door'; see 'Return of the Fourth Horseman.'

52 World Health Organization, *Bridging the Gaps: World Health Report 1995* (Geneva: WHO, 1995); World Bank, *Investing in Health: World Development Report 1993* (New York: Oxford University Press, 1993).

53 Murray and Lopez, *Global Burden of Disease* (using what has emerged in public health

literature as Disability Adjusted Life Years (DALYs) to measure morbidity and mortality of selected communicable and non-communicable diseases in various regions of the world and finding the developing world, especially Africa, to be lagging behind other regions).

54 The pros and cons of each of the dominant theoretical schools is discussed under the rubric of 'the wealth and poverty of theory.' See below at 102–7.

55 I borrowed this expression from Richard Falk, with whose arguments on a humane world order I completely concur. See Falk, *Law in an Emerging Global Village* at 29.

56 The constitution of the WHO defines health as 'a state of complete physical, mental and social well-being and not merely the absence of disease or infirmity.' See Constitution of the World Health Organization 1946 (Preamble) *World Health Organization: Basic Documents*, 43rd ed., (Geneva: WHO, 2001).

57 The legal powers of the WHO to adopt conventions, regulations, and non-binding guidelines are contained in Articles 19–23 of its constitution.

58 'Making the World Health Organization Work: A Legal Framework for Universal Access to the Conditions for Health' (1992) 18 Am. J. of Law & Med. 301.

59 'Health,' in O. Schachter and C.C. Joyner, eds., *United Nations Legal Order*, vol. 2 (New York: Cambridge University Press, 1995) 859.

60 'The Future of the World Health Organization'; 'Return of the Fourth Horseman'; 'International Law and Global Public Health.'

61 'International Law and Global Public Health' at 15. I agree with Fidler, especially his caveat that this critique of WHO does not mean that international law will solve today's public health problems, but is intended rather to encourage the WHO to integrate useful legal strategies in its work and take relevant international legal development more seriously.

62 A. Kiss and D. Shelton, *International Environmental Law* (New York: Transnational Publishers, Inc., 1991); P.W. Birnie and A.E. Boyle, *International Law and the Environment* (Oxford: Clarendon Press, 1992).

63 World Bank, *Investing in Health*.

64 In this sense I agree with P. Ellis that 'the qualitative approach helps us to understand people as they interact in various social contexts and to define social reality from their own experience, perspective and meaning rather than from that of the researcher alone ... It raises hitherto unasked questions, the answers to which afford deeper and sharper insights into how and why people participate as they do in a variety of social processes.' Quoted in J. Kitts and J.H. Roberts, *The Health Gap: Beyond Pregnancy and Reproduction* (Ottawa: International Research Development Centre, 1996) 37. See also, World Health Organization, *Qualitative Research for Health Programmes* (Geneva: WHO, Division of Mental Health and Prevention of Substance Abuse, 1996).

65 See Murray and Lopez, *Global Burden of Disease*.

66 W. Foege, 'Foreword,' Murray and Lopez, *Global Burden of Disease*.

67 See Pan American Health Organization, *Health in the Americas*, vols. 1 & 2 (Washington, DC: PAHO, 1998).

68 See 'Introduction,' *The Right to Health in the Americas: A Comparative Constitutional Study*, ed. H.L. Fuenzalida and S.S. Connor (Washington, DC: Pan American Health Organization, 1989.

69 For a detailed overview of critical legal scholarship, see D. Held, *Introduction to Critical Theory: Horkheimer to Habermas* (London: Hutchinson, 1980); D. Kairys, ed., *The Politics of Law: A Progressive Critique*, 3rd ed. (New York: Basic Books, 1998).

70 See generally, L. Nader, 'The Anthropological Study of Law' (1965) 67 American Anthropologist Pt. 2 (Special Issue) 3; C. Geertz, 'Local Knowledge: Fact and Law in Comparative Perspective,' in C. Geertz, ed. *Further Essays in Interpretive Anthropology* (New York: Basic Books, 1989).

71 F.G. Snyder, 'Law and Development in the Light of Dependency Theory' (1980) 14 Law & Society Rev. 723; D.M. Trubek, 'Towards a Social Theory of Law: An Essay on the Study of Law and Development' (1972) 82 Yale Law Journal 1.

Chapter 2: The Paradox of a Global Village in a Divided World

1 The Constitution of the World Health Organisation 1946 (Preamble), *World Health Organization: Basic Documents*, 43rd ed. (Geneva: World Health Organization, 2001) 1.

2 See L.C. Chen et al., 'Health as a Global Public Good,' in *Global Public Goods: International Co-operation in the 21st Century*, ed. Inge Kaul, et al. 384 (New York: UNDP/ Oxford University Press, 1999).

3 I. Kaul et al., 'Defining Global Public Goods,' in *Global Public Goods*, 2.

4 Because of the complexities of globalization, I will explore its health implications in two levels of inquiry within the rubric of what I explore as 'globalization of poverty.' See below, 32–40.

5 For a discussion of 'neighbourhood values' from a global perspective, see *Our Global Neighborhood: The Report of the Commission on Global Governance*, co-chaired by I. Carlsson and S. Ramphal (New York: Oxford University Press, 1995) 48.

6 Nobel Laureate Joseph Stiglitz has explored globalization and its contradictions in his seminal work *Globalization and Its Discontents* (New York: Norton, 2003).

7 See below 35–40.

8 United Nations Development Programme, *Human Development Report 1997* (New York: Oxford University Press, 1997) 7.

9 United Nations Development Program, *Human Development Report 1998* (New York: Oxford University Press, 1998) 29–30.

10 World Bank, *World Development Report 1993: Investing in Health* (New York: Oxford University Press, 1993).

11 J.M. Last, *Public Health and Human Ecology* (Stamford, CT: Appleton & Lange, 1998) 338. .

12 Apart from income disparities, multilateral institutions use other criteria to classify countries: gross national product (GNP), infant mortality, life expectancy at birth, and disability adjusted life years (DALYs).

13 To avoid the controversy that surrounds the use of the terms 'First World' and 'Third World,' I prefer to use the term 'South-North' in discussing contemporary global disparities. See generally I.L. Head, *On a Hinge of History: The Mutual Vulnerability of South and North* (Toronto: University of Toronto Press, in association with International Development Research Centre, 1991).

14 *The End of the Third World* (New York: St Martins Press, 1993) 45.

15 The South Commission, *The Challenge of the South* (New York: Oxford University Press, 1990) 1.

16 Ibid.

17 G.H. Brundtland, 'A Call for Healthy Development,' in *World Health Organization Report on Infectious Diseases: Removing Obstacles to Healthy Development* (Geneva: WHO, 1999) 66.

18 World Health Organization, *The World Health Report 1995: Bridging the Gaps* (Geneva: WHO, 1995) 1.

19 Ibid.

20 The World Health Organization, the World Bank, and the Harvard School of Public Health have jointly commissioned the global burden of disease study: a comprehensive assessment of mortality and disability from diseases, injuries, and risk factors in 1990 and projected to 2020. Measuring the disease burden by mortality and morbidity using Disability Adjusted Life Years DALYs, the study divided the world into eight regions: established market economies (EMEs), formerly socialist economies of Europe (FSEs), India, China, Other Asia and Islands, Sub-Saharan Africa, Latin America and the Caribbean, and Middle Eastern Crescent. See generally, C.J.L. Murray and A. Lopez, eds., *The Global Burden of Disease and Injury Series* (Geneva: WHO, 1996).

21 Ibid.

22 I use 'his,' 'her,' 'she,' and 'he' all through this book not in a gendered sense but generically.

23 *World Health Report 1995: Bridging the Gaps* 2.

24 This part draws from a paper I published in the (Spring 2000) 7 (2) Indiana Journal of Global Legal Studies 603 entitled 'Global Village, Divided World: South-North Gap and Global Health Challenges at Century's Dawn.' The article was in response to D.P. Fidler's 'Neither Science Nor Shamans: Globalization of Markets and Health in the Developing World' (1999) 7 Indiana Journal of Global Legal Studies 191.

25 For an extensive discourse of how the phenomenon of globalization affects people in

different parts of the world, see T.L. Friedman, *The Lexus and the Olive Tree* (New York: Anchor Books, 2000).

26 D.Y. and D. Bettcher, 'The Globalization of Public Health I: Threats and Opportunities' (1998) 88 American J. of Public Health 735.

27 K. Lee and R. Dodgson, 'Globalization and Cholera: Implications for Global Governance' (Apr.–June 2000) 6 (2) Global Governance 213 at 214.

28 Lee and Dodgson define globalization as 'a process that is changing the nature of human interaction across a range of social spheres, including the economic, political, social, technological, and environmental. This process is globalizing in the sense that many *boundaries hitherto separating human interaction are being increasingly eroded. These boundaries – spatial, temporal, and cognitive – can be described as the dimensions of globalization.*' 'Globilization and Cholera' at 215. According to David P. Fidler, 'globalization refers to processes or phenomena that undermine the ability of the sovereign state to control what occurs in its territory.' See 'The Globalization of Public Health: Emerging Infectious Diseases and International Relations' (1997) 7 Indiana J. of Global Legal Studies 11. Gordon R. Walker and Mark A. Fox argue that 'the key feature which underlies the concept of globalization ... is the *erosion or irrelevance of national boundaries* in markets which can truly be described as global.' 'Globalization: An Analytical Framework' (1996) 3 Indiana J. of Global Legal Studies 375.

29 D. Held et al., *Global Transformations: Politics, Economics and Culture* (Cambridge: Polity Press, 1999) 16.

30 J.A. Scholte, *Globalization: A Critical Introduction* (New York: St Martin's Press, 2000) 45.

31 R.O. Keohane and J.S. Nye, 'Introduction,' *Governance in a Globalizing World*, ed. Joseph S. Nye and John D. Donahue (Washington, DC: Brookings Institution Press, 2000) 2.

32 Scholte, *Globalization* at 16.

33 Lee and Dodgson, 'Globalization and Cholera' at 215.

34 D. Held and A. McGrew, 'Introduction,' in D. Held and A. McGrew, eds., *Governing Globalization: Power, Authority and Global Governance* (Cambridge: Polity Press, 2002) 2.

35 R. Keily, 'Globalisation, (Post-)Modernity and the Third World,' in *Globalisation and the Third World*, ed. R. Keily and P. Marfleet (London and New York: Routledge, 1998) 2 citing M. Waters, *Globalization* (London: Routledge, 1995).

36 A. Giddens, *The Consequences of Modernity* (London: Polity Press, 1990); R. Robertson, *Globalization: Social Theory and Global Culture* (London: Sage, 1992). The two scholars differ on the scope of the progression of globalization from the fifteenth century. Giddens posits globalization squarely within modernity; Robertson identifies other variables that are global in nature. See also Held and McGrew, *Governing Globalization* at 2 (asserting that 'different historical forms of globalization can be identified,

including the epoch of world discovery in the early modern period, the era of European empires and the present era shaped by the neoliberal global economic project').

37 Thucydides, *History of the Peloponnesian War*, chapter 48, discussed in detail by J. Longrigg, 'Epidemic, Ideas and Classical Athenian Society,' in *Epidemics and Ideas*, ed. Terence Ranger and Paul Slack (Cambridge: Cambridge University Press, 1992) 21.

38 Keohane and Nye, 'Introduction' at 2.

39 I explore this argument in detail in subsequent chapters dealing with the origin of multilateral cooperation in the field of public health. See chapters 3 and 4 below.

40 I am interested in the human right to health less in terms of the intense debate between the schools of universalism and cultural relativism, but rather in terms of the impact of poverty and underdevelopment on an effective articulation of a viable right to health in international law.

41 International Covenant on Economic, Social and Cultural Rights, G.A. Res. 2200, U.N. GAOR, 21st Sess., Supp. No. 16, Art. 2(1), at 49, U.N.Doc. A/6316 (1966).

42 U.N. Convention on the Rights of the Child, G.A. Res. 44/25, U.N. GAOR, Supp. No. 49, at 167, U.N. Doc. A/44/49 (1989).

43 The Constitution of World Health Organisation 1946 (Preamble) 1.

44 B. Toebes, 'Towards an Improved Understanding of the International Human Right to Health' (1999) 21 Human Rights Quarterly 661 (arguing that although it is often asserted that all human rights are interdependent, interrelated, and of equal importance, in practice, Western states and NGOs have tended to treat economic, social, and cultural rights as if they were less important than civil and political rights).

45 K. Tomaseveski, 'Health,' in *United Nations Legal Order*, vol. 2, ed. O. Schachter and C.C. Joyner (Cambridge: Cambridge University Press, 1995) 859.

46 For a critique of justiciability as the dominant criterion to determine the viability of right to health, see V. Leary, 'Justiciability and Beyond: Complaint Procedures and the Right to Health' (1995) 55 Review of the International Commission of Jurists (Special Issue on Economic, Social and Cultural Rights and the Role of Lawyers) 89. For a critique of the Western liberal approach to human rights based on John Locke's social contract philosophy, see M. Mutua, 'The Banjul Charter and the African Cultural Fingerprint: An Evaluation of the Language of Duties' (1995) 35 Virginia J. of Int'l Law 340 and 'The Ideology of Human Rights' (1996) 36 Virginia J. of Int'l Law 589.

47 See for instance Ruth Roemer's contribution, 'The Right to Health Care,' in *The Right to Health in the Americas*, ed. H.L. Fuenzalida-Puelma and S.S. Connor (Washington, DC: Pan-American Health Organisation, 1989) 17, arguing that the phrase 'right to health' is absurd because it connotes the guarantee of perfect health. For a good summary of the confusion in literature on the right to health, health care, health status, medicare, and healthy conditions, see V. Leary, 'The Right to Health in International Human Rights Law' (1994) 1 (1) Health & Human Rights 25.

48 See generally, 'Towards a New Understanding of the International Human Right to Health'; Leary, 'Right to Health'; D.P. Fidler, *International Law and Infectious Diseases* (Oxford: Clarendon Press, 1999) 169 and 'International Law and Global Public Health' (1999) 48 University of Kansas Law Rev. 40; L. Gostin and J. Mann, 'Towards a Human Rights Impact Assessment for the Formulation and Evaluation of Public Health Policies' (1994) 1 Health & Human Rights 59; L. Gostin and Z. Lazzarini, *Human Rights and Public Health in the Aids Pandemic* (Oxford and New York: Oxford University Press, 1997); S.D. Jamar, 'The International Human Right to Health' (1994) 22 Southern Univ. Law Rev. 1.

49 For a recent intellectual account of these linkages from a development perspective, see A. Sen, *Development as Freedom* (New York: Anchor Books, 1999) stating, inter alia, that the constitutive role of freedom relates to the importance of substantive freedoms in enriching human life. Substantive freedoms include elementary capabilities such as being able to avoid starvation, undernourishment, escapable morbidity, and premature mortality, as well as the freedoms associated with being literate and numerate and enjoying political participation and uncensored speech.

50 Here Leary follows Ronald Dworkin's theory of rights as expounded in *Taking Rights Seriously* (Cambridge: Harvard University Press, 1978). Dworkin argued that when something is categorized as a right, it trumps other claims or goods; Leary argues that the use of rights language in relation to health emphasizes the importance of health and health status. It does indicate that health issues are of special importance given the impact of health on the life and survival of individuals. Leary, 'The Right to Health' at 36.

51 Leary, 'The Right to Health.' The work of the U.S.-based Physicians for Human Rights underscores the interdependence of all human rights. For instance, detention under inhuman conditions or torture inevitably affects the health of the person(s) detained or tortured. For documentation of these linkages by the Physicians for Human Rights, see *The Taliban's War on Women: Health and Human Rights Crisis in Afghanistan* (Boston and Washington, DC: Physicians for Human Rights, 1998); A. Chapman and L. Rubenstein, eds., *Human Rights and Health: The Legacy of Apartheid* (New York: American Association for the Advancement of Science and Physicians for Human Rights, 1998) (discussing deaths in detention, racial discrimination in the health sector, and segregation in medical education under the apartheid system in South Africa).

52 See L. Gostin and J. Mann, 'Towards the Development of a Human Rights Impact Assessment for the Formulation and Evaluation of Public Health Policies' (1994) 1 Health & Human Rights 59.

53 Ibid.

54 Ibid.

55 Fidler, 'International Law and Global Public Health' at 40.

56 See the decision of the Inter-American Human Rights Commission in the Yanomami Indians Case 7615, Inter-American Commission on Human Rights 24 OEA/Ser.L/v/ 11.66, doc.10 rev.1 (1985). The commission ruled that the Brazilian government's road construction project in the Amazon violated the right of the Yanomami Indians to preservation of their health as enshrined in Article XI of the American Declaration of Human Rights. In both permitting the massive penetration into the Indians' territory of outsiders carrying contagious diseases that have infected the Indians and its failure to provide essential medical care to the affected Indians, the government of Brazil violated their right to health.

57 The World Health Organization's Primary Health Care and its 1977 Alma-Ata Declaration on Health for All provides a benchmark against which to evaluate a government's provision of basic public health services and information. The WHO's Health for All policy stressed public health education on prevention and control of diseases, adequate food and nutrition, safe water supplies and basic sanitation, maternal and child health, immunization against major infectious diseases, prevention and control of endemic diseases, appropriate treatment for common diseases and injuries, and provision of essential drugs. See Fidler, 'International Law and Global Public Health' at 45, citing A.L. Taylor, 'Making the World Health Organization Work: A Legal Framework for Universal Access to the Conditions for Health' (1992) 18 Am. J. of Law & Medicine 301 at 315.

58 Basic factors affecting health would include other social, economic, and cultural rights affecting the right to health – education, housing, safe working environments, food and nutrition.

59 'Economic and Social Rights and the Right to Health' (An Interdisciplinary Discussion Held at Harvard Law School, September 1993) 36.

60 For a critique of the weak enforcement regime of human rights in international law generally, see M. Mutua, 'Looking Past the Human Rights Committee: An Argument for De-Marginalizing Enforcement' (1998) 4 Buffalo Human Rights Law Rev. 211 (arguing that many official international human rights bodies such as the Human Rights Committee are weak, timid, and ineffectual).

61 'The Right to the Highest Attainable Standard of Health' (General Comment No. 14, Committee on Economic, Social and Cultural Rights, 4 July 2000 E/C.12/2000/4).

62 The International Bill of Rights collectively refers to the Universal Declaration of Human Rights 1948, the International Covenant on Civil and Political Rights 1966, and the International Covenant on Economic, Social and Cultural Rights 1966.

63 'The Right to the Highest Attainable Standard of Health' (General Comment No.14).

64 Ibid.

65 A. Attaran, 'Human Rights and Biomedical Research Funding for the Developing World: Discovering State Obligations Under the Right to Health' 4 (1) Health and Human Rights 26.

66 For an articulation of emerging global issues that threaten to dislocate a rigid state-model international system, see M.W. Zacher, 'The Decaying Pillars of the Westphalian Temple: Implications for International Order and Governance,' in *Governance without Government: Order and Change in World Politics*, ed. J.N. Rosenau and Ernst-Otto Czempiel (Cambridge: Cambridge University Press, 1992) 58.

67 L. Henkin, *The Age of Rights* (New York: Columbia University Press, 1990) 44.

68 Attaran, 'Human Rights and Biomedical Research Funding' at 35.

69 Henkin, *Age of Rights* 45 argues that wealthy states are morally obligated and should be legally obligated to help the poorer states to give effect to some socio-economic rights – rights to food, housing, education, health care, and an adequate standard of living – through financial aid and without forcible intervention. See also M.C.R. Craven, *The International Covenant on Economic, Social and Cultural Rights: A Perspective on Its Development* (Oxford: Oxford University Press, 1995) 376.

70 R.E. Robertson, 'Measuring State Compliance with the Obligation to Devote the Maximum Available Resources to Realizing Economic, Social and Cultural Rights' (1994) 16 Human Rights Quarterly 693.

71 Leary, 'The Right to Health' at 46.

72 Ibid.

73 See World Health Organization United Nations Children's Fund, *Alma-Ata Declaration on Primary Health Care*, 12 September 1978 (hereafter Declaration of Alma Ata).

74 H. Fuenzalida-Puelma and S.S. Connor, eds., *The Right to Health in the Americas* (Washington, DC: PAHO, 1989) 603.

75 Fidler, 'Neither Science Nor Shamans' at 204–6; D.P. Fidler, 'A Kinder, Gentler System of Capitulations? International Law, Structural Adjustment Policies, and the Standard of Liberal, Globalized Civilization' (2000) 35 Texas International Law Journal 327.

76 S. Cleary, *Structural Adjustment in Africa*, quoted in *Structurally Adjusted Africa: Poverty, Debt and Basic Needs*, ed. Devid Simon (London: Pluto Press, 1995) 3.

77 B.K Campbell and J. Loxley, eds., *Structural Adjustment in Africa* (Houndmills, Basingstroke, UK: Macmillan, 1989) 41.

78 Simon, ed., *Structurally Adjusted Africa* at 3.

79 D.E. Sahn et al., *Structural Adjustment Reconsidered: Economic Policy and Poverty in Africa* (Oxford: Oxford University Press, 1997) 254. For opposing perspectives on SAPs, see generally M. Chossudovsky, *The Globalization of Poverty: Impacts of IMF and World Bank Reforms* (Penang, Malaysia: Third World Network, 1997); R. Keily and P. Manfleet, eds. *Globalisation and the Third World* (London: Routledge, 1998) 32; G.A Cornia et al., eds. *Africa's Recovery in the 1990s: From Stagnation and Adjustment to Human Development* (Basingstoke: Macmillan, 1992); W. vam Geest, ed., *Negotiating Structural Adjustment in Africa* (New York: UNDP, 1994); R. Lensink, *Structural Adjustment in Sub-Saharan Africa* (New York: Addison-Wesley, 1996).

80 Chossudovsky, *Globalization of Poverty* at 37.

81 Ibid.

82 Ibid.

83 Ibid.

84 See generally, R.F. Whalley and T.J. Hashim, *A Textbook of World Health: A Practical Guide to Global Health Care* (New York: CRC Press/Partheneon, 1995).

85 WHO, *Removing Obstacles to Healthy Development* at 65. See also Whalley Hashim, *Textbook of World Health*, for a similar observation on the disease implication of reckless construction of dams.

86 R. Falk, 'The Coming Global Civilization: Neo-Liberal or Humanist?' in *Legal Visions of the 21st Century: Essays in Honour of Judge Christopher Weeramantry*, ed. Antony Anghie and G. Sturgess, 15 (The Hague: Kluwer, 1998). For Falk's extensive critique of the present world order and his proposal for a humane world order, see *On Humane Governance: Toward a New Global Politics* (College Park: Pennsylvania State University Press, 1995).

87 Falk, 'The Coming Global Civilization' at 15.

88 World Bank, *Sub-Saharan Africa: From Crisis to Sustainable Growth* (Washington, DC: World Bank, 1989) 62.

89 See K. Mickelson, 'Rhetoric or Rage: Third World Voices in International Legal Discourse' (1998) 16 Wisconsin International Law Journal 353 (asserting, inter alia, that to the extent that a broader Third World approach to international law is recognized at all, it is ordinarily characterized as essentially reactive in nature).

90 For a clear articulation of these developmental prerequisites in the context of health promotion, see Ottawa Charter for Health Promotion 1986 (Adopted at the first International Conference on Health Promotion, Ottawa, Canada, 21 November 1986). For a discussion of the Ottawa Charter from a broad public health as opposed to a medical perspective, see J. Mann et al., 'Health and Human Rights' (1994) 1 (1) Health & Human Rights 7. The World Health Report issued annually by the World Health Organization has articulated most of the issues outlined by the Ottawa Charter; see, for instance, *The World Health Report, 1995: Bridging the Gaps; The World Health Report, 1996: Fighting Disease, Fostering Development* (Geneva: WHO, 1996); *The World Health Report, 1997: Conquering Suffering, Enriching Humanity* (Geneva: WHO, 1997) (each reporting in varying lengths the impact of food insecurity, inadequate housing, poor sanitation and environmental degradation, illiteracy, political conflicts, and civil wars on human health.

91 I.L. Head, 'The Contribution of International Law to Development' (1987) 25 Canadian Yearbook of International Law 29 at 33.

92 Ibid.

93 Brundtland, 'A Call for Healthy Development' at 66.

94 Falk, 'The Coming Global Civilization' at 15.

95 L. Nader, 'The Anthropological Study of Law,' *American Anthropology* (1965) 67 at 25. For a further exploration of this theme from the law and anthropology school of thought, see C. Geertz, 'Local Knowledge: Fact and Law in Comparative Perspective,' in *Further Essays in Interpretive Anthropology* (New York: Basic Books, 1989).

96 See, for instance, F.G. Snyder, 'Law and Development in the Light of Dependency Theory' (1980) 14 Law & Society Rev. 723.

97 D.M. Trubek, 'Towards a Social Theory of Law: An Essay on the Study of Law and Development' (1972) 82 Yale Law Journal 1. Trubek's view radically departs from the theory of Max Weber, whose concern was to explain the influence and role of the Western legal system in the triumph of capitalism in Europe. See M. Weber, *Economy and Society*, vols. 1 and 2, ed. G. Roth and C. Wittich (Berkeley and Los Angeles: University of California Press, 1978). For a recent critique of the Weberian conception of legitimacy of law and the legal system, see O.C. Okafor, 'The Concept of Legitimate Governance in the Contemporary International Legal System' (1997) 44 Netherlands Int'l Law Rev. 33. For a discussion of competing social models of mental health care from Western and non-Western perspectives, see S. Salzberg, 'The Social Model of Mental Health Care and Law in Comparative Context' (1993) Proceedings of Congress of the World Federation for Mental Health.

98 See, for instance, T. Mkandawire and C.C. Soludo, *Our Continent, Our Future: African Perspectives on Adjustment* (Ottawa: International Development Research Council, in conjunction with the Council for the Development of Social Science Research in Africa, 1999).

99 Ibid.

100 World Bank, *Sub-Saharan Africa* 62. For a recent discussion of the social impact of its policies by the bank, see D. Marayan et al. eds., *The Voices of the Poor Crying Out for Change* (Washington, DC: World Bank, 2000).

101 Head, *On a Hinge of History* at 215.

102 D. Held and A. McGrew, *Globalization/Anti-Globalization* (Cambridge: Polity Press, 2002).

103 Stiglitz, *Globalization and Its Discontents*.

Chapter 3: Mutual Vulnerability and Globalization of Public Health in the Global Neighbourhood

1 Most of the public health literature lumps emerging and re-emerging infectious diseases together as 'emerging infectious diseases' (EIDs). The U.S. Centres for Disease Control and Prevention (CDC) defines EIDs as 'diseases of infectious origin whose incidence in humans has increased within the past two decades or threatens to increase in the near future.' See CDC, *Addressing Emerging Infectious Disease Threats: A Prevention Strategy for the United States* (Atlanta, GA: CDC, 1994) 1. See also

World Health Organization, *World Health Report 1996: Fighting Disease, Fostering Development* (Geneva: WHO, 1996) 15. This definition includes completely new diseases that have emerged and previously known diseases that have either re-emerged in their traditional locations or emerged in new parts of the world.

2 H. Nakajima, 'Global Disease Threats and Foreign Policy' (1997) 4 (1) Brown J. of World Affairs 319.

3 Within socio-economic and environmental factors that contribute to transboundary spread of EIDs, Fidler mentions social unrest and war, environmental degradation, changes in human behaviour, urbanization, and poverty. See D.P. Fidler, 'Return of the Fourth Horseman: Emerging Infectious Diseases and International Law' (1997) 81 Minnesota Law Rev. 771.

4 *House Report No. 706: Hearings Before the Committee on Foreign Relations, House of Representatives, 70th US Congress*, Washington, DC, House Report No. 706, January 1928, stating, inter alia, that 'it has been observed that many deadly diseases, once considered to be indigenous to the Tropics may be and are carried to the Temperate Zones by various transmitting agencies, and there seem to become indigenous with no diminution in their virulence ... Hence, *each nation in more or less degree must become the keeper of its brother nations; this as a matter of self-protection if for no other reason*' (my emphasis) quoted in Nakajima, 'Global Disease Threats' at 319.

5 Thucydides, in the *History of the Peloponnensian War*, suggested that plaque originated from Ethiopia and spread through Egypt and Libya before it arrived in Athens in 430 BC, as a result of movement of troops during the war. J.N. Hays, *The Burdens of Disease: Epidemics and Human Response in Western History* (New Brunswick, NJ: Rutgers University Press, 1998) 39, argues that most historians now say that the Black Death had its origins in the reservoir of infection found in Central Asia, not far from Lake Issyk Kul in what is today known as Kyrgyzstan. See also Nakajima, 'Global Disease Threats' at 320, stating that plague from Asia reaced Italy in 1347 after it spread from Mongolia across Asia. The path of the Black Death followed international travel and trading routes, and subsequently spread to Europe and North Africa. See generally, S. Watts, *Epidemics and History: Disease, Power and Imperialism* (New Haven, CT: Yale University Press, 1997) 1–25; D. Porter, *Health, Civilization and the State: A History of Public Health from Ancient to Modern Times* (London and New York: Routledge, 1999) 31–4.

6 G. Berlinguer, 'Health and Equity as a Primary Global Goal' (1999) 42 (4) Development (Responses to Globalization: Rethinking Health and Equity) 17 at 18.

7 Porter, *Health, Civilization and the State* at 46; see also Berlinguer, 'Health and Equity' at 18 arguing that the discovery (or conquest) of America by Europeans – a turning point in history – also meant the transition from the separation of peoples and diseases to mutual interchange and communication. Until that time, differences in environmental conditions and nutritional patterns, in social and cultural organization, and in

the presence or absence of biological agents and vectors of transmissible diseases had produced markedly different epidemiological trends in the Old and New Worlds. Indeed smallpox, measles, and yellow fever did not exist in the Americas, while syphilis was unknown in Eurasia and Africa. For a detailed discussion of disease exchanges between continents, especially after the conquest of the Americas by Europeans, see A.W. Crosby, *The Columbian Exchange: Biological and Cultural Consequences of 1492* (Westport, CT: Greenwood Press, 1972) and *Ecological Imperialism: The Biological Expansion of Europe, 900–1900* (Cambridge: Cambridge University Press, 1986).

8 See ibid. For a good historical account of the decimation of Native Indian populations by smallpox in the post-Columbus Americas, as well as the complex interaction of the disease with populations in the Old and New Worlds, see Watts, *Epidemics and History* at 89–121; Porter, *Health, Civilization and the State* at 46–7.

9 Hays, *The Burdens of Disease* at 7.

10 W.H. McNeill, *Plagues and Peoples* (New York: Doubleday, 1976) 257.

11 Hippocrates, who lived in the Greek Island of Cos, is often widely cited (not without controversy) in public health literature as the founder of modern medicine. Porter, in at 15 argued that Hippocrates probably lived some time between 460 and 361 BC. His ancient biographers, including Aristotle and Plato, praised him as a great and honoured physician, but it is uncertain whether he authored any of the collection of essays and text known as the Hippocratic Corpus. The Corpus was compiled by many authors, and absorbed the traditions of many of the Greek medical communities. Hippocratic medicine radically departed from the religious and mystical traditions of healing and stressed that disease was a natural event, not caused by supernatural forces. H. Zinsser, in *Rats, Lice and History: A Chronicle of Pestilence and Plagues* (New York: Black Dog and Leventhal, 1963) at 112 observed that Hippocrates was probably not the first great physician of antiquity. It is likely that many skilful and sagacious medical men practised in ancient Egypt where, according to Herodotus, physicians were even more highly specialized than they are today, since they often limited themselves to a single organ of the body. There were dentists, as well as internists and surgeons. Hippocrates, however, is the first great physician from whom we have records and writings, which show an approach to medical problems entirely analogous to our own.

12 Hays, *The Burdens of Disease* at 8.

13 Zinsser, *Rats, Lice and History* at 111.

14 N. Goodman, *International Health Organizations and Their Work* (London: Churchill and Livingstone, 1971) 27.

15 For a history of the concept of quarantine, see B. Mafart and J.L. Perret, 'History of the Concept of Quarantine' (March 1998) 58 Medicine Tropicale 14–20 (defining quarantine as a concept developed by society to protect against the outbreak of contagious disease). Goodman, *International Health Organizations* at 29 states that the word 'quarantine' is derived from the forty-day (*quaranta*) isolation period imposed at Ven-

ice in 1403 and said to be based on the period during which Jesus and Moses had remained in isolation in the desert. Paul Slack's 'Introduction' in *Epidemics and Ideas: Essays on the Historical Perception of Pestilence*, ed. P. Slack and T. Ranger (Cambridge: Cambridge University Press, 1992) at 15 noted that quarantine practices began in Italian city states in the fifteenth century.

16 See Goodman, *International Health Organizations* at 27–9, also summarized by D.P. Fidler, *International Law and Infectious Diseases* (Oxford: Clarendon Press, 1999) 26.

17 Ibid.

18 N. Howard-Jones, *The Scientific Background of the International Sanitary Conferences, 1851–1938* (Geneva: World Health Organization, 1975) 11, quoting the English translation from J.P. Papon, *De la Peste ou les epoques ce fleau et les moyens de s'en preserver*, vol. 2 (Paris, 1800). Howard-Jones stated further that very similar precautions were prescribed in the quarantine regulations promulgated by the French Minister of Commerce in 1835. Article 614 stated that where there was need for surgical intervention, a surgical student should be 'invited' to be incarcerated with the patient – students presumably being more expendable than doctors. The latter had to be separated from patients with 'contagious' diseases by 'at least twelve metres.' If the patient was too ill to approach the limit of this no-man's land the doctor would prescribe supposedly suitable remedies on the basis of the report made by the student.

19 Shakespeare, *Romeo and Juliet*, Act V. Scene ii.

FRIAR JOHN: Going to find a bare-foot brother out,
One of our order, to associate me,
Here in this city visiting the sick,
And finding him, the 'searchers' of the town,
Suspecting that we both were in a house
Where an infectious pestilence did reign,
Seal'd up the doors and would not let us forth;
So that my speed to Mantua was stay'd.

('Searchers of the town' are defined in the note as 'officers of the town responsible for public health during a plague' (New York: Dover Thift Editions, 1993).

20 *International Health Organizations* at 27.

21 Ibid.

22 J. Siddiqi, *World Health and World Politics: The World Health Organization and the UN System* (London: Hurst & Co., 1995) 14 arguing that 'the new ease of travel and trade also transformed hitherto foreign epidemic diseases such as cholera into European scourges. One early response of European states to limit the spread of cholera involved the quarantining of shipping at different ports for months at a time. Arbitrary and unequal quarantine regulations at various ports inevitably created great burdens on the

international trade of ... maritime nations such as Britain and France, whose fear of economic collapse overwhelmed their dread of imported disease and led them to support ... international action to relieve shipping from the burdensome shackles of quarantine regulations.'

23 Siddiqi, *World Health*. Also, Howard-Jones, *Scientific Background of the International Sanitary Conferences* at 11 stated that while the elaborate precautions of quarantine imposed intolerable constraints upon travellers, what governments found most irksome were the often disastrous hindrances to international commerce, and it was this concern that finally prompted the European nations to meet to discuss to what extent these onerous restrictions could be lifted without undue risk to the health of their populations. If, in the old colonial days, it was true that 'trade follows the flag,' it was equally true that the first faltering steps towards international health cooperation followed trade.

24 The states included Italian city states then known as the four papal states: Sardinia, Tuscany, and the Two Sicilies. Others were Austria, Great Britain, Greece, Portugal, Russia, Spain, and France – the convenor and host.

25 In this section, I am only concerned with mutual vulnerability as a motivating factor in the evolution of multilateral health cooperation. I shall explore the politics, frustrations, and shortcomings of regulating the cross-border spread of diseases, which were manifest in most of the international sanitary conferences held from 1851 to the early twentieth century, in the chapter 4 under the rubric 'vulnerability of multilateralism.'

26 Paris in 1851, Paris in 1859, Constantinople in 1866, Vienna in 1874, Washington in 1881, Rome in 1885, Venice in 1892, Dresden in 1893, Paris in 1894, and Venice in 1897.

27 See Fidler, *International Law and Infectious Diseases* at 24.

28 Ibid.

29 Ibid.

30 Howard-Jones, *Scientific Background of the International Sanitary Conferences* at 65.

31 Ibid.

32 Ibid.

33 Ibid.

34 The International Sanitary Bureau is the precursor of the Pan-American Sanitary Bureau and the present Pan-American Health Organization (PAHO).

35 According to Fidler, *International Law and Infections Diseases* at 24 the intensity of efforts continued in the twentieth century as the predominantly European efforts of the later half of the nineteenth century were joined by the diplomatic activity in the Americas to control infectious diseases.

36 Siddiqi, World Health at 20, stating that the reason for OIHP's intransigence is unclear even to leading scholars in the field like Norman Howard-Jones, who observed in *International Public Health between the Two World Wars: The Organizational Prob-*

lems (Geneva: WHO, 1978) 73 that there was a remarkable overlap in the membership of the OIHP (based in Paris) and the Health Organization of the League of Nations (based in Geneva), and so it was strange that a majority of member states in each organization were making proposals in Geneva that they themselves would later reject in Paris.

37 Fidler, *International Law and Infectious Diseases* at 24.

38 Within the Americas, the 1905 Inter-American Sanitary Convention imposed notification duties for cases of cholera, plague, and yellow fever. In 1924 the Pan-American Sanitary Code provided for bi-weekly notification of ten specific diseases and such other diseases as the Pan-American Sanitary Bureau might add, and also for immediate notification of 'plague, cholera, yellow fever, smallpox, typhus, or any other dangerous contagion liable to spread through ... international commerce.' See Articles 3–4, Pan American Sanitary Code 1924.

39 Ibid.

40 Ibid.

41 For a definition of emerging and re-emerging infectious diseases by WHO and CDC, see CDC, *Addressing Emerging Infectious Disease Threats*; WHO, *World Health Report, 1996.*

42 See National Science and Technology Council Committee on International Science, Engineering, and Technology Working Group on Emerging and Re-Emerging Infectious Diseases, *Infectious Diseases: A Global Health Threat* (Washington, DC: CISET, 1995) 14 (hereafter CISET Report). Some of the diseases in the list published by CISET includes Ebola hemorrhagic fever (1977), Legionnaire's disease (1977), toxic shock syndrome (1981), lyme disease (1982), acquired immunodeficiency syndrome (AIDS) (1983), and Brazilian hemorrhagic fever (1984). The CISET Report was adopted by the WHO in *The World Health Report 1996* at 112. For a discussion of the CISET report from an international legal perspective, see Fidler, 'Return of the Fourth Horseman: Emerging Infectious Diseases and International Law.'

43 See CISET Report identifying about twenty re-emerging infections, including rabies, dengue and dengue hemorrhagic fever, yellow fever, malaria, plague, schistosomiasis, diphtheria, tuberculosis, and cholera.

44 Fidler, 'Return of the Fourth Horseman' at 779–80.

45 See WHO, *World Health Report 1996* at 1.

46 Ibid.

47 Ibid.

48 I focus on tuberculosis and malaria not because they are the most important or unique among the emerging and re-emerging infectious diseases listed in the CISET Report, but simply because it is impossible to discuss in detail all the new and old diseases that are emerging and re-emerging across national boundaries. Tuberculosis and malaria are used as examples to rethink the dynamics of mutual vulnerability.

49 WHO, *World Health Report 1996* at 26–7.

50 '*Tuberculosis*, WHO Fact Sheet No. 104 (Revised April 2000), available online at http://www.who.int/inf-fs/fac104.html (accessed 28 July 2000).

51 *World Health Report 1996*, at 27.

52 L.O. Gostin, 'The Resurgent TB Epidemic in the Era of AIDS: Reflections on Public Health, Law and Society' (1995) 54 Maryland Law Review 1.

53 *World Health Report 1996* at 27. For the linkage of tuberculosis and HIV-AIDS, see WHO/UN Aids Programme, *A Deadly Partnership: Tuberculosis in the Era of HIV* (Geneva: WHO and UNAIDS, 1996).

54 World Health Organization, *Guidelines for the Management of Drug-Resistant Tuberculosis* (Geneva: WHO, 1998) 7.

55 *World Health Report 1996*, at 28. The WHO recommends the directly observed treatment short-course (DOTS) – an inexpensive strategy that involves detection of TB cases through low-cost sputum smear tests followed by six to eight months of treatment with a combination of inexpensive drugs.

56 Ibid.

57 Fidler, 'Return of the Fourth Horseman' at 780–1 quoting a statement of Dr Margaret H. Hamburg, Health Commissioner of New York City, in 'Emerging Infections: A Significant Threat to the Nation's Health: Hearings Before the Senate Committee on Labor and Human Resources' (104th US Congress, 1995).

58 Fidler, 'Return of the Fourth Horseman.' See also A.S. Fauci, 'Tuberculosis Morbidity: United States' (1995) Journal of American Medical Association 788.

59 *World Health Report 1996* at 28.

60 See H. Branswell, 'Drug-Resistant Strains of TB Global Threat, WHO Warns,' *Recorder and Times* (Brockville, ON), 24 March 2000, quoting Dr Howard Njoo, director for tuberculosis-prevention and control at Health Canada's Laboratory Centre for Disease and Control. Dr Njoo, inter alia, was quoted as arguing that 'TB bacilli don't respect borders,' and that Canada is not immune. It is spreading round the world and certainly Canada is affected by that spread.

61 R. Bedell, 'Tuberculosis Is a Canadian Problem,' *Globe and Mail* (Toronto), 21 March 2000. On TB and the risk of infection through air travel generally, see World Health Organization, *Tuberculosis and Air Travel: Guidelines for Prevention and Control* (Geneva: WHO, 1998).

62 See 'Drug-Resistant Tuberculosis Is Rising in Areas Once Deemed under Control,' *Wall Street Journal* (Washington, DC), 24 March 2000.

63 See generally, World Health Organization, *WHO Report 2003: Global Tuberculosis Control: Surveillance, Planning, Financing* (Geneva: WHO, 2003).

64 *World Health Report 1996*, at 47.

65 Ibid.

66 Ibid. See also WHO, *Severe Falciparum Malaria: Transactions of the Royal Society of*

Tropical Medicine and Hygiene, vol. 94, supplement 4 (Geneva: WHO, 2000) stating, inter alia, that 'any patient with malaria who is unable to swallow tablets, has any evidence of vital organ dysfunction, or a high parasite count is at increased risk of dying. The exact risk depends on the degree of abnormality, age, background immunity, and access to appropriate treatment.'

67 For a distinction between 'imported malaria' and 'airport malaria,' see N.G. Gratz et al., 'Why Aircraft Disinsection?' (2000) 78 Bulletin of the WHO, 995 stating that 'the most direct evidence of transmission of disease by mosquitoes imported on aircraft is the occurrence of airport malaria, i.e. cases of malaria in and near international airports, among persons who have not recently travelled to areas where the disease is endemic or who have not recently received blood transfusions. Airport malaria should be distinguished from imported malaria among persons who contract the infection during a stay in an area of endemicity and subsequently fall ill.'

68 G. Capdevila, 'Malaria-Carrying Mosquitoes Hitch Rides on Air Planes' *Inter Press*, 22 August 2000.

69 WHO, *Removing Obstacles to Healthy Development: WHO Report on Infectious Diseases* (Geneva: WHO, 1999) 50.

70 WHO Regional Office for Europe, *Strategy to Roll Back Malaria in the WHO European Region* (Copenhagen: WHO, 1999) 6. Gratz et al., 'Why Aircraft Disinsection' at 998 argue that airport malaria is particularly dangerous in that physicians generally have little reason to suspect it. This is especially true if there has been no recent travel to areas where malaria is endemic.

71 See Gratz, 'Why Aircraft Disinsection' for a detailed discussion of individual cases of airport malaria in Europe as well as useful references and a review of public health literature that explore the problem.

72 WHO Regional Office for Europe, *Strategy to Roll Back Malaria* at 6.

73 Ibid.

74 WHO, *Removing Obstacles to Healthy Development*, at 52 using data from Behrens, *Travel Morbidity in Ethnic Minority Travellers*.

75 'Outbreak Not Contained: West Nile Virus Triggers a Re-evaluation of Public Health Surveillance,' *Scientific American* April 2000, 20.

76 The US Centers for Disease Control and Prevention (CDC), *Preventing Emerging Infectious Diseases: A Strategy for the 21st Century* (Atlanta, GA: CDC, 1998) 3. Since I have dealt with the twin issues of poverty and underdevelopment in the preceding chapter, the focus of my analysis of these factors here is on global travel.

77 Lifson identified eight similar factors that contribute to the spread of dengue across the world. These include international travel, urbanization, population growth, crowding, poverty, inadequate sanitation facilities, weak public health infrastructure, and lack of sustained support for disease-control measures. See Alan Lifson, 'Mosquitoes, Models, and Dengue' (1996) 347 Lancet 1201.

78 WHO, *World Health Report 1996* at 17.

79 Fidler, 'Return of the Fourth Horseman' at 965.

80 Ibid.

81 Ibid.

82 Ibid., quoting L. Garret, 'The Return of Infectious Disease' (Jan.–Feb. 1996) Foreign Affairs 66, who noted the 1918–19 global influenza pandemic that killed 22 million people and thus queries 'how many more victims could a similarly lethal strain of influenza claim in 1996, when some half a billion passengers will board airline flights?'

83 Ibid.

84 D. Yach and D. Bettcher, 'The Globalization of Public Health II: The Convergence of Self-Interest and Altruism' (1998) 88 American J. of Public Health 738.

85 Institute of Medicine, *America's Vital Interest in Global Health: Protecting Our People, Enhancing Our Economy, and Advancing Our International Interests* (Washington, DC: National Academy Press, 1994).

86 Ibid.

87 I borrowed this expression from Yach and Bettcher, 'Globalization of Public Health II' at 738.

88 Nakajima, 'Global Disease Threats' at 330.

Chapter 4: Vulnerability of Multilateralism and Globalization of Public Health in the Global Neighbourhood

1 *World Health and World Politics: The World Health Organization and the UN System* (London: Hurst & Co., 1995) 2.

2 D.P. Fidler, 'Microbialpolitik: Infectious Diseases and International Relations' (1998) 14 American University Int'l Law Rev. 5.

3 N. Howard-Jones, *The Scientific Background of the International Sanitary Conferences 1851–1938* (Geneva: WHO, 1975) 12.

4 Ibid.

5 Ibid.

6 For a discussion of the submission of Menis, see ibid. at 12.

7 For a discussion of the submission of Sutherland, see Ibid. at 12.

8 Miasmists argued that diseases were caused locally by filth and foul air. This is the traditional Hippocratic view. See J. Longrigg, 'Epidemic, Ideas and Classical Athenian Society,' in *Epidemics and Ideas: Essays on the Historical Perception of Pestilence*, ed. T. Ranger and P. Slack (Cambridge: Cambridge University Press, 1992) 36.

9 Contagion theorists argued that diseases were transmitted directly from an infected person to a healthy person. See Pullan, 'Plague and Perceptions of the Poor in Early Modern Italy,' in *Epidemics and Ideas* at 101.

10 *Scientific Background of the International Sanitary Conferences* at 16. See also Siddiqi,

World Health at 15 stating that 'while the official objective of the first Conference was stated as the desire to regulate in a uniform way the quarantine and lazarettos in the Mediterranean, the national motives for participation were primarily political and commercial, with public health being merely an accidental issue. The primacy of concerns about shipping over those about public health was no secret ...'

11 Siddiqui, *World Health.*

12 D.P. Fidler, *International Law and Infectious Diseases* (Oxford: Clarendon Press, 1999) 25.

13 D. Kennedy, 'Primitive Legal Scholarship' (1986) 27 Harvard International Law J. 1; A. Rubin, 'International Law in the Age of Columbus' (1992) 39 Netherlands International Law Rev. 5; A. Anghie, 'Francisco de Vitoria and the Colonial Origins of International Law' (1996) 5 Social & Legal Studies 321; A. Nussbaum, *A Concise History of the Law of Nations* (New York: Macmillan, 1954).

14 See A.W. Crosby, *The Columbian Exchange: Biological and Cultural Consequences of 1492* (Westport, CT: Greenwood Press, 1972).

15 See Anghie, 'Francisco de Vitoria'; Rubin, 'Internatiolnal Law' for a detailed discussion of the interaction between the Spaniards and American Indians and how Francisco De Vitoria, a leading international legal scholar of the time, rationalized that interaction legally.

16 P. Malanczuk, *Akehurst's Modern Introduction to International Law,* 7th ed. (London and New York: Routledge, 1997) 13.

17 M. Bedjaoui, *Towards a New International Economic Order* (Paris: UNESCO, 1979) 48.

18 Ibid. at 49–50.

19 For an ingenious discussion of the triumph of positivism in nineteenth-century international law, see A. Anghie, 'Finding the Peripheries: Sovereignty and Colonialism in Nineteenth-Century International Law' (1999) 40 Harvard International Law Journal 1.

20 Ibid.

21 This question is beyond the scope of this study. However, it has been the subject of detailed inquiry by leading international scholars from the developing world. See R.P. Anand, *New States and International Law* (Delhi: Vikas Ltd., 1972), arguing that in the nineteenth century Asian states were incapacitated to play any active role in the development of international law during the most creative period of its history, and that many rules of international law that emerged in the nineteenth century were explicitly devised to facilitate the economic exploitation of non-European territories; T.O. Elias, *Africa and the Development of International Law,* 2nd rev. ed. (The Hague: Martinus Nijhoff, 1988) arguing that African peoples were excluded in the deliberations at the Berlin Conference 1884–5, where Africa was partitioned among the leading European powers: France, Britain, and Germany; C.F. Amarasinghe, *State Responsibility for Injury to Aliens* (1967), cited in I.L. Head, 'The Contribution of

International Law to Development' (1987) 25 Canadian Yearbook of International
Law 29 at 31, arguing that international law in its early stages was developed by states
that had more or less similar standards of economic development, and that accepted
the colonial principle. This makes it natural for some of the new states to challenge
some rules of international law.

22 These questions logically follow Antony Anghie's well-founded observation that 'the
question of the enduring effects on non-European societies of the history of exclusion
is related to the issue of the legacy of the nineteenth-century for the discipline as a
whole.' See Anghie, 'Finding the Peripheries' at 73.

23 I.L. Head, *On a Hinge of History: The Mutual Vulnerability of South and North* (Toronto: University of Toronto Press, in association with the International Development
Research Centre, 1991) 10, arguing that 'the North has discovered the South many
times, and it has given the South a variety of names sometimes in error. Curiosity,
greed, fear, evangelic fervour, the zeal to civilize: the motivation for contact has ranged
from the loftiest to the most base. The North assumed that modernization is desirable,
and has thus interpreted Northern dominance as earned. Records of the odysseys of
discovery were written by or about the adventurers, not by those discovered.'

24 E. Said, *Orientalism* (New York: Vintage Books, 1978) 2.

25 Ibid.

26 D.P. Fidler, 'A Kinder, Gentler System of Capitulations? International Law, Structural
Adjustment Policies, and the Standard of Liberal, Globalized Civilization' (2000) 35
Texas Law J. 327 (defining capitulations basically as a system of extraterritorial jurisdiction and power wielded by European states and the United States in the territories
of non-European countries, and categorizing the Structural Adjustment Policies of the
World Bank and the IMF as capitulatory in nature. Fidler argues further that past and
present capitulatory regimes were are supported by international law, and that the
standards of civilization supporting capitulation were visible in nineteenth-century
international law).

27 Preamble to the Constitution of the World Health Organization, as adopted by the
International Health Conference, New York, USA, 19–22 June 1946 *World Health
Organization: Basic Documents*, 43rd ed. (Geneva: WHO, 2001) 1.

28 Ibid.

29 For a text of this Resolution see WHO, *Handbook of Resolutions and Decisions of the
World Health Assembly and the Executive Board*, Vol. 2, *1973–1984* (Geneva: WHO,
1985) 397.

30 A similar resolution, WHA34.38, was passed by the World Health Assembly in May
1981 requesting the WHO director-general to continue collaboration with the secretary general of the United Nations and with other governmental and non-governmental organizations in establishing a broad and authoritative international committee of
scientists and experts for the comprehensive study and elucidation of the threat of

thermonuclear war and its potentially baneful consequences for the life and health of peoples of the world. For a text of Resolution WHA34.38, see WHO, *Handbook of Resolutions and Decisions*, at 397–8.

31 World Health Organization, *Effects of Nuclear War on Health and Health Services: Report of the International Committee of Experts in Medical Sciences and Public Health to Implement Resolution WHA34.38* (Geneva: WHO, 1984). The World Health Assembly adopted this report in May 1983 by Resolution WHA36.28.

32 This was ironical because the end of the Cold War in the early 1990s would be expected to have facilitated global consensus on effective non-proliferation of nuclear weapons.

33 Although advisory opinions of the International Court of Justice are not legally binding, they nonetheless serve as authoritative and persuasive interpretations of treaty and customary international law on issues within the competence of the UN General Assembly and specialized agencies of the United Nations system.

34 See Speech of Ms Lini, 46th World Health Assembly: Summary Records of Committees, 260, WHA46/1993/REC/3 (12 May 1993) (hereafter Summary Records). In support of Vanuatu, the delegate of Zambia argued that requesting an opinion from the International Court of Justice was a 'gesture that would have tremendous impact on the world's nuclear status. As the prevention of nuclear proliferation merely served to maintain or even increase the nuclear arsenals of the nuclear countries while hindering other states from obtaining such weapons, the focus should be on their complete abolition.' See Summary Records at 259.

35 Ibid. at 259.

36 Speech of Mr Boyer, US delegate to the 46th World Health Assembly, Summary Records at 273.

37 *Legality of the Use by a State of Nuclear Weapons in Armed Conflict, Advisory Opinion* (1996) ICJ Reports 4 at 66 (WHO Opinion). I am concerned here not with whether the court's ruling/opinion was rightly decided or given *per incuriam*, but with the South-North dimension of the debate at the 46th World Health Assembly that preceded its journey to the ICJ. International legal scholars are sharply polarized on whether the opinion expressed by the court was right or wrong. In a recent volume, Laurence Boisson de Chazournes and Philippe Sands have dealt with the divergent views of eminent international lawyers on the soundness or otherwise of the nuclear weapons decisions of the International Court of Justice: see *International Law, the International Court of Justice and Nuclear Weapons* (Cambridge: Cambridge University Press, 1999) (with contributions from Richard Falk, Thomas Franck, Virginia Leary, David Kennedy, M. Koskenniemi, George Abi Saab, and others).

38 International law as a defensive ontological discipline compelled lawyers to defend the very existence of their discipline by debating whether international law is law, politics, or morality. See T.M. Franck, *Fairness in International Law and Institutions* (Oxford: Clarendon Press, 1995) 6.

39 International law as a creative post-ontological discipline enables lawyers to ask questions about the fairness of international law and its effectiveness/legitimacy in regulating emerging global issues. See Franck, *Fairness in International Law*.

40 Here I remain a student of Thomas M. Franck, whose fairness discourse argues that 'international law has matured into a complete legal system covering all aspects of relations among states ... The challenge of space exploration has joined with the degradation of the earth's environment ... to entice or compel individuals and governments to think in terms of our common destiny: to counter humanity as a single gifted but greedy species, sharing a common, finite, and endangered speck of the universe ... These factors have drawn humanity into a circle, seized our attention, and empowered the law makers.' See *Fairness in International Law*.

41 A. L'hirondel and D. Yach, 'Develop and Strengthen Public Health Law' (1998) 51 World Health Statistics Quarterly 79.

42 See generally, D.P. Fidler, 'Return of the Fourth Horseman: Emerging Infectious Diseases and International Law' (1997) 81 Minnesota Law Rev. 771, and *International Law and Infectious Diseases* at 21, arguing that 'historically once public health problems entered the realm of the international system, states turned to international law as a tool to develop common rules, institutions and values.'

43 Allyn Taylor, in a seminal article published in 1992, asserted that 'WHO has had only limited success in stimulating national implementation of universal health service programs, in part because the organization has paid insufficient attention to the role *that legislation* can play in the Health for All Strategy.' See A.L. Taylor, 'Making the World Health Organization Work: A Legal Framework for Universal Access to the Conditions of Health' (1992) 18 American J. of Law & Medicine 302. Fidler argues that 'the WHO is facing an international legal tsunami that will require a sea change in its attitude towards international law. WHO's lack of interest in international law does not reflect the historical experience of states and international health organizations prior to World War II. While WHO has been accused of focusing too little on international law, international relations prior to World War II were plagued by too much international health law.' See D.P. Fidler, 'The Future of the World Health Organization: What Role for International Law' (1998) 31 Vanderbilt J. of International Law 1079. See also K. Tomasevski, 'Health,' in *United Nations Legal Order*, vol. 2 (ed. O. Schachter and C.C. Jones Cambridge: Cambridge University Press, 1995) 859 (arguing that the WHO's Eighth General Programme of Work covering the period 1990–5 does not even mention international law. The paucity of health law developed by the WHO could lead to an impression that health protection is not susceptible to legal regulation were it not for its expansion elsewhere, including the United Nations, both in quantity and in the range of issues it covers).

44 Article 19 of the Constitution of the World Health Organization, *World Health Organization: Basic Documents*, 43rd ed. (Geneva: World Health Organization, 2000) 7.

45 Fidler, 'Future of the World Health Organization' at 1087.

46 On treaty making by states in international law, see *Vienna Convention on the Law of Treaties 1969* (1969) 8 I.L.M 679; D.J. Harris, *Cases and Materials on International Law*, 5th ed. (London: Sweet & Maxwell, 1997) 765; I. Brownlie, *Principles of Public International Law*, 4th ed. (Oxford: Clarendon Press, 1990) 603.

47 W.R. Sharpe, 'The New World Health Organization' (1947) 41 American J. of Int'l Law 509. For a study of international legislative process of international organizations 'by which an increasingly substantial amount of international law is steadily being created,' see P.C. Szasz, *Selected Essays on Understanding International Institutions and the Legislative Process* (Ardsley, NY: Transnational, 2001); E. Kwakwa, 'Some Comments on Rule Making at the World Intellectual Property Organization' (2002) 12 (1) Duke Journal of International Law 179; E. Kwakwa, 'Institutional Perspectives of International Economic Law,' in *Perspectives in International Economic Law*, ed. A.H. Qureshi (The Hague: Kluwer Law International, 2002) 45–62.

48 See my discussion of Hippocrates and the influence he had on modern medicine and epidemiology, chapter 3, note 13.

49 D.P. Fidler, 'International Law and Global Public Health' (1999) 48 University of Kansas Law Rev. 1 at 15. See also Tomasevski 'Health' at 859 (strongly critiquing the WHO's overt bias in favour of non-binding and non-legal norms built upon ethical rather than legal principles, and also submitting that an important reason for that bias the traditional reluctance of the medical profession to submit itself to the rule of law. Beginning in the eighteenth century, medical associations developed codes of professional behaviour. Self-regulation presumes the exclusion of lay persons, thus reinforcing the traditional paternalism of the medical profession, dating back to the Hippocratic Oath: the assumption that whatever a physician decides is, by definition, correct).

50 Taylor, 'Making the World Health Organization Work' at 303. See also A. Lakin, 'The Legal Powers of the World Health Organization' (1997) 3 Medical Law International 23 (discussing the underdeveloped but potentially influential normative function of the WHO and whether the Organization could more effectively utilize its constitutional legal powers to pursue its role as director and advocate of international health).

51 Fidler, 'The Future of the World Health Organization' at 1099.

52 Ibid.

53 OR 13 1948 (Records of the First World Health Assembly, 1948) 77. Sir Wilson Jameson was responding to legal issues and reservations raised by U.S. membership of the WHO.

54 L'hirondel and Yach, at 83 have identified international human rights law, international environmental law, international trade law, law of the sea, international maritime law, intellectual property law, law of bioethics, as areas of international law relevant to WHO's global health mandate. Fidler's *International Law and Infectious*

Diseases creates similar linkages between global infectious disease threats and international trade law, international environmental law, international humanitarian law, and international human rights.

55 Fidler, 'International Law and Global Public Health' at 1 and 57.

56 World Health Organization, *International Health Regulations, 1969*, 3rd annotated ed. (Geneva: WHO, 1983).

57 For detailed provisions of the IHR on the obligation to notify the WHO of outbreaks of these diseases and the sharing of epidemiological information contained in the notifications to other member states, see Articles 2–13 of the IHR.

58 Fidler, *International Law and Infectious Diseases* at 61, stating that the IHR seek to provide WHO member states with maximum protection against the importation of infectious diseases. To achieve this objective, the IHR establish a global surveillance system for the diseases subject to the regulations, require certain types of health-related capabilities at ports and airports of member states, and set out disease-specific provisions for the covered diseases.

59 Article 14(2) IHR.

60 Article 14(3) IHR.

61 Article 15 IHR.

62 Ibid.

63 Article 17 IHR.

64 Article 18 IHR.

65 Article 19 IHR.

66 Article 66(1) IHR.

67 Article 66(3) IHR.

68 Article 77(1) IHR.

69 Article 77(2) IHR.

70 D.L. Heymann, 'The International Health Regulations: Ensuring Maximum Protection with Minimum Restriction' 13 (unpublished manuscript, Program Materials on Law and Emerging and Re-Emerging Infectious Diseases, Annual Meeting of the American Bar Association, 1996) (on file with the author).

71 Ibid.

72 A.L. Taylor, 'Controlling the Global Spread of Infectious Diseases: Towards a Reinforced Role for the International Health Regulations (1997) 33 Houston Law Rev. 1327 at 1348 citing Heymann, 'International Health Regulations' See also L. Garret, 'The Return of Infectious Diseases,' *Foreign Affairs* (Jan.–Feb. 1996) 73–4 (stating that India lost almost two billion dollars as result of excessive measures following the plague outbreak).

73 See European Commission, *Decision 97/878/EC, (1997)* at 64; European Commission, *Decision 98/84/EC* at 43.

74 See Fidler, *International Law and Infectious Diseases* at 80.

75 A.T. Price-Smith, *The Health of Nations: Infectious Disease, Environmental Change, and their Effects on National Security and Development* (Cambridge, MA: MIT Press, 2002) 18.

76 'The Truth about SARS,' *Time* (Canadian Edition), 5 May 2003, 13.

77 Ibid.

78 According to B. Velimirovic, 'Do We Still Need International Health Regulations?' (1976) 133 J. of Infectious Diseases 478 at 481, 'Is there much sense in the mainte-nance of rules if they are not observed – if they are disregarded or more or less system-atically broken – without any consequences for those who deviate.'

79 Ibid., arguing that the IHR lags behind medical, trade, and travel advances.

80 (Emphasis added). See 'International Public Health Law: An Overview,' in *Oxford Textbook of Public Health*, vol. 1, ed. S.S. Fluss (Oxford: Oxford University Press, 1996) 371.

81 P. Dorolle, 'Old Plagues in the Jet Age: International Aspects of Present and Future Control of Communicable Diseases' (1969) WHO Chronicle 105.

82 Ibid., quoting E. Roelsgaard, 'Health Regulations and International Travel' (1974) 28 WHO Chronicle 265. See also Fidler, *International Law and Infectious Diseases* at 68 (stating that the WHO constitution does not provide for any sanction against a mem-ber state that fails to comply with a binding regulation enacted under Article 21).

83 WHO, *Revision and Updating of the International Health Regulations*, WHA Resolu-tion 48.7, 48th World Health Assembly, 12 May 1995.

84 Fidler, *International Law adn Infectious Diseases* at 70, citing *Communicable Diseases Prevention and Control: New, Emerging and Re-Emerging Infectious Diseases*, WHA Res-olution 48.13, 48th World Health Assembly, 12 May 1995.

85 Taylor, 'Controlling the Global Spread of Infectious Diseases' at 1346.

86 WHO, *The International Response to Epidemics and Application of the International Health Regulations: Report of a WHO Informal Consultation*, UN Doc. WHO/EMC/IHR 96.1 (1995).

87 'Controlling the Global Spread of Infecious Diseases' at 1350.

88 Since I do not intend to deal with all the changes proposed by the expert committee, I focus on just two of the changes: reporting of syndrome instead of diseases, and the need for the WHO to use information on outbreaks obtained from other reliable sources if a country fails to report an outbreak directly to the organization.

89 T.W. Grein et al., 'Rumours of Disease in the Global Village: Outbreak Verification' (2000) 6 Emerging Infectious Diseases 97.

90 Ibid.

91 ProMed maintains ProMed-mail: a free electronic mail list with subscribers from over 150 countries. Subscribers numbering over 15,000 report and discuss outbreaks of infectious diseases. For a discussion of ProMed-mail, see J. Woodall, 'Outbreak Meets the Internet: Global Epidemic Monitoring by ProMED-Mail' (1997) 1 SIM

Quarterly: Newsletter of the Society for the Internet in Medicine<http://www.
cybertas.demon.co.UK/Simq/issue1/papers.html>

92 View of Dr Johan Giesecke, Professor of Epidemiology, Karolinska Institute of Public
    Health, Stockholm, Sweden, and formerly head of the IHR Revision Team at the
    WHO, Geneva. (Interview with the author, Geneva, 30 April 2000).

93 I have recently explored the key proposals of the WHO IHR revision process, as well
    as the relevance of international law in global disease surveillance. See O. Aginam,
    'International Law and Communicable Diseases' (2002) 80 (12) Bulletin of the
    World Health Organization 946–51.

94 Taylor, 'Controlling the Global Spread of Infectious Diseases' at 1357 (stating that
    new monitoring mechanisms are now widely used by UNECSO, WIPO, ILO,
    UNEP and the UN Human Rights Commission).

95 See generally, Fidler, 'Future of the World Health Organization' at 1079.

96 Fidler, *International Law and Infectious Diseases* at 73 (stating that the IHR Provi-
    sional Draft proposes expanding notification duties without confronting the
    dilemma of financial and technological resources facing the developing world).

97 Although I will address this argument in detail in the concluding chapter where I dis-
    cuss a proposal for a global health fund, I have also dealt with it in another forum
    with respect to compliance with the WHO's International Health Regulations. See
    O. Aginam, 'Are We Our Brother's and Sister's Keepers: Africa and Public Health
    Challenges in a Divided World' (unpublished; paper presented at the Berkeley/Stan-
    ford Joint Center for African Studies Spring Conference, 'Health & Society in
    Africa,' 24 April 1999, Stanford University) (on file with the author).

98 World Bank, *World Development Report, 1993: Investing in Health* (New York:
    Oxford University Press, 1993) 7.

99 Ibid.

100 D.P. Fidler, 'Mission Impossible? International Law and Infectious Diseases' (1996)
    10 Temple International & Comparative Law J. 493 at 500.

101 T.M. Franck, *The Power of Legitimacy Among Nations* (New York: Oxford University
    Press, 1990) 3.

102 In this context, I use 'incentives' broadly to include tangible benefits – financial,
    technical and human resources – and intangible benefits – health as a global public
    good – as well as the relevance of enlightened self-interest as humanity is confronted
    with an avalanche of South-North dangers. Although Thomas Franck posits his
    entire treatise on determinacy as the primary reason why states obey international
    law, he also notes that the international system must strive to tackle fair global distri-
    bution of 'scarce but moderate resources.' See T.M. Franck, *Fairness in International
    Law and Institutions* (Oxford: Clarendon Press, 1995) 95.

103 O. Schachter, 'Towards a Theory of International Obligation' (1968) 6 Virginia J. of
    International Law 301 (enumerating the following basis of obligation in interna-

tional legal scholarship: consent of states, customary practice, a sense of 'rightness' – the juridical conscience, natural law and natural reason, social necessity, the will/consensus of the international community, direct intuition, common purposes of the participants, effectiveness, sanctions, systemic goals, shared expectations as to authority, and rules of recognition).

104 L. Henkin, *How Nations Behave: Law and Foreign Policy* (New York: Columbia University Press, 1979) 49. For the IHR, it is a matter of argument whether the advantages of observance – the formulation of maximum health measures by the WHO – outweigh the disadvantages – trade, and other economic embargoes that could cost a country billions of dollars.

105 See generally, Franck, *Fairness in International Law.*

106 During the EU ban of fresh fish from East Africa as a result of a cholera outbreak in three East African countries, the WHO exercised its global health mandate by issuing a strong statement condemning the ban as a punitive measure not based on any sound epidemiological principles. The WHO statement influenced the EU to lift the ban and to settle the case that was already heading to the dispute settlement panel of the World Trade Organization. See WHO, 'Director-General Says Food Import Bans Are Inappropriate for Fighting Cholera,' WHO Press Release WHO/24, February 1998.

107 World Health Assembly, Resolution WHA52.18 *Towards a WHO Framework Convention on Tobacco Control*, Geneva, World Health Organization, 1999.

108 C.L.J. Murray and A.D Lopez, eds., *The Global Burden of Disease* (Cambridge, MA: Harvard School of Public Health on behalf of the World Health Organization and The World Bank, 1996), C.L. Murray and A.D. Lopez, 'Alternative Projections of Mortality and Disability by Cause 1990–2020: Global Burden of Disease Study' (1997) 349 Lancet 1498.

109 Ibid. See also A.L. Taylor, 'An International Regulatory Strategy for Global Tobacco Control' (1996) 21 Yale J. of International Law 257 (stating that the absence of effective domestic regulation of tobacco in developing countries has created a lucrative opportunity for transnational tobacco companies to target such countries. In many of the poorer states, aggressive tobacco promotion by the tobacco industry and Western states simply overwhelms underfunded national tobacco control efforts).

110 G.N. Connoly, 'Worldwide Expansion of the Transnational Tobacco Industry' (1992) 2 Journal of the National Cancer Institute 29.

111 D.P. Fidler, 'Neither Science Nor Shamans: Globalization of Markets and Health in the Developing World' (1999) 7 Indiana J. of Global Legal Studies 191 at 201.

112 A.L. Taylor and D. Bettcher, 'WHO Framework Convention on Tobacco Control: A Global Good for Public Health' (2000) 78 (7) Bulletin of the World Health Organization 920 at 923 citing C.L.J. Murray and A.D. Lopez, 'Assessing the Burden of Disease that can be Attributed to Specific Risk Factors,' in WHO, *Report of Ad Hoc*

Committee on Health Research Relating to Future Intervention Options, Investing in Health Research and Development (Geneva: WHO, 1996).

113 Ibid.

114 WHO, 'Health Consequences of Tobacco,' in WHO, *The World Health Report 1999: Making a Difference* (Geneva: WHO, 1999) 66.

115 Ibid.

116 Ibid. For a more detailed study of tobacco smoke on children, see WHO, Tobacco Free Initiative, *International Consultation on Environmental Tobacco Smoke (ETS) and Child Health (Consultation Report)*, 11–14 January 1999 (Geneva: WHO–Tobacco Free Initiative, 1999) enumerating the following: respiratory health and middle ear disease, pneumonia, worsening of asthma, foetal growth, sudden infant death syndrome (SIDS), neuro-developmental effects, cardiovascular effects, and childhood cancers as the medical effects of tobacco smoke on children.

117 Zimbabwe, Malawi, Kenya, and many other countries in Africa, and in South and Central America, are tobacco growing and exporting countries. The WHO is now holding talks with the Food and Agriculture Organization of the United Nations (FAO) and the World Bank to develop an effective and workable crop substitution policy for these countries. Detailed scientific study as well as financial and technical assistance is needed to substitute other cash crops for tobacco in these countries.

118 The aim of these two related trade rules is to prevent discrimination against imported goods in the domestic markets of WTO member states. Based on the national treatment principle, a WTO member state shall not treat a foreign company less favourably than its national companies and shall accord imported goods or goods made by foreign companies the same treatment it gives to goods manufactured by national companies. Based on the most favoured-nation principle, a WTO member state shall extend the best tariffs and policies it gives to a trading partner to all other WTO member countries.

119 Thailand – Restrictions on Importation of and Internal Taxes on Cigarettes, Adopted November 7 1990, GATT Doc. DS10/R, BISD 37S/200.

120 Taylor Bettcher, 'WHO Framework Convention on Tobacco Control' at 924. Dr Douglas Bettcher led the Framework Convention on Tobacco Control Team at WHO headquarters, Geneva. Dr Allyn Taylor was the external legal adviser, WHO Tobacco Free Initiative. See also Taylor, 'An International Regulatory Strategy for Global Tobacco Control' at 257 (arguing that the tobacco multinationals have focused not only on gaining entry into closed national markets throughout the world, but also on blocking the imposition of national regulations that restrict the advertising or sale of cigarettes. Political pressure by major Western tobacco-exporting states, particularly the United States, has forced open markets and expanded advertising in importing countries. Western pressure has also led to a number of

changes in the developing and newly industrialized countries that have reduced the price and increased the demand for cigarettes).

121 World Health Assembly, 'Towards a WHO Framework Convention on Tobacco Control,' WHA Resolution 52.18 (1999).

122 See for instance, D. Bodansky, *What Makes International Agreements Effective? Some Pointers to the WHO Framework Convention on Tobacco Control*, FCTC Technical Briefing Series, WHO/NCD/TFI/99.4 (Geneva: WHO, 1999) and *The Framework-Protocol Approach*, FCTC Technical Briefing Series, WHO/NCD/TFI/99.1 (Geneva: WHO, 1999); L. Joossens, *Improving Public Health Through an International Framework Convention on Tobacco Control*, FCTC Technical Briefing Series WHO/NCD/TFI/99.2 (Geneva: WHO, 1999); INFACT, *Mobilizing NGOs and the Media Behind the International Framework Convention on Tobacco Control: Lessons From the Code on Marketing of Breast-Milk Substitutes and Conventions on Landmines and the Environment*, FCTC Technical Briefing Series WHO/NCD/TFI/99.3 (Geneva: WHO, 1999), and A.M. Halvorssen, *The Role of National Institutions in Developing and Implementing the WHO Framework Convention on Tobacco Control*, FCTC Technical Briefing Series WHO/NCD/TFI/99.5 (Geneva: WHO, 1999).

123 WHO, 'Elements of a WHO Framework Convention on Tobacco Control,' A/FCTC/WG1/6 (1999).

124 WHO, 'Subjects of Possible Protocols and Their Relation to the Framework Convention on Tobacco Control,' A/FCTC/WG1/3 (1999).

125 BBC News, 'Key Anti-Smoking Treaty Adopted,' BBC News Online, 21 May 2003 <http://news.bbc.co.uk> (accessed 21 May 2003); A. Langley, *New York Times*, 'Anti-Smoking Treaty Is Adopted by 192 Nations,' http://www.nytimes.com (accessed 21 May 2003).

126 The WHO has stated that 'since about 1950, more than 70,000 scientific articles have left no scientific doubt that prolonged smoking is an important cause of premature mortality and disability world-wide.' See WHO, *The World Health Report 1999* at 66. See also World Bank, *Curbing the Epidemic: Governments and the Economics of Tobacco Control* (Washington, DC: World Bank, 1999).

127 G.H. Brundtland, speech at Seminar on Tobacco Industry Disclosures, WHO, Geneva, 20 October 1998 (on file with the author). See also Taylor, 'An International Regulatory Strategy for Global Tobacco Control' at 257 (stating that the global tobacco epidemic is international in origin, has international repercussions, and necessitates collaborative, multilateral action).

128 WHO Director-General Gro Harlem Brundtland, speech at the WHO's International Conference on Global Tobacco Control Law: Towards a WHO Framework Convention on Tobacco Control, New Delhi, India, 7 January 2000 (on file with the author).

129 For a full text of the Ozone Convention, see (1987) 26 International Legal Materials 1529.

130 According to A. Kiss and D. Shelton, *International Environmental Law* (New York: Transnational Publishers, 1991) at 231, 'Ozone is a form of oxygen, containing one more atom than the oxygen breathed in the atmosphere. Ozone produces harmful consequences at certain altitudes, particularly on plants. In contrast, stratospheric ozone, whose strongest concentrations are found between 20 and 25 kilometres above earth, filters a part of the sun's ultraviolet radiation which otherwise would cause harm to different forms of life on earth.'

131 Ibid. at 232, citing a study by the United Nations Environment Programme (UNEP), and also A.K. Biswas, *The Ozone Layer* (1979), state that because all living beings have lived under the protection of the ozone layer, and the ozone plays a critical life-support role for all living beings on earth, its depletion risks an increase in the number of human skin cancers, harm to eyes, and other unforeseen biological consequences.

132 Ibid. at 232, observing that 'the main cause for reduction of the ozone layer is the utilization of chlorofluorocarbons ... The emissions of chlorofluorocarbons, if they continue at 1977 levels, will result within twenty years in a five percent reduction in the ozone layer.'

133 R. Benedick, *Ozone Diplomacy* (Cambridge: Harvard University Press 1998).

134 Patricia W. Birnie and Alan Boyle, *Basic Documents on International Law and the Environment* (Oxford: Clarendon Press, 1995) 211.

135 Article 2.

136 For a text of the Montreal Protocol, see (1987) 26 International Legal Materials 1550. The Montreal Protocol came into force on 1 January 1989.

137 The London Amendments to the Montreal Protocol entered into force on 19 August 1992.

138 Birnie and Boyle, *Basic Documents on International Law and the Environment* at 211.

139 Kiss and Shelton in the 1994 supplement to their treatise asserted that 'for the first time an international environmental treaty called for financial transfers from industrialized to developing countries.' *International Environmental Law (1994 Supplement)* (New York: Transnational Publishers, 1994) 125.

140 Ibid.

141 Ibid.

142 P.W. Birnie and A. Boyle, *International Law and the Environment* (Oxford: Clarendon Press, 1992) 411.

143 For a full text of the Instrument Establishing the Global Environmental Facility, see (1994) 33 International Legal Materials 1273.

144 Kiss and Shelton, *International Environmental Law* at 47.

145 For a text of the recommendations of the Rio Conference, see the United Nations, *Report of the UNCED* (June 1992).

146 United Nations Framework Convention on Climate Change, New York, 9 May 1992; reproduced in 31 International Legal Materials (1992).

147 United Nations Convention on Biological Diversity, Nairobi, 22 June 1992; reproduced in (1992) 31 International Legal Materials 818.
148 Non-Legally Binding Authoritative Statement of Principles for a Global Consensus on the Management, Conservation and Sustainable Development of all Types of Forests, 13 June 1992, A/CONF.151/6/Rev.1; reproduced in 31 International Legal Materials (1992).
149 Agenda 21 is a volume with 40 chapters and 115 topics covered in 800 pages. It is divided into four main parts covering socio-economic dimensions, conservation and resource management, civil society participation, and implementation mechanisms.
150 *Basic Documents on International Law and the Environment* 666. *See* also, Kiss Shelton, *International Environmental Law* at 47 (stating that GEF is intended to assist developing countries in addressing four global environmental issues: climate change, stratospheric ozone depletion, loss of biological diversity, and pollution of international waters).
151 For a detailed discussion of GEF, see R. Ricupero, 'Chronicle of a Negotiation: The Financial Chapter of Agenda 21' (1993) 4 Colorado J. of Int'l Environmental Law & Policy 81, D. Reed, ed., *The GEF: Sharing Responsibility for the Biosphere* (Washington, DC: World Wide Fund for Nature, 1993).

Chapter 5: Case Study: Global Malaria Policy and Ethno-Pharmacological/ Traditional Medical Therapies for Malaria in Africa

1 Ethnomedicine is defined as 'the study of different ways in which people of various cultures perceive and cope with illness, including making a diagnosis and obtaining therapy,' see H. Fabrega, 'The Need for an Ethnomedical Science' (1975) Vol. 189 Science No. 4207 at 969.
2 The World Health Organization defines traditional medicine as including 'diverse health practices, approaches, knowledge and beliefs incorporating plant, animal, and/ or mineral based medicines, spiritual therapies, manual techniques and exercises applied singularly or in combination to maintain well-being, as well as to treat, diagnose or prevent illness.' See WHO, *WHO Traditional Medicine Strategy, 2002–2005* (Geneva: WHO, 2002) at 7. See also WHO, *WHO General Guidelines for Methodologies on Research and Evaluation of Traditional Medicine* (Geneva: WHO/EDM/ TRM, 2000) (defining traditional medicine as the 'sum total of the knowledge, skills, and practices based on the theories, beliefs and experiences, indigenous to different cultures, whether explicable or not, used in the maintenance of health as well as in the prevention, diagnosis, improvement or treatment of physical and mental illnesses'). The terms complementary, alternative, and non-conventional medicine are used interchangeably with traditional medicine in many countries. For a discussion of complementary and alternative medicine specifically, see D. Eisenberg, 'Exploring Complimentary and Alternative Medicine,' The Richard and Hinda Rosenthal Lectures, 2001 (Washington, DC, Institute of Medicine).

3 Reacting to the question, what is ethnopharmacology?, P. A.G.M. De Smet, in his famous work *Herbs, Health and Healers: Africa as Ethnopharmacological Treasury* (Berg en Dal, The Netherlands: Afrika Museum, 1999) 11 states that 'from time immemorial, man has valued the plant kingdom and animal kingdom as sources of bioactive products ... Some of these traditional plant and animal substances are purely magical. They have no relevant pharmacological (i.e. drug-like) effects, which can be produced in a laboratory setting. Many substances have a measurable pharmacological action, however, which corresponds well to their traditional application. The scientific discipline, which explores this pharmacological basis of traditional drugs and poisons is called ethnopharmacology. Its focus ranges from the first-hand observation of native drug practices (by early travellers and anthropologists) through the identification of crude ingredients and their constituents (by botanists, zoologists and chemists) to the evaluation of wanted and unwanted drug effects (by pharmacologists and toxicologists).'

4 F. Staugard, *Traditional Medicine in Botswana* (Gaborone: Ipelegeng Publishers, 1985) 5. See also U. Wassermann, 'Traditional Medicine and the Law' (1984) 18 J. of World Trade Law 155 (asserting that 'Europeans and North Americans are often inclined to think of traditional medicine only in terms of witchcraft, spiritism, laying on of hands, or with a slightly less condescending attitude of homeopathy and such more embracing systems as India's *ayurveda* or Moslem *Unani* medicine').

5 Staugard, *Traditional Medicine* at 5.

6 I. Sindiga, 'African Ethnomedicine and Other Medical Systems,' in *Traditional Medicine in Africa*, ed. I. Sindiga (Nairobi: East African Publishers, 1995) 16, citing British scholar E.E. Evans-Pritchard, *Witchcraft, Oracle and Magic among the Azende* (Oxford: Oxford University Press, 1937) as an example of such perspective of African disease aetiology.

7 De Smet, *Herbs, Health and Healers* at 11.

8 The 1972 World Health Assembly Resolution WHA29.72 noted the huge manpower reserve constituted by traditional medical practitioners. The 1977 World Health Assembly Resolution WHA30.49 called on member states to explore the utilization of traditional medicine in their health care systems. The 1978 World Health Assembly Resolution WHA31.33 noted the medicinal value of medicinal plants in the health systems of many developing countries.

9 For a discourse of the challenges of the legal protection of traditional medicine, *see* R. Wilder, 'Protection of Traditional Medicine,' Commission on Macroeconomics and Health, Working Paper Series No. 4, July 2001; U. Wassermann, 'Traditional Medicine and the Law.' I have explored the challenges of integrating traditional medical therapies into the global malaria policy framework in O. Aginam, 'From the Core to the Peripheries: Multilateral Governance of Malaria in a Multi-Cultural World' (2002) 3 (1) Chicago J. of International Law 87.

10 For a recent detailed global strategy on the interaction of traditional, alternative, and complementary medicine and the formal health care system, see WHO, *WHO Traditional Medicine Strategy, 2002–2005* (Geneva: WHO, 2002).

11 O. Akerele, 'The Best of Both Worlds: Bringing Traditional Medicine up to Date' (1987) 24 (2) Social Science and Medicine 117. For a study of ethno-medicine across various societies in the developing world, see K. Appiah-Kubi, *Man Cures, God Heals: Religion and Medical Practice Among the Akans of Ghana* (Totawa, NJ: Allanheld & Osmun, 1981); C. Leslie and A. Young, *Paths to Asian Medical Knowledge* (Berkeley and Los Angeles: University of California Press, 1992); T. Dummer, *Tibetan Medicine and Other Holistic Health-Care Systems* (London and New York: Routledge, 1988); H.M. Said, *Medicine in China* (Karachi: Hanidard Academy, 1965); G.E. Simpson, *Yoruba Religion and Medicine in Ibadan* (Ibadan: Ibadan University Press, 1980).

12 E.B. Weiss, *In Fairness to Future Generations: International Law, Common Patrimony, and Intergenerational Equity* (New York: United Nations University/Transnational Publishers, 1989) 266. See generally, M.M. Iwu and J.C. Wootton, *Advances in PhytoMedicine*, vol. 1 (Amsterdam: Elsevier, 2002).

13 D.R. Phillips, *Health and Health Care in the Third World* (New York: Longman, 1990) 75 defines medical pluralism as 'the existence and use of a wide range of sources of medical care, traditional and modern, static and evolving.'

14 J.M. Janzen, *The Quest for Therapy: Medical Pluralism in Lower Zaire* (Berkeley: University of California Press, 1978); H. Fabrega, 'A Complimentary on African Systems of Medicine,' in *African Health and Healing Systems: Proceedings of a Symposium*, ed. P.S Yoda (Los Angeles: Crossroads, 1982).

15 O. Ampofo and J.D. Johnson-Romauld, 'Traditional Medicine and Its Role in the Development of Health Services in Africa,' Technical Discussions of the 25th, 26th and 27th Sessions of the WHO Regional Office for Africa (Brazzaville, Congo: WHO, 1987) 51.

16 M.M. Iwu, 'Preface,' in P.A.G.M De Smet, *Herbs, Health and Healers* at 9.

17 J.S Mbiti, *African Religions and Philosophy* (London: Heinemann, 1969) 169. See also Ampofo and Johnson-Romauld, 'Traditional Medicine' at 15 (arguing that in Africa, disease is not just a malfunctioning of the body or an organ but essentially a rupture of life's harmony with nature).

18 Phillips, *Health and Health Care* at 81.

19 In Africa, according to Mbiti, the individual's needs, rights, joys, and sorrows are woven into a social tapestry that denies singular individuality. Traditional medical practitioners symbolize the hopes of society; hopes of good health, protection and security from evil forces, prosperity and good fortune, and ritual cleansing when harm or impurities have been contracted. See Mbiti, *African Religions* 141 and 171.

20 Ogbu Kalu has argued that 'crucial to indigenous traditions is a religious cosmology with an awareness of the integral and whole relationship of symbolic and material life.

Ritual practices of the cosmological ideas which underpin society cannot be separated from the daily round of subsistence practices ... By sacralizing nature, indigenous worldviews purvey an ideology which is at once more eco-sensitive, eco-musical and devoid of the harsh flutes of those who see nature as a challenge to be conquered, exploited and ruled. They see the environment not in terms of competing interests but as the playing field on which all other interests intersect.' See O. Kalu, 'The Gods Are to Blame' (unpublished) Proceedings of the 6th International Congress on Ethnobiology, Whakatana, New Zealand, 24–6 November 1998, quoted by Iwu, 'Preface: Symbols of Power and Health,' in De Smet, *Herbs, Health and Healers* at 9.

21 I use the term 'indigenous populations' in this context to refer broadly to populations in any society or community (especially in the developing world) that serve as customary custodians of bio-diversity and bio-medical resources available in that society or community, as opposed to the use of the term in the North American legal context to refer to Native Indian populations.

22 For some works that explore indigenous knowledge from intellectual property perspectives, see Wilder, 'Protection of Traditional Medicine'; E. Da Costa Silva, 'The Protection of Intellectual Property for Local and Indigenous Peoples' (1995) 17 European Intellectual Property Rev. 546; A Gutterman, 'The North-South Debate Regarding the Protection of Intellectual Property' (1993) 23 Wake Forest Law Rev. 89; R.M. Gdbaw and T.J. Richard, *Intellectual Property Rights: Global Consensus, Global Conflict* (Boulder, CO: Westview Press, 1998); M. Bowman, ed., *International Law and Conservation of Biological Diversity* (London: Kluwer Law International 1996).

23 R. Falk, *Law in an Emerging Global Village: A Post-Westphalian Perspective* (New York: Transnational Publishers, 1998) 29. For a recent exploration of this theme in an international colloquium of experts, see Bioresources Development and Conservation Programme, *Report of the International Conference on Traditional Medicine in HIV/AIDS and Malaria*, 5–7 December 2000, Abuja, Nigeria; available online at http:// www.bioresources.org (accessed 30 March 2001).

24 For an extensive discussion of this conundrum, see D.P. Fidler 'Neither Science nor Shamans: Globalization of Markets and Health in the Developing World' (1999) Indiana J. of Global Leg. Stud. 191.

25 P. Trigg and A. Kondrachine, 'The Global Malaria Control Strategy' in World Health: Unied against Malaria (The Magazine of the WHO) May–June 1998) 4.

26 Ibid.

27 WHO, *The World Health Report 1999: Making a Difference* (Geneva: WHO, 1999) 49. For a detailed discussion of the economic analysis of malaria control, see C. Goodman et al., *Economic Analysis of Malaria Control in Sub-Saharan Africa* (Geneva: Global Forum for Health Research, 2000). See also the detailed scholarly studies on the impact of disease and ill-health (including malaria) on economic development undertaken by the WHO Commission on Macroeconomics and Health of the Harvard

Center for International Development and the World Health Organization under the pioneering leadership of J.D. Sachs, available online at http://www.cid.harvard.edu (acessed 10 June 2001).

28 For a general overview of WHO's Roll Back Malaria project, see http://www.who.int/ rbm (accessed 20 March 2001).

29 WHO, *World Health Report 1999* at 52.

30 Ibid.

31 *Medicines for Malaria Venture*, Press Release, 3 November 1999 Geneva: WHO, 1999.

32 For general information about MMV and how it operates, see http://www.mmv.org (accessed 2 April 2003).

33 Medicines for Malaria Venture Press Release 3 Nov. 1999.

34 G. Yamey, 'Global Campaign to Eradicate Malaria' (2001) 322 British Medical Journal 1191 (stating that the Roll Back Malaria Campaign has had two major successes. First, it has built an impressive partnership of the United Nations and development agencies, the World Bank and International Monetary Fund, governments, the private sector, researchers, and non-governmental organizations. Second, it has raised the visibility of a neglected disease – one that causes at least 3,000 deaths a day and that slows down economic growth by 1.3 per cent per year in endemic areas).

35 This part of the study is based on the interviews I conducted among rural populations in Southeastern Nigeria in December 2000.

36 The interviews were conducted in Ekwulobia, a rural community located about 120 kilometres from Enugu – the capital of the former Eastern Region of Nigeria. Choice of the community was informed by the fact that the author was born there, speaks the same mother tongue as residents (Igbo language), and understands their cultures and customs. They never perceived the author as a foreigner, but rather felt at ease to answer all of the questions put to them. Also, malaria is endemic in this community, as in most parts of tropical Africa.

37 The two traditional healers and almost all the interviewees within the group requested anonymity. To protect their privacy, I shall use only coded names where necessary as opposed to their real names. The Western-trained physician I interviewed is IPS Okafor, medical director, St Victoria Hospital and Maternity, Ekwulobia.

38 WHO, *Qualitative Research for Health Programmes* (Geneva: WHO, Division of Mental Health and Prevention of Substance Abuse, 1996) 12.

39 Ibid.

40 J. Okafor, 'Issues in African Biodiversity No.3: Identification, Utilization, and Conservation of Medicinal Plants in Southeastern Nigeria,' Biodiversity Support Program Publication Database 1999 (unpublished; on file with the author).

41 The symptoms each of them described to me correspond almost exactly to the symptoms that Western medical science associates with malaria. See, for instance, WHO, *Management of Severe Malaria: A Practical Handbook*, 2nd ed. (Geneva: WHO, 2000) 1.

42 I was also informed of this by IPS Okafor, medical director, St Victoria Hospital, Ekwulobia, Nigeria, in an interview held on 18 December 2000. Okafor stated that about 40 per cent of his malaria patients are brought to the clinic with severe and sometimes life-threatening cerebral malaria after having visited traditional healers in search of therapies or trying self-help without success.

43 L.A. Salako, 'An African Perspective,' in *World Health: United Against Malaria* (*The Magazine of the World Health Organization* (May–June 1998) 24.

44 R. Arazu, Interview in *The Torch* (Biannual Publication of the Students of Bigard Memorial Seminary, Enugu, Nigeria), Special Edition on Healing and Exorcism: Implications and Realities, 120 (Dec. 2000–June 2001) 38.

45 Chinua Achebe, *Things Fall Apart* (New York: Anchor Books, 1994). Achebe's work is the most vivid account of the pre-colonial world-view and culture of the Ibo ethnic group in popular art and, by extension, that of most pre-colonial African societies.

46 *Ibid.* 75–6, 85–6 (emphasis added).

47 For an extensive exposé of these terms and their application to global issues, see R. Falk, 'The Making of Global Citizenship,' in *Global Visions: Beyond the New World Order*, ed. J. Brecher (Boston: South End Press, 1993) 39; Falk, *Law in an Emerging Global Village*.

48 Falk, *Law in an Emerging Global Village*, at 218.

49 Ibid. at 216.

50 Ibid. at 206 citing approvingly Jürgen Habermas, *The Theory of Communicative Action*, 2 vols. (Boston: Beacon Press, 1984, 1989).

51 Ibid., citing M. Koskenniemi, *From Apology to Utopia: The Structure of International Legal Argument* (Helsinki: Finnish Lawyers' Publishing Group, 1989).

52 Ibid., 206–7.

53 See Resolutions of the World Health Assembly on traditional medicine.

54 WHO, *The World Health Report 2000: Health Systems, Improving Performance* (Geneva: WHO, 2000) 5.

55 Ibid.

56 D. Nabarro and E.M. Taylor, 'The Roll Back Malaria Campaign' (26 June 1998) 280 Science 2067. Also available online at: www.science.org.

57 Yamey, 'Global Campaign' at 1192.

58 This proposal is not entirely novel, because many countries have since initiated a process of harmonizing traditional medical therapies with Western medicine. This is done by incorporating aspects of traditional healing practices, mainly with herbs and roots that are scientifically proven to have medicinal value as part of the national health care systems. See for instance, J.I. Durodola, *Scientific Insights into Yoruba Traditional Medicine* (Owerri and New York: Trado-Medic Books, 1986) (analysing aspects of Yoruba traditional medicine in Western Nigeria for which scientific evaluation has been made); S. Nadasen, *Public Health Law in South Africa* (Durban: Butterworths, 2000)

32–7 (analysing the legal framework for incorporation of alternative/traditional medicine as part of health care in South Africa); M. Last and G.L. Chavundika, eds., *The
Professionalisation of African Medicine* (Manchester: Manchester University Press,
1986) (giving a useful overview of the prospects and ambiguities of traditional medicine across African societies); Wassermann, 'Traditional Medicine and the Law' (analysing the different systems of interaction between traditional and modern medicine
within countries). For an articulation of the challenges of integrating traditional medicine into national health care systems, see WHO, WHO Traditional Medicine Strategy 2002–2005.

59 N. Roht-Arriaza, 'Of Seeds and Shamans: The Appropriation of the Scientific and
Technical Knowledge of Indigenous and Local Communities' (1996) 17 Michigan J.
of International Law 919 at 921. For an insightful discussion of bio-piracy, see I.
Mgbeoji, 'Patents and Traditional Knowledge of the Uses of Plants: Is a Communal
Patent Regime Part of the Solution to the Scourge of Bio Piracy?' (2001) 9 (1) Indiana
J. of Global Legal Studies 163.

60 Ibid.

61 Ibid.

62 Ibid.

63 Ibid.

64 The World Health Organization correctly observed that 'without critical assessment of
what should be integrated and what should not, we risk developing a health care system that costs more, is less safe, and fails to address the management of chronic disease
in a publicly responsible manner.' See WHO, Traditional Medicine Strategy 2002–
2005. at 20.

65 I have given an overview of the theories of modernization, development, dependency,
and anthropological study of law, the basis of obligation in international law, the post-
colonial discourse of the nineteenth-century infectious disease diplomacy, and a critique of the Westphalian model of statehood in the preceding chapters.

66 E. Bodenheimer, *Jurisprudence* (Cambridge: Harvard University Press, 1974) 12.

67 Mark W. Zacher and Richard A. Matthew, 'Liberal International Theory: Common
Threads, Divergent Strands,' in *Controversies in International Relations Theory: Realism
and the Neo-Liberal Challenge*, ed. C.W. Kegley (New York: St Martin's, 1995) 107.
See generally, A. Hasenclever et al., *Theories of International Regimes* (Cambridge:
Cambridge University Press, 1997).

68 Hedley Bull, *The Anarchical Society: A Study of Order in World Politics*, 2nd ed. (London: Macmillan, 1995) 23.

69 D. Fidler, *International Law and Infectious Diseases* (Oxford: Clarendon Press, 1999)
296.

70 Ibid.

71 Zacher and Matthew, 'Liberal International Theory' at 109.

72 Ibid.
73 Kant, *Perpetual Peace*, trans. L.W. Beck (Indianapolis: Bobbs-Merrill, 1957).
74 Bull, *Anarchical Society* at 310. Zacher and Matthew, 'Liberal International Theory' at 112, state that 'while Kant's commitment to progress in international relations is indisputable, his image of the ultimate form that universal peace would assume has been the subject of disagreement. Whether one reads in Kant a future world of co-operative states or some form of world government, it is clear that, like earlier liberals, he accepted a strong, but gradually diminishing role for power relations and the use of force.'
75 Fidler, *International Law and Infectious Diseases* at 297.
76 See, for instance, WHO, Tobacco Industry Strategies to Undermine Tobacco Control Activities at the World Health Organization: Report of the Committee of Experts on Tobacco Industry Documents (Geneva: WHO, July 2000); P.J. Hilts, *Smokescreen: The Truth behind Tobacco Industry Cover-Up* (Reading, MA: Addison-Wesley Co., 1996).
77 B.S. 'Chimni, 'Marxism and International Law: A Contemporary Analysis' (6 February 1999) Economic & Political Weekly 337 (stating that despite the critical role international law has come to play in building and sustaining the contemporary international system, Marxists have entirely neglected its study. While an attempt was made in the former Soviet Union to articulate a Marxist approach to international law, its content was dictated less by Marxism-Leninism than by the need to rationalize Soviet foreign policy).
78 Zacher and Matthew, 'Liberal International Theory' at 108.
79 For a detailed application of critical theory to emerging and re-emerging infectious disease threats, see P. Farmer, 'Social Inequalities and Emerging Infectious Diseases' (1996) 2 Emerging Infectious Diseases 259.
80 Chimni, 'Marxism and International Law' at 339.
81 R. Devetak, 'Critical Theory,' in *Theories of International Relations*, ed. S. Burchill & A. Linklater (London: Macmillan, 1996) 145.
82 Fidler, *International Law and Infectious Diseases* at 298.
83 With some caveats I am a student of Thomas Franck, whose influential works explore the distributive and procedural dimensions of fairness in the interaction between states. See T.M. Franck, *Fairness in International Law and Institutions* (Oxford: Clarendon Press, 1995).
84 Ibid. 7.
85 Ibid.
86 Ibid.
87 J.N. Rosenau, *Along the Domestic-Foreign Frontier: Exploring Governance in a Turbulent World* (Cambridge: Cambridge University Press, 1997) 5.
88 Ibid.

Chapter 6: In Search of Prophylaxis: Communitarian Globalism and Multilateral Disease Non-Proliferation Facility

1 T.M. Franck, *Fairness in International Law and Institutions* (Oxford: Clarendon Press, 1995) 12.

2 World Bank, *World Development Report 1993: Investing in Health* (New York: Oxford University Press, 1993).

3 J.M. Last, *Public Health and Human Ecology* (Stamford, CT: Appleton & Lang, 1998) 348.

4 See 'Global Health Challenges,' Report of a Symposium by the Liu Centre for the Study of Global Issues, Vancouver, Canada, 5 March 1999 at 10, stating that protocols for an effective global surveillance system properly fall within the ambit of the World Health Organization but would likely depend for financing and co-leadership on the World Bank. In global health terms, such a system will depend for its effectiveness upon the enthusiastic participation of all UN members. The need is so great, and the benefits so demonstrable, that political support should be vigorously sought and leadership by the WHO and the World Bank actively encouraged.

5 The Joint United Nations Programme on HIV/AIDS (UNAIDS) is a partnership between the United Nations Children's Fund (UNICEF), the World Health Organization (WHO), the United Nations Development Programme (UNDP), the United Nations Educational, Scientific and Cultural Organization (UNESCO), the United Nations Population Fund (UNFPA), and the World Bank. The WHO's Roll Back Malaria Campaign is a partnership between the World Health Organization, the United Nations Development Programme, the United Nations Children's Fund, and the World Bank.

6 See my critique of the WHO's Roll-Back Malaria partnership on similar grounds, above chapter 5.

7 M. Larkin, 'Global Aspects of Health and Health Policy in Third World Countries,' in *Globalisation and the Third World*, ed. R. Keily and P. Marfleet (London and New York: Routledge, 1998) 104–5. For a recent criticism of the uncontrollable power of international financial institutions, especially the World Bank and the International Monetary Fund, from an international legal perspective, see A. Anghie, 'Time Present and Time Past: Globalization, International Financial Institutions and the Third World' (2000) 32 New York J. of Int'l Law & Politics 243.

8 World Bank, *World Development Report 1993* at 5. For evidence of another significant shift by the World Bank towards poverty alleviation, see the recent report, *Voices of the Poor Crying Out for Change*, ed. D. Narayan et al. (Washington, DC: World Bank, 2000) (discussing, inter alia, the impact of poverty on health care and vulnerability of the poor to a deluge of socio-economic risks).

9 *World Development Report 1993*.

10 Ibid.
11 Ibid. at 106.
12 Ibid.
13 Ibid.
14 This proposal was made before the Geneva-based Global Fund to Fight AIDS, Tuberculosis and Malaria (GFATM) was set up. I will assess the GFATM subsequently in this chapter, including ways to improve its effectiveness.
15 Commission on Health Research for Development, *Health Research: Essential Link to Equity and Development* (Oxford: Oxford University Press, 1990) 29.
16 *World Health Report 1993* at 166.
17 UNDP, *Human Development Report 1998* at 37.
18 J.D. Sachs, 'A New Global Commitment to Disease Control in Africa' (May 2001) 7 Nature Medicine 521.
19 Ibid.
20 Ibid.
21 Ibid. at 522. Sachs cites the example of Bill Gates, whose $750 million aid to the Global Fund for Children's Vaccines reinvigorated programs for childhood immunization and stirred the conscience of international agencies, resulting in a better coordinated Global Alliance for Vaccines and Immunization (GAVI).
22 See Speech by Kofi Annan to the African Summit on HIV/AIDS, Tuberculosis and other Related Infectious Diseases, Abuja, Nigeria, 24–7 April 2001 (on file with the author). Also available online at UN website http://www.un.org/News/Press/docs/2001/SGSM7779R1.doc.htm (accessed 10 May 2001).
23 Ibid.
24 Ibid.
25 Ibid.
26 ABUJA Declaration on HIV/AIDS, Tuberculosis and other Related Infectious Diseases, OAU/SPS/ABUJA/3, made pursuant to the African Summit on HIV/AIDS, Tuberculosis and other Related Infectious Diseases, 24–7 April 2001.
27 Ibid.
28 Ibid.
29 K. Annan, 'Poverty: Biggest Enemy of Health in the Developing World,' Speech to the 54th World Health Assembly, Geneva, Switzerland, 17 May 2001 (on file with the author). Also available online at http://www.un.org/News/Press/docs/2001/sgsm7808.doc.htm (accessed 25 May 2001).
30 G.H. Brundtland, Speech at the 54th World Health Assembly Technical Briefing, 'Scaling Up Action to Tackle Illness Associated with Poverty: The Global Fund for AIDS and Health,' Geneva, 15 May 2001 (on file with the author). Also available online at http:www.who.int/director-general/speeches/20.../20010515_wha54technicalbriefing.en.htm (accessed 25 May 2001).

31 See 'Global Crisis-Global Action,' Declaration of Commitment on HIV/AIDS adopted by the United Nations General Assembly Special Session, New York, 25–7 June 2001 (on file with the author); also available online at http://www.un.org/ga/aids/coverage/FinalDeclarationHIVAIDS.html (accessed 4 July 2001).

32 Ibid.

33 'Final Statement of the 2001 G-8 Summit,' Genoa, Italy, Sunday, 22 July 2001 (on file with the author), available online at http://www.washingtonpost.com/wp-dyn/articles/A33436-2001Jul22.html (accessed 23 July 2001). For the most recent G8 commitment to the Global Fund to Fight AIDS, Tuberculosis and Malaria, see 'Health: A G8 Action Plan,' 2003 G8 Summit Documents, Evian, France (reaffirming their support for the Global Health Fund, and reiterating the commitment of G8 countries to fight against AIDS, tuberculosis, and malaria as agreed in Okinawa through further actions in such areas as institutional building, public-private partnerships, human resource development, research activities and promotion of public health at the community level). For a critical assessment of the commitment of the G8 to global health, see R. Labonte et al., *Fatal Indifference: The G8, Africa and Global Health* (Lansdowne, South Africa: University of Cape Town Press, 2004).

34 R. Brugha and G. Walt, 'A Global Health Fund: A Leap of Faith' (21 July 2001) 323 British Medical J. 152 (exploring the Global Health Fund in comparison with the challenges of other public-private partnerships like the Global Alliance for Vaccines and Immunization, GAVI). See also T. Richards, 'New Global Fund' (Editorial) (2 June 2001), 322 British Medical J. 1321; G. Yamey, 'WHO in 2002: Faltering Steps Towards Partnerships' (23 November 2002) 325 British Medical J. 1236; K. Buse and G. Walt, 'Public-Private Partnerships: Part II – What Are the Health Issues for Global Governance' (2000) 78 (5) Bulletin of the World Health Organization 699.

35 This does not mean that specialized agencies of the United Nations like the World Health Organization will have no formal or informal links with the fund. The various mandates and expertise of these organizations make them important players on global health issues. What is being suggested is a framework that is more participatory and inclusive of all the relevant actors and stakeholders.

36 C.J.L. Murray and A. Lopez, *The Global Burden of Disease* (Cambridge: Harvard University Press, 1996).

37 For some proposals made on the governance of the Global Fund, see generally, Global Health Council, 'A Discussion of Issues Relating to Governance of the Global Fund to Fight AIDS, Tuberculosis and Malaria,' November 2001 (unpublished), available online www.globalfundatm.org (accessed 30 March 2003); R. Drew, 'The Global Fund for AIDS, Tuberculosis and Malaria: Accountability, Eligibility, Technical Review and Advice' (Discussion Paper by HealthLink Worldwide) November 2001 (Unpublished) available online at www.globalfundatm.org (accessed 30 March 2003).

38 G.H. Brundtland, 'Scaling-Up Action to Tackle Illness Associated with Poverty: The

Global Fund for AIDS and Health,' Speech at the Technical Briefing Session of the 54th World Health Assembly, Geneva, 15 May 2001, available online at http://www.who.int/director-general/speeches/20.../20010515_wha54technicalbriefing.en.htm (accessed 25 May 2001).

39 See Sachs, 'New Global Commitment to Disease Control.'

40 See Brundtland, Speech.

41 Ibid.

42 See Sachs, 'New Global Commitment to Disease Control.'

43 Ibid.

44 Ibid.

45 Ibid.

46 For detailed information on the Global Fund to Fight AIDS, Tuberculosis and Malaria, see http://www.globalfundatm.org (accessed 2 July 2003). See also N.K. Poku, 'The Global AIDS Fund: Context and Opportunity' (2002) 23 Third World Quarterly 283 (articulating the facets of the governance challenge facing the Fund); A.L. Taylor, 'Public-Private Partnerships for Health: The United Nations Global Fund on AIDS and Health' (2002) 35 John Marshall Law Rev. 400.

47 http://www.globalfundatm.org/faq_gfund.html (accessed 2 July 2003).

48 Ibid.

49 The executive director of UNAIDS and the director-general of the WHO serve as ex-officio members of the GFATM board.

50 Most of these seats have alternates and will therefore rotate among countries in the region.

51 For a complete list of the GFATM Board and their constituencies, visit the Fund website, www.globalfundatm.org (last accessed 2 July 2003).

52 See generally, S. Ramsay, 'Global Fund Makes Historic First Round of Payments' (News), 4 May 2002, 359 The Lancet 158.

53 See www.globalfundatm.org/qa.html (accessed 3 July 2003).

54 Tim France, et al., 'The Global Fund: Which Countries Owe How Much?', unpublished paper, 21 April 2002, available on the websites of Health and Development Networks, www.hdnet.org and Aidspan, www.aidspan.org (on file with the author).

55 Ibid.

56 Ibid.

57 Poku, 'The Global Aids Fund' (discussing some of the complexities of donor fatigue in the governance of the GFATM).

58 'No person can give that which he does not have.' See H.C. Black, *Black's Law Dictionary*, 6th ed. (St Paul, MN: West Publishing Co., 1990) 1037. Can a developing country have a voting right to authorize disbursement of funds that it never contributed?

59 On proposals for quality control in Public-Private Partnerships on global health governance, see K. Buse and A. Waxman, 'Public-Private Health Partnerships: A Strategy for

WHO' (2001) 79 (8) Bulletin of the WHO 748; Buse and Walt, 'Public-Private Health Partnerships: Part II' K. Buse and G. Walt, 'Globalisation and Multilateral Public-Private Health Partnerships: Issues for Health Policy,' in *Health Policy in a Globalising World*, ed. K. Lee, K. Buse, and S. Fustukian (Cambridge: Cambridge University Press, 2002) 41.

60 G.H. Brundtland, 'Globalization as a Force for Better Health,' Lecture at the London School of Economics, London, UK, 16 March 2001 (on file with the author), also available online at http://www.who.int/director-general/speeches/2001/eng.../ 20010316_lselecturelondon.en.htm (accessed 25 June 2001). For an exploration of global health challenges from globalization and self-interest perspectives, see D. Yach and D. Bettcher, 'The Globalization of Public Health, II: The Convergence of Self-Interest and Altruism' (1998) 88 Am. J. of Pub. Health 738.

61 World Bank, *World Development Report 1993* at 6–7.

62 The Ottawa Charter for Health Promotion, 1986 provides, inter alia, that health promotion is not just the responsibility of the health sector, but goes beyond health lifestyles to well-being.

63 The WHO/UNICEF Alma-Ata Declaration on Primary Health Care 1978, inter alia, provides that Primary Health Care forms an integral part of a country's health system and of the overall social and economic development of the community. See WHO/ UNICEF Declaration on Primary Health Care 1978.

64 Health determinants include (non-exhaustively), biological, behavioural, environmental, health system, socioeconomic factors, sociocultural factors, aging of the population, science and technology, information and communication, gender, equity, and social justice. See G. Pinet, 'Health Challenges of the 21st Century: A Legislative Approach to Health Determinants' (1998) 49 International Digest of Health Legislation 131.

65 L. Garrett, Betrayal of Trust: The Collapse of Global Public Health (New York: Hyperion, 2000) 590.

66 See 'Global Health Challenges,' Report of a Symposium by the Liu Centre, at 12.

67 I use the term 'global civil society' not in a restrictive sense that merely refers to nongovernmental organizations, but in the broad sense suggested by Paul Wapner as 'that domain of associational life that exists above the individual and below the state yet across state boundaries through which people experience the virtues of sociality and represent themselves in a social context.' See P. Wapner, 'The Normative Promise of Nonstate Actors: A Theoretical Account of Global Civil Society,' in *Principled World Politics: The Challenge of Normative International Relations*, ed. P. Wapner and L. Ruiz (Lanham, MD: Rowman & Littlefield 2000) 261 at 266.

68 Ibid.

69 Ibid.

70 Y.H. Ferguson and R.W. Mansbach, 'Global Politics at the Turn of the Millennium:

Changing Bases of "Us" and "Them,"' Proceedings of the 1999 International Studies Association (Malden, MA: Blackwell, 1999) 77.

71 R. Falk, *Law in an Emerging Global Village* (New York: Transnational Publishers, 1998) 33.

72 Ibid.

73 Many multilateral institutions including the United Nations organs and specialized agencies grant observer status to civil society organizations. Article 71 of the Constitution of the World Health Organization provides that the WHO may, on matters within its competence, arrange for consultation and cooperation with non-governmental international organizations, and with the consent of the Government consult with national organizations, governmental or non-governmental. See generally, *Principles Governing Relations between the World Health Organization and Non-Governmental Organizations*, Resolution WHA40.25 adopted by the Fortieth World Health Assembly, reproduced in World Health Organization, *Basic Documents* (Geneva: WHO, 1996) 74.

74 See Wapner and Ruiz, *Principled World Politics* at 262.

75 See Falk, *Law in an Emerging Global Village* at 35. For a persuasive argument in favour of new global governance structures in the millennium, see G. Smith and M. Naim, *Altered States: Globalization, Sovereignty and Governance* (Ottawa: IDRC, 2000).

76 For some recent exposition of the normative and theoretical bases of the involvement of non-state actors in governance of multilateral issues, see R. A. Matthew, 'Social Responses to Environmental Change,' in *Environmental Change, Adaptation and Security*, ed. S.C. Lonergan, 17 (The Hague: Kluwer, 1999); P. Wapner, *Environmental Activism and World Civic Politics* (New York: SUNY Press, 1996); R. Falk, 'Global Civil Society, Perspectives, Initiatives, Movements' (1998) 26 Oxford Development Studies 99; R. Falk, 'The Making of Global Citizenship,' in *Global Visions: Beyond the New World Order*, ed. J. Brecher, 39 (Boston: South End Press, 1993); Y.H. Ferguson and R.W. Mansbach, 'Beyond Inside/Outside: Political Space and Westphalian States in a World of Polities' (1996) 2 Global Governance 261; J. Mathews, 'Power Shift' (1997) 76 Foreign Affairs 50.

77 Falk, *Law in an Emerging Global Village* at 38.

78 H.G. Brundtland, 'Globalization as a Force for Better Health,' Lecture at the London School of Economics, 16 March 2001 (on file with the author).

79 Garret, *Betrayal of Trust* at 585 (emphasis added).

80 (London: Macmillan, 1997).

81 Ibid. at 1–2.

Bibliography

Books

Achebe, C. *Things Fall Apart*. New York: Anchor Books, 1994.

Anand, R.P. *New States and International Law*. Delhi: Vikas Ltd., 1972.

Appiah-Kubi, K. *Man Cures, God Heals: Religion and Medical Practice among the Akans of Ghana*. Totawa, NJ: Allenheld & Osmun, 1981.

Arnold, G. *The End of the Third World*. New York: St Martin's Press, 1993.

Basch, P.F. *A Textbook of International Health*. Oxford: Oxford University Press, 1990.

Bedjaoui, M. *Towards a New International Economic Order*. Paris: UNESCO, 1979.

Benedick, R. *Ozone Diplomacy*. Cambridge: Harvard University Press, 1991.

Birnie, P.W. and A. Boyle. *Basic Documents on International Law and the Environment*. Oxford: Clarendon Press, 1995.

– *International Law and the Environment*. Oxford: Clarendon Press, 1992.

Black, H.C. *Black's Law Dictionary*. 6th ed. St Paul, MN: West Publishing Co., 1990.

Bodenheimer, E. *Jurisprudence*. Cambridge: Harvard University Press, 1974.

Boisson de Chazournes, L., and P. Sands. *International Law, the International Court of Justice and Nuclear Weapons*. Cambridge: Cambridge University Press, 1999.

Bowman, M. ed. *International Law and Conservation of Biological Diversity*. London: Kluwer Law International, 1996.

Brownlie, I. *Principles of Public International Law*. 4th ed. Oxford: Clarendon Press, 1990.

Bull, H. *The Anarchical Society: A Study of Order in World Politics*. 2nd ed. London: Macmillan, 1995.

Campbell, B.K., and J. Loxley. *Structural Adjustment in Africa*. Houndmills, Basingstoke, UK: Macmillan, 1989.

Chapman, A., and R. Rubenstein. *Human Rights and Health: The Legacy of Apartheid*. New York: American Association for the Advancement of Science and Physicians for Human Rights, 1998.

Chossudovsky, M. *The Globalisation of Poverty: Impacts of IMF and World Bank Reforms.* Penang, Malaysia: Third World Network, 1997.

Cook, R.J., B.M. Dicken, and M.F. Fathalla. *Reproductive Health and Human Rights.* Oxford: Oxford University Press, 2003.

Commission on Global Governance. *Our Global Neighbourhood: The Report of the Commission on Global Governance.* New York: Oxford University Press, 1995.

Cornia, G.A. et al., eds. *Africa's Recovery in the 1990s: From Stagnation and Adjustment to Human Development.* Basingstoke, UK: Macmillan, 1992.

Craven, M.C.R. *The International Covenant on Economic, Social and Cultural Rights: A Perspective on Its Development.* Oxford: Oxford University Press, 1995.

Crosby, A.W. *The Columbian Exchange: Biological and Cultural Consequences of 1492.* Westport, CT: Greenwood Press, 1972.

– *Ecological Imperialism: The Biological Expansion of Europe, 900–1900.* Cambridge: Cambridge University Press, 1986.

De Smet, P.A.G.M. *Herbs, Health and Healers: Africa as Ethnopharmacological Treasury.* Berg en Dal, The Netherlands: Africa Museum, 1999.

Dummer, T. *Tibetan Medicine and Other Holistic Health-Care Systems.* London and New York: Routledge, 1988.

Durodola, J.I. *Scientific Insights into Yoruba Traditional Medicine.* Owerri and New York: Trado-Medic Books, 1986.

Dworkin, R. *Taking Rights Seriously.* Cambridge: Harvard University Press, 1978.

Elias, T.O. *Africa and the Development of International Law.* 2nd rev. ed. The Hague: Martinus Nijhoff, 1988.

Evans-Pritchard, E.E. *Witchcraft, Oracle and Magic among the Azende.* Oxford: Oxford University Press, 1937.

Falk, R.A. *Law in an Emerging Global Village: A Post-Westphalian Perspective.* New York: Transnational Publishers, 1998.

– *On Humane Governance: Towards a New World Politics.* College Park: Pennsylvania State University Press, 1995.

– *Predatory Globalization: A Critique.* Oxford: Blackwell Publishers, 1999.

Fidler, D.P. *International Law and Infectious Diseases.* Oxford: Clarendon Press, 1999.

Ford Foundation. *Globalization, Health Sector Reform, Gender and Reproductive Health.* New York: Ford Foundation, 2001.

Frank, T.M. *Fairness in International Law and Institutions.* Oxford: Clarendon Press, 1995.

– *The Power of Legitimacy among Nations.* New York: Oxford University Press, 1990.

Friedman, T.L. *The Lexus and the Olive Tree.* New York: Anchor Books, 2000.

Fuenzalida-Puelma, H.L., and S.S. Connor, eds. *The Right to Health in the Americas: A Comparative Constitutional Study.* Washington, DC: Pan-American Health Organization, 1989.

Garrett, L. *Betrayal of Trust: The Collapse of Global Public Health.* New York: Hyperion, 2000.

- *The Coming Plague: Newly Emerging Diseases in a World Out of Balance*. New York: Farrar, Strauss & Giroux, 1994.

Gdbaw, R.M., and T.J. Richard. *Intellectual Property Rights: Global Consensus, Global Conflict*. Boulder, CO: Westview Press, 1998.

Geest, W., ed. *Negotiating Structural Adjustment in Africa*. New York: UNDP, 1994.

Giddens, A. *The Consequences of Modernity*. London: Polity Press, 1990.

Goodman, C., et al. *Economic Analysis of Global Malaria Control in Sub-Saharan Africa*. Geneva: Global Forum for Health Research, 2000.

Goodman, N.M. *International Health Organizations and Their Work*. 2nd ed. London: Churchill Livingstone, 1977.

Gostin, L. *Public Health Law: Power, Duty, Restraint*. Berkeley: University of California Press, 2001.

Gostin, L., and Z. Lazzarini. *Human Rights and Public Health in the AIDS Pandemic*. Oxford and New York: Oxford University Press, 1997.

Habermas, J. *The Theory of Communicative Action*. Boston: Beacon Press, 1981; 1986.

Harris, D.J. *Cases and Materials on International Law*. 5th ed. London: Sweet & Maxwell, 1997.

Hasenclever, A., et al., eds. *Theories of International Regimes*, Cambridge: Cambridge University Press, 1997.

Hays, J.N. *The Burdens of Disease: Epidemics and Human Response in Western History*. New Brunswick, NJ: Rutgers University Press, 1998.

Head, I.L. *On a Hinge of History: The Mutual Vulnerability of South and North*. Toronto: University of Toronto Press, in association with the International Development Research Centre, 1991.

Held, D. *Introduction to Critical Theory: Horkheimer to Habermas*. London: Hutchinson, 1980.

Held, D., and A. McGrew, eds. *Globalization/Anti-Globalization*. Cambridge: Polity Press, 2002.

- *Governing Globalization: Power, Authority and Global Governance*. Cambridge: Polity Press, 2002.

Held, D., et al. *Global Transformations: Politics, Economics and Culture*. Cambridge: Polity, 1999.

Henkin, L. *The Age of Rights*. New York: Columbia University Press, 1990.

- *How Nations Behave: Law and Foreign Policy*. New York: Columbia University Press, 1979.

Hilts, P.J. *Smokescreen: The Truth behind the Tobacco Industry Cover-Up*. Reading, MA: Addison-Wesley, 1996.

Howard-Jones, N; *International Public Health between the Two World Wars: The Organizational Problems*. Geneva: WHO, 1978.

- *The Scientific Background of the International Sanitary Conferences 1851–1938*. Geneva: WHO, 1975.

Iwu, M.M., and J.C. Wootton. *Advances in PhytoMedicine*. Vol. 1. Amsterdam: Elsevier, 2002.

Janzen, J.M. *The Quest for Therapy: Medical Pluralism in Lower Zaire*. Berkeley: University of California Press, 1978.

Kairys, D., ed. *The Politics of Law: A Progressive Critique*. 3rd ed. New York: Basic Books, 1998.

Kant, I. *Perpetual Peace*. Trans. L.W. Beck. Indianapolis: Bobbs-Merrill, 1957.

Kaul, I., et al., eds. *Global Public Goods: International Co-operation in the 21st Century*. New York: UNDP/Oxford University Press, 1999.

Keily, R., and P. Marfleet, eds. *Globalisation and the Third World*. London: Routledge, 1998.

Kiss, A., and D. Shelton, eds. *International Environmental Law*. New York: Transnational Publishers, 1991.

– *International Environmental Law* (1994 Supplement). New York: Transnational Publishers, 1994.

Kitts, J., and J.H. Roberts. *The Health Gap: Beyond Pregnancy and Reproduction*. Ottawa: IDRC, 1996.

Koskenniemi, M. *From Apology to Utopia: The Structure of International Legal Argument*. Helsinki: Finnish Lawyers' Publishing Group, 1989.

Labonte, R., et al. *Fatal Indifference: The G8, Africa and Global Health*. Lansdowne, South Africa: University of CapeTown Press, 2004.

Last, J.M. *A Dictionary of Epidemiology*. 3rd ed. New York: Oxford University Press, 1995.

– *Public Health and Human Ecology*. 2nd ed. Stamford, CT: Appleton & Lange, 1998.

Last, M., and G.L. Chavundika, eds. *The Professionalisation of African Medicine*. Manchester: Manchester University Press, 1986.

Lensink, R. *Structural Adjustment in Sub-Saharan Africa*. New York: Addison-Wesley, 1996.

Leslie, C., and A. Young. *Paths to Asian Medical Knowledge*. Berkeley and Los Angeles: University of California Press, 1992.

MacLuhan, M., and B.R. Powers. *The Global Village: Transformations in World Life and Media in the 21st Century*. New York: Oxford University Press, 1992.

Malanczuk, P. *Akehurst's Modern Introduction to International Law*. 7th ed. London and New York: Routledge, 1997.

Mbiti, J.S. *African Religions and Philosophy*. London: Heinemann, 1969.

McNeill, W.H. *Plagues and Peoples*. New York: Doubleday, 1976.

Mkandawire, T., and C.C. Soludo. *Our Continent, Our Future: African Perspectives on Adjustment*. Ottawa: International Development Research Council in conjunction with Council for the Development of Social Science Research in Africa, CODESSRIA, 1999.

Murray, C.J.L., and A. Lopez. *The Global Burden of Disease*. Cambridge: Harvard University Press, 1996.

– *The Global Burden of Disease and Injury Series.* Geneva: WHO, 1996.

Nadasen, S. *Public Health Law in South Africa.* Durban: Butterworths, 2000.

Narayan, D., et al. *Voices of the Poor Crying Out for Change.* Washington, DC: World Bank, 2000.

Nef, J. *Human Security and Mutual Vulnerability: The Global Political Economy of Development and Underdevelopment.* 2nd ed. Ottawa: IDRC, 1999.

Nussbaum, A. *A Concise History of the Law of Nations.* New York: Macmillan, 1954.

Nye, J.S., and D.D. Donahue, eds. *Governance in a Globalizing World.* Washington, DC: Brookings Institution Press, 2000.

Phillips, D.R. *Health and Health Care in the Third World.* New York: Longman, 1990.

Physicians for Human Rights. *The Taliban's War on Women: Health and Human Rights Crisis in Afghanistan.* Boston and Washington, DC: Physicians for Human Rights, 1998.

Porter, D. *Health, Civilization and the State: A History of Public Health from Ancient to Modern Times.* London and New York: Routledge, 1999.

Price-Smith, A.T. *The Health of Nations: Infectious Disease, Environmental Change, and Their Effects on National Security and Development.* Cambridge, MA: MIT Press, 2002.

Rawls, J. *A Theory of Justice.* Rev. ed. Cambridge: Harvard University Press, 1999.

Reed, D. ed. *The GEF: Sharing Responsibility for the Biosphere.* Washington, DC: World Wide Fund for Nature, 1993.

Robertson, R. *Globalization, Social Theory and Global Culture.* London: Sage, 1992.

Rosenau, J.N. *Along the Domestic-Foreign Frontier: Exploring Governance in a Turbulent World.* Cambridge: Cambridge University Press, 1997.

Rotblat, J. *World Citizenship: Allegiance to Humanity.* London: Macmillan, 1997.

Said, E. *Orientalism.* New York: Vintage Books, 1978.

Said, H.M. *Medicine in China.* Karachi: Hanidard Academy, 1965.

Sahn, D.E., et al. *Structural Adjustment Reconsidered: Economic Policy and Poverty in Africa.* Oxford: Oxford University Press, 1997.

Schachter, O., and C.C. Joyner, eds. *United Nations Legal Order.* Vol. 2. New York: Cambridge University Press, 1995.

Scholte, J.A. *Globalization: A Critical Introduction.* New York: St Martin's Press, 2000.

Sen, A. *Development as Freedom.* New York: Anchor Books, 1999.

Siddiqi, J. *World Health and World Politics: The World Health Organization and the United Nations System.* London: Hurst & Co, 1995.

Simon, D., et al., eds. *Structurally Adjusted Africa: Poverty, Debt and Basic Needs.* London: Pluto Press, 1995.

Simpson, G.E. *Yoruba Religion and Medicine in Ibadan.* Ibadan: Ibadan University Press, 1980.

Smith, G., and M. Naim. *Altered States: Globalization, Sovereignty and Governance.* Ottawa: IDRC, 2000.

Sohn, L. and T. Buergenthal, eds. *The Movement of Persons across Borders*. Washington, DC: American Society of International Law; Studies in Transnational Legal Policy No. 23, 1992.

Stiglitz, J.E. *Globalization and Its Discontents*. New York: Norton, 2003.

Stuagard, F. *Traditional Medicine in Botswana*. Gaborone: Ipelegang Publishers, 1985.

Szasz, P.C. *Selected Essays on Understanding International Institutions and the Legislative Process*. Ardsley, NY: Transnational Publishers, 2001.

South Commission. *The Challenge of the South*. Oxford: Oxford University Press, 1990.

Thucydides. *History of the Peloponnesian War*. Trans. R. Warner. Harmondsworth: Penguin Books, 1954.

Wapner, P. *Environmental Activism and World Civic Politics*. New York: SUNY Press, 1996.

Waters, M. *Globalization*. London: Routledge, 1995.

Watkins, K., ed. *Oxfam Poverty Report*. Oxford: Oxfam, 1995.

Watts, S. *Epidemics and History: Disease, Power and Imperialism*. New Haven, CT: Yale University Press, 1997.

Weber, M. *Economy and Society*, vols. 1 and 2. Ed. G. Roth, and C. Wittich. Berkeley and Los Angeles: University of California Press, 1978.

Weiss, E.B. *In Fairness to Future Generations: International Law, Common Patrimony, and Intergenerational Equity*. New York: United Nations University/Transnational Publishers, 1989.

Whalley, R.F., and T.J. Hashim. *A Textbook of World Health: A Practical Guide to Global Health Care*. New York: CRC Press/Partheneon, 1995.

World Health Organization. *Management of Severe Malaria: A Practical Handbook*. 2nd ed. Geneva: WHO, 2000.

Zinsser, H. *Rats, Lice and History: A Chronicle of Pestilence and Plagues*. New York: Black Dog and Leventhal, 1963.

Articles, Book Chapters, and Conference Papers

Aginam, O. 'Are We Our Brother's and Sister's Keepers: Africa and Public Health Challenges in a Divided World.' Proceedings of Berkeley/Stanford Joint Center for African Studies Spring Conference, Stanford University, 24 April 1999.

– 'From the Core to the Peripheries: Multilateral Governance of Malaria in a Multi-Cultural World' (2002) 3 (1) Chicago Journal of International Law 87.

– 'Global Village, Divided World: South-North Gap and Global Health Challenges at Century's Dawn' (2000) 7 Indiana J. of Global Legal Studies 603.

– 'International Law and Communicable Diseases' (2002) 80 (12) Bulletin of the World Health Organization 946.

Akerele, O. 'The Best of Both Worlds: Bringing Traditional Medicine up to Date' (1987) 24 (2) Social Science and Medicine 177.

Ampofo, O. and J.D. Johnson-Romauld. 'Traditional Medicine and Its Role in the Development of Health Services in Africa.' Technical Discussions of the 25th, 26th and 27th Sessions of the WHO Regional Office for Africa (Brazaville, Congo: WHO 1957) 51.

Anand, R.P. 'Development and Environment: The Case of Developing Countries' (1980) 24 Indian J. of International Law 1.

Anghie, A. 'Finding the Peripheries: Sovereignty and Colonialism in Nineteenth-Century International Law' (1999) 40 Harvard International Law J. 1.

– 'Francisco de Vitoria and the Colonial Origins of International Law' (1996) 5 Social & Legal Studies 321.

– 'Time Present and Time Past: Globalization, International Financial Institutions and the Third World' (2000) 32 New York J. of International Law & Politics 243.

Attaran, A. 'Human Rights and Biomedical Research Funding for the Developing World: Discovering State Obligations Under the Right to Health' 4 (1) Health & Human Rights 26.

Berlinguer, G. 'Health and Equity as a Primary Global Goal' (1999) 42 (4) Development. (Responses to Globalization – Rethinking Health and Equity) 17.

Brugha, R., and G. Walt. 'A Global Health Fund: A Leap of Faith?' (21 July 2001) 323 British Medical J. 152.

Buse, K., and A. Waxman. 'Public-Private Partnerships: A Strategy for WHO' (2001) 79 (8) Bulletin of the World Health Organization 748

– 'Public-Private Health Partnerships: Part II – What Are the Health Issues for Global Governance' (2000) 78 (5) Bulletin of the World Health Organization 699

Buse, K., and G. Walt. 'Globalisation and Multilateral Public-Private Partnerships: Issues for Health Policy.' In *Health Policy in a Globalising World*, ed. K. Lee, K. Buse, and S. Fustukian, 41. Cambridge: Cambridge University Press, 2002.

Chen, L.C., et al. 'Health as a Global Public Good.' In *Global Public Goods: International Co-operation for the 21st Century*, ed. I. Kaul, 384. New York: UNDP/Oxford University Press, 1999.

Chimni, B.S. 'Marxism and International Law: A Contemporary Analysis' (6 February 1999) Economic & Political Weekly 337.

Connoly, G.N. 'Worldwide Expansion of the Transnational Tobacco Industry' (1992) 2 J. of the National Cancer Institute 29.

Da Costa Silva, E. 'The Protection of Intellectual Property for Local and Indigenous Peoples' (1995) 17 European Intellectual Property Rev. 546.

Devetak, R. 'Critical Theory.' In *Theories of International Relations*, ed. S. Burchill and A. Linklater, 145. London: Macmillan, 1996.

Dorolle, P. 'Old Plaques in the Jet Age: International Aspects of Post and Future Control of Communicable Diseases' (1969) WHO Chronicle 105.

Fabrega, H. 'A Complimentary on African Systems of Medicine.' In *African Health and*

Healing Systems: Proceedings of a Symposium, ed. P.S. Yoda, 238. Los Angeles: Cross-
roads, 1982.
– 'The Need for an Ethnomedical Science' (1975) 189 Science 969.
Falk, R. 'The Coming Global Civilization: Neo-Liberal or Humanist.' In *Legal Visions of
the 21st Century: Essays in Honour of Judge Christopher Weeramantry,* ed. A. Anghie and
G. Sturgess, 15. The Hague: Kluwer Law International, 1998.
– 'Global Civil Society, Perspectives, Initiatives, Movements' (1998) 26 Oxford Develop-
ment Studies 99.
– 'The Making of Global Citizenship.' In *Global Visions: Beyond the New World Order,* ed.
J. Brecher, 39. Boston: South End Press, 1993
Farmer, P. 'Social Inequalities and Emerging Infectious Diseases' (1996) 2 Emerging Infec-
tious Diseases 259.
Fauci, A.S. 'Tuberculosis Morbidity: United States' (1995) J. of the American Medical
Association 788.
Ferguson, Y.H., and R.W. Mansbach. 'Beyond Inside/Outside: Political Space and West-
phalian States in a World of Politics (1996) 2 Global Governance 261.
– 'Global Politics at the Turn of the Millennium: Changing Bases of "Us" and "Them"'
Proceedings of the 1999 International Studies Association. Malden, MA: Blackwell, 1999)
77.
Fidler, D.P. 'The Future of the World Health Organization: What Role for International
Law' (1998) 31 Vanderbilt J. of Transnational Law 1079.
– 'The Globalization of Public Health: Emerging Infectious Diseases and International
Relations' (1997) 5 (1) Indiana J. of Global Legal Studies 1.
– 'The Globalization of Public Health: The First 100 Years of International Health Diplo-
macy' (2001) 79 (9) Bulletin of the World Health Organization 842.
– 'International Law and Global Public Health' (1999) 48 University of Kansas Law
Rev. 1.
– 'A Kinder, Gentler System of Capitulations? International Law, Structural Adjustment
Policies, and the Standard of Liberal, Globalized Civilization' (2000) 35 Texas Interna-
tional Law J. 327.
– 'Microbialpolitik: Infectious Diseases and International Relations' (1998) 14 American
University International Law Rev. 1.
– 'Mission Impossible? International Law and Infectious Diseases' (1996) 10 Temple
International & Comparative Law J. 493.
– 'Neither Science Nor Shamans: Globalization of Markets and Health in the Developing
World' (1999) 7 Indiana J. of Global Legal Studies 191.
– 'Return of the Fourth Horseman: Emerging Infectious Diseases and International Law'
(1997) 81 Minnesota Law Rev. 771.
Fluss, S.S. 'International Public Health Law: An Overview.' In *Oxford Textbook of Public
Health.* Vol. 1. Ed. R. Detels, 371. Oxford: Oxford University Press, 1996.

France, T., et al. 'The Global Fund: Which Countries Owe How Much' (21 April 2001) Unpublished Manuscript by Health and Development Networks, and AIDSPAN, available online at www.hdnet.org and www.aidspan.org.

Garret, L. 'The Return of Infections Disease' (Jan.–Feb. 1996) Foreign Affairs.

Geertz, C. 'Local Knowledge: Fact and Law in Comparative Perspective.' In *Further Essays in Interpretive Anthropology*, 1 New York: Basic Books, 1989.

Gostin, L. 'The Resurgent TB Epidemic in the Era of AIDS: Reflections on Public Health, Law and Society' (1995) 54 Maryland Law Rev. 1.

Gostin, L., and J. Mann. 'Towards the Development of a Human Rights Impact Assessment for the Formulation and Evaluation of Public Health Policies' (1994) 1 Health & Human Rights 59.

Gratz, N.G. 'Why Aircraft Disinsection' (2000) 78 International J. of Public Health 995.

Grein, T.W., et al. 'Rumours of Disease in the Global Village: Outbreak Verification' (2000) 6 Emerging Infectious Diseases 97.

Gutterman, A. 'The North-South Debate Regarding the Protection of Intellectual Property' (1993) 23 Wake Forest Law Rev. 89.

Head, I.L. 'The Contribution of International Law to Development' (1987) 25 Canadian Yearbook of International Law 29.

Jamar, S.D. 'The International Human Right to Health' (1994) 22 Southern Univ. Law Rev. 1.

Kalu, O.U. 'The Gods Are to Blame.' Unpublished Proceedings of the 6th International Congress on Ethnobiology, Whakatana, New Zealand, 24–6 November, 1998.

Keily, R. 'Globalisation, (Post-)Modernity and the Third World.' In *Globalisation and the Third World*, ed. R. Keily and P. Marfleet, 2. London/New York: Routledge, 1998.

Kennedy, D. 'Primitive Legal Scholarship' (1986) 27 Harvard International Law J. 1.

Kwakwa, E. 'Institutional Perspectives of International Economic Law.' In *Perspectives in International Economic Law*, ed. A.H. Qureshi, 45. The Hague: Kluwer Law International, 2002.

– 'Some Comments on Rulemaking at the World Intellectual Property Organization' (2002) 12 Duke J. of Comparative and International Law 179.

Lakin, A. 'The Legal Powers of the World Health Organization' (1997) 3 Medical Law International 23.

Larkin, M. 'Global Aspects of Health and Health Policy in Third World Countries.' In *Globalisation and the Third World*, R. Keily and P. Marfleet, 104. London: Routledge, 1998) 104

Leary, V. 'Justiciability and Beyond: Complaint Procedures and the Right to Health' (1995) 55 Rev. of the International Commission of Jurists 89.

– 'The Right to Health in International Human Rights Law' (1994) 1 Health & Human Rights 25.

Lee, K., and R. Dodgson. 'Globalization and Cholera: Implications for Global Governance' (2000) 6 (2) Global Governance 213.

L'hirondel A., and D. Yach. 'Develop and Strengthen Public Health Law' (1998) 51 World Health Statistics Quarterly 79.

Lifson, A. 'Mosquitoes, Models, and Dengue' (1996) 347 Lancet 1201.

Longrigg, J. 'Epidemic, Ideas and Classical Athenian Society,' In *Epidemics and Ideas: Essays on the Historical Perception of Pestilence*, ed. T. Ranger and P. Slack, 21. Cambridge: Cambridge University Press, 1992.

Mafart, B., and J.L. Perret. 'History of the Concept of Quarantine' (March 1998) 58 Medicine Tropicale 14.

Mann, J., et al. 'Health and Human Rights' (1994) 1 (1) Health & Human Rights 7.

Matthew, R.A. 'Social Responses to Environmental Change.' In *Environmental Change: Adaptation and Security*, ed. S.C. Lonergan, 17. The Hague: Kluwer, 1999.

Matthews, J. 'Power Shift' (1997) 76 Foreign Affairs 50.

Mgbeoji, I. 'Patents and Traditional Knowledge of the Uses of Plants: Is a Communal Patent Regime Part of the Solution to the Scourge of Bio Piracy?' (2001) 9 (1) Indiana J. of Global Legal Studies 163.

Mickelson, K. 'Rhetoric or Rage: Third World Voices in International Legal Discourse' (1998) 16 Wisconsin International Law J. 353.

Murray, C.J.L., and A. Lopez. 'Alternative Projections of Mortality and Disability by Cause, 1990–2020: Global Burden of Disease Study' (1997) 349 Lancet 1498.

Mutua, M. 'The Banjul Charter and the African Cultural Fingerprint: An Evaluation of the Language of Duties' (1995) 35 Virginia J. of International Law 340.

– 'The Ideology of Human Rights' (1996) 36 Virginia J. of International Law 586.

– 'Looking Past the Human Rights Committee: An Argument for De-Marginalizing Enforcement' (1998) 4 Buffalo Human Rights Law Rev. 211.

– 'What Is TWAIL.' *Proceedings of the 94th Annual Meeting of American Society of International Law*. Washington, DC: ASIL, 2000.

Nabarro, D., and E.M. Taylor. 'The Roll Back Malaria Campaign' (26 June 1998) 280 Science 2067.

Nader, L. 'The Anthropological Study of Law', (1965) 67 American Anthropologist 25.

Nakajima, H. 'Global Disease Threats and Foreign Policy' (1997) 4 (1) Brown J. of World Affairs 319.

Okafor, J. 'Issues in African Biodiversity No.3: Identification, Utilization and Conservation of Medicinal Plants in Southeastern Nigeria' Biodiversity Support Program Publication Database, 1999.

Okafor, O.C. 'The Concept of Legitimate Governance in the Contemporary International Legal System' (1997) 44 Netherlands International Law Rev. 33.

Pinet, G. 'Health Challenges of the 21st Century: A Legislative Approach to Health Determinants' (1998) 49 International Digest of Health Legislation 131.

Plotkin, B.J., and A.M. Kimball. 'Designing the International Policy and Legal Framework for the Control of Infectious Diseases: First Steps' (1997) 3 Emerging Infectious Diseases 1.

Poku, N.K. 'The Global AIDS Fund: Context and Opportunity' (2002) 23 Third World Quarterly 283.

Pullan, B. 'Plague and Perceptions of the Poor in Early Modern Italy.' In *Epidemics and Ideas: Essays on the Historical Perception of Pestilence*, ed. T. Ranger and P. Slack, Cambridge: Cambridge University Press, 1992.

Ramsay, S. 'Global Fund Makes Historic First Round of Payments' (2002) 359 Lancet 158.

Richards, T. 'New Global Health Fund' (Editorial) (2 June 2001) 322 British Medical J. 1321.

Ricupero, R. 'Chronicle of a Negotiation: The Financial Chapter of Agenda 21' (1993) 4 Colorado J. of International Environmental Law & Policy 81.

Robertson, R.E. 'Measuring State Compliance with the Obligation to Devote the Maximum Available Resources to Realizing Economic, Social and Cultural Rights' (1994) 16 Human Rights Quarterly 693.

Roemer, R. 'The Right to Health Care.' In *The Right to Health in the Americas: A Comparative Constitutional Study*, ed. H.L. Fuezalida-Puelma and S.S. Connor, 17 Washington, DC: Pan-American Health Organisation, 1989.

Roht-Arriaza, N. 'Of Seeds and Shamans: The Appropriation of the Scientific and Technical Knowledge of Indigenous and Local Communities' (1996) 17 Michigan J. of International Law 919.

Rubin, A. 'International Law in the Age of Columbus' (1992) 39 Netherlands International Law Rev. 5.

Sachs, J. 'A New Global Commitment to Disease Control in Africa' (May 2001) Nature Medicine 521.

Salako, L.A. 'An African Perspective.' *World Health: United against Malaria, The Magazine of World Health Organization* (May–June 1998): 24.

Salzberg, S. 'The Social Model of Mental Health Care and Law in Comparative Context.' Proceedings of World Congress, World Federation for Mental Health (August, 1993).

Schachter, O. 'Towards a Theory of International Obligation' (1968) 6 Virginia J. of International Law 301.

Sharpe, W.R. 'The New World Health Organization' (1947) 41 Am. J. of International Law 509.

Sindiga, I. 'African Ethnomedicine and Other Medical Systems.' In *Traditional Medicine in Africa*, ed. I. Sindiga, 16. Nairobi: East African Publishers, 1995.

Snyder, F.G. 'Law and Development in the Light of Dependency Theory' (1980) 14 Law & Society Rev. 723.

Taylor, A.L. 'Controlling the Global Spread of Infectious Diseases: Towards a Reinforced Role for the International Health Regulations' (1997) 33 Houston Law Rev. 1327.

– 'An International Regulatory Strategy for Global Tobacco Control' (1996) 21 Yale J. of International Law 257.

– 'Making the World Health Organization Work: A Legal Framework for Universal Access to the Conditions for Health' (1992) 18 American J. of Law & Medicine 301.

– 'Public-Private Partnerships for Health: The United Nations Global Fund on AIDS and Health' (2002) 35 John Marshall Law Rev. 400.

Taylor, A.L., and D. Bettcher. 'WHO Framework Convention on Tobacco Control: A Global Good for Public Health' (2000) 78 (7) International J. of Public Health 920.

Toebes, B. 'Towards an Improved Understanding of the International Human Right to Health' (1999) 21 Human Rights Quarterly 661.

Tomaseveski, T. 'Health.' In *United Nations Legal Order*, vol. 2 eds. O. Schachter and C.C. Joyner, 859 New York: Cambridge University Press, 1995.

Trigg, P., and A. Kondrachine. 'The Global Malaria Control Strategy.' *World Health: The Magazine of the World Health Organization* (May–June 1998) 4.

Trubek, D. 'Towards a Social Theory of Law: An Essay on the Study of Law and Development' (1972) 8 Yale Law J. 1.

Velimirovic, B. 'Do We Still Need International Health Regulations?' (1976) 133 J. Infectious Diseases 478.

Walt, G. 'Globalization of International Health' (1998) 351 Lancet 434.

Walker, G.R., and M.A. Fox. 'Globalization: An Analytical Framework' (1996) 3 Indiana J. of Global Legal Studies 375.

Wapner, P. 'The Normative Promise of Non-State Actors: A Theoretical Account of Global Civil Society.' In *Principled World Politics: The Challenge of Normative International Relations*, ed. P. Wapner and R. Lester, 261 Lanham: Rowman & Littlefield, 2000.

Wasserman, U. 'Traditional Medicine and the Law' (1984) 18 J. of World Trade Law 155.

Wilder, R. 'Protection of Traditional Medicine.' Working Paper Series No. 4, July 2001. WHO Commission on Macroeconomics and Health.

Woodall, J. 'Outbreak Meets the Internet: Global Epidemic Monitoring by Pro-MED Mail' (1997) 1 SIM Quarterly: Newsletter of the Society for the Internet in Medicine 1.

Woodward, D., et al. 'Globalization and Health: A Framework for Analysis and Action' (2001) 79 (9) Bulletin of the World Health Organization 875.

Yach, D., and D. Bettcher. 'The Globalization of Public Health I: Threats and Opportunities' (1998) 88 American J. of Public Health 735.

– 'The Globalization of Public Health II: The Convergence of Self-Interest and Altruism' (1998) 88 American J. of Public Health 738.

Yamey, G. 'Global Campaign to Eradicate Malaria' (2001) 322 British Medical J. 1191.

– 'WHO in 2002: Faltering Steps Towards Partnerships' (2002) 325 British Medical J. 1236.

Zacher, M.W. 'The Decaying Pillars of the Westphalian Temple: Implications for International Order and Governance.' In *Governance Without Government: Order and Change in World Politics*, ed. J.N. Rosenau and C. Ernst-Otto, 58. Cambridge: Cambridge University Press, 1992.

– 'Global Epidemiological Surveillance: International Co-Operation to Monitor Infectious Diseases.' In *Global Public Goods: International Co-operation in the 21st Century*, ed. I. Kaul, 266. New York: UNDP and Oxford University Press, 1999.

Zacher, M.W., and R. Matthew. 'Liberal International Theory: Common Threads, Divergent Strands.' In *Controversies in International Relations Theory: Realism and the Neo-Liberal Challenge*, ed. C.W. Kegley, 107. New York: St Martin's, 1995.

Reports of Multilateral Institutions, Symposium/Conference Reports, Web (Internet), Secondary and Miscellenous Documents

Annan, K. 'Poverty: Biggest Enemy of Health in Developing World.' Speech to the 54th World Health Assembly, Geneva, Switzerland, 17 May 2001. http://www.un.org/News/Press/docs/2001/sgsm7808.doc.htm.

Arazu, R. Interview in *The Torch* (Biannual Publication of the Students of Bigard Memorial Seminary, Enugu, Nigeria), 120 (Dec. 2000–June 2001), Special issue on Healing and Exorcism: Implications and Realities, 38.

BBC News. 'Key Anti-Smoking Treaty Adopted,' BBC News Online, 21 May 2003, http://news.bbc.co.uk/2/hi/health/3046223.stm (accessed 21 May 2003).

Bedell, R. *'Tuberculosis Is a Canadian Problem.' Globe and Mail* (Toronto), 21 March 2000.

Bioresources Development and Conservation Programme (BDCP). *Report of the International Conference on Traditional Medicine in HIV/AIDS and Malaria*, 5–7 December 2000; available online at http://www.bioresources.org (accessed 30 March 2001).

Bodansky, D. *The Framework-Protocol Approach*. FCTC Technical Briefing Series, WHO/NCD/FTI/99.1. Geneva: WHO, 1999.

– *What Makes International Agreements Effective? Some Pointers to the WHO Framework Convention on Tobacco Control*. FCTC Technical Briefing Series, WHO/NCD/FTI/99.4. Geneva: WHO, 1999.

Branswell, H. *Drug-Resistant Strains of TB Global Threat, WHO Warns. Recorder and Times* (Brockville, ON), 24 March 2000.

Brundtland, G.H. 'Globalization as a Force for Better Health.' Lecture at the London School of Economics, 16 March 2001.

– 'Scaling Up Action to Tackle Illness Associated with Poverty: The Global Fund for AIDS and Health.' Speech at the 54th World Health Assembly Technical Briefing, Geneva, 15 May 2001, available online at http://www.who.int/director-general/speeches/20…/20010515_wha54technicalbriefing.en.htm.

Capdevila, G. 'Malaria-Carrying Mosquitoes Hitch Rides on Air Planes.' Inter-Press Service. 22 August 2000.

Commission on Health Research for Development. *Health Research: Essential Link to Equity and Development*. Oxford: Oxford University Press, 1990.

Committee on Economic, Social and Cultural Rights (High Commission for Human Rights) *The Right to the Highest Attainable Standard of Health*. General Comment No. 14. 4 July 2000.

Editorial Commentary. 'Outbreak Not Contained: West Nile Virus Triggers a re-evaluation of Public Health Surveillance.' Scientific American (April 2000) 20.

General Agreement on Tariffs & Trade (GATT Panel), *Thailand-Restrictions on Importation of and Internal Taxes on Cigarettes*, Adopted November 7, 1990, GATT Doc. DSID/R, BISD 375/200.

G-8 Summit. 'Final Statement of 2001 G-8 Summit.' Genoa, Italy, 22 July 2001, available online at http://www.washingtonpost.com/wp-dyn/articles/A33436-2001Jul22.html (accessed 23 July 2003).

Halvorssen, A.M. *The Role of National Institutions in Developing and Implementing the WHO Framework Convention on Tobacco Control*. FCTC Technical Briefing Series, WHO/NCD/TFI/99.5. Geneva: WHO, 1999.

Harvard Law School. 'Economic and Social Rights and the Right to Health.' An Interdisciplinary Discussion held at Harvard Law School, September 1993.

INFACT. *Mobilizing NGOs and the Media behind the International Framework Convention on Tobacco Control: Lessons From the Code Marketing of Breast-Milk Substitutes and Conventions on Landmines and the Environment*. FCTC Technical Briefing Series, WHO/NCD/TFI/99.5. Geneva: WHO, 1999.

International Conference on Health Promotion, *Ottawa Charter for Health Promotion*, 21 November 1986. http://www/who.dk/policy/ottawa.htm (accessed 8 April 2001)

International Covenant on Economic, Social and Cultural Rights, G.A. Res. 2200, U.N. GAOR 21st sess. Supp. No. 16, U.N. Doc. A/6316 (1986).

International Court of Justice, *Legality of the Use by a State of Nuclear Weapons in Armed Conflict* (Advisory Opinion) 1996 ICJ Reports 4.

Joossens, L. *Improving Public Health Through an International Framework on Tobacco Control*. FCTC Technical Briefing Series, WHO/NCD/TFI/99.5. Geneva: WHO, 1999.

Langley, A. 'Anti-Smoking Treaty Is Adopted by 192 Nations,' *New York Times*, 21 May 2003, www.nytimes.com/2003/05/21/international/21CND-TOBA.html (accessed 21 May 2003).

Liu Centre for the Study of Global Issues. *Global Health Challenges*. Report of a Symposium Organized by the Liu Centre, University of British Columbia, Vancouver, 5 March 1999.

National Science and Technology Council Committee on International Science, Engineering and Technology Working Group on Emerging and Re-Emerging Infectious Diseases (CISET). *Infectious Diseases: A Global Health Threat.* Washington, DC: CISET, 1995.

Pan-American Health Organization (PAHO). *Health in the Americas,* vols. 1 and 2. Washington, DC: PAHO, 1998.

United Nations. *Report of the UNCED.* New York: UNCED, June 1992.

United Nations Development Programme. *Human Development Report, 1997.* New York and Oxford: Oxford University Press, 1997.

– *Human Development Report, 1998.* New York and Oxford: Oxford University Press, 1998.

United Nations, *The Rights to the Highest Attainable Standard of Health,* General Comment No. 14, Committee on Economic, Social and Cultural Rights, 4 July 2000 E/ C.12/2000/4.

United Nations, UN Convention on the Rights of the Child, G.A. Res. 44/25, U.N. GADR, Sup. No. 49 at 167, U.N. Doc. A/44/49(1989).

United States Centres for Disease Control (CDC). *Addressing Emerging Infectious Disease Threats: A Prevention Strategy for the United States.* Atlanta, GA: CDC, 1994.

United States Centres for Disease Control (CDC). *Preventing Emerging Infectious Diseases: A Strategy for the 21st Century.* Atlanta, GA: CDC, 1998.

United States Congress. *Emerging Infections: A Significant Threat to the Nation's Health, Hearings Before the Senate Committee on Labor and Human Resources.* Washington, DC: 104th US Congress, 1995.

United States House of Representatives. *House Report No. 706: Hearings Before the Committee on Foreign Relations, House of Representatives, 70th US Congress.*

United States Institute of Medicine. *America's Vital Interest in Global Health: Protecting Our People, Enhancing Our Economy, and Advancing Our International Interests.* Washington, DC: National Academy Press, 1994.

Vienna Convention on the Law of Treaties 1969 (1969) 8 I.L.M. 679.

World Bank. *Curbing the Epidemic: Governments and the Economics of Tobacco Control.* Washington, DC: The World Bank, 1999.

– *World Development Report, 1993: Investing in Health.* New York: Oxford University Press, 1993.

– *Sub-Saharan Africa: From Crisis to Sustainable Growth.* Washington, DC: The World Bank, 1989.

World Health Organization. *World Health Report, 1995: Bridging the Gaps.* Geneva: WHO, 1995.

– *Effects of Nuclear War on Health and Health Services: Report of the International Committee of Experts in Medical Sciences and Public Health to Implement Resolution WHA34.38.* Geneva: WHO, 1984.

– *Guidelines for the Management of Drug-Resistant Tuberculosis.* Geneva: WHO, 1998.

– *Handbook of Resolutions and Decisions of the World Health Assembly and the Executive Board*. Vol. 2. 1973–1984. Geneva: WHO, 1985.
– *International Health Regulations*. 3rd annotated ed. Geneva: WHO, 1983.
– *The International Response to Epidemics and Application of the International Health Regulations: Report of a WHO Informal Consultation*. Geneva: WHO, 1995.
– *Medicines for Malaria Venture*. Press Release, 3 November 1999. Geneva: WHO, 1999.
– *Qualitative Research for Health Programmes*. Geneva: WHO, Division of Mental Health and Prevention of Substance Abuse, 1996.
– *Removing Obstacles to Healthy Development: Report on Infectious Diseases*. Geneva: WHO, 1999.
– *World Health Organization: Basic Documents*. 43rd ed. (Geneva: WHO, 2001.
– *Report of Ad Hoc Committee on Health Research Relating to Future Intervention Options, Investing in Health Research and Development*. Geneva: WHO, 1996.
– *Severe Falciparum Malaria: Transactions of the Royal Society of Tropical Medicine & Hygiene*, vol. 94, supplement 4. Geneva: WHO, 2000.
– *Tobacco Industry Strategies to Undermine Tobacco Control Activities at the World Health Organization: Report of the Committee of Experts on Tobacco Industry Documents*. Geneva: WHO, 2000.
– *Tuberculosis*, WHO Fact Sheet No. 104 (Revised April 2000); available online at http://www.who.int/inf-fs/fac104.html.
– *Tuberculosis and Air Travel: Guidelines for Prevention and Control*. Geneva: WHO, 1998.
– *WHO Report 2003: Global Tuberculosis Control: Surveillance, Planning, Financing*. Geneva: WHO, 2003.
– *WHO Traditional Medicine Strategy, 2002–2005*. Geneva: WHO, 2002.
– *World Health Report, 1996: Fighting Disease, Fostering Development*. Geneva: WHO, 1996.
– *World Health Report, 1997: Conquering Suffering, Enriching Humanity.* Geneva: WHO, 1997.
– *The World Health Report, 1999: Making a Difference*. Geneva: WHO, 1999.
– *The World Health Report, 2000: Health Systems, Improving Performance*. Geneva: WHO, 2000.
World Health Organization (Regional Office for Europe). *Strategy to Roll Back Malaria in the WHO European Region*. Copenhagen: WHO, 1999.
World Health Organization, Tobacco Free Initiative. *Report of International Consultation on Environmental Tobacco Smoke (ETS) and Child Health*, 11–14 January 1999. Geneva: WHO – Tobacco Free Initiatives, 1999.
World Health Organization/UN Programme on AIDS (WHO/UNAIDS). *A Deadly Partnership: Tuberculosis in the Era of HIV*. Geneva: WHO/UNAIDS, 1996.
World Health Organization/UNICEF, '*Alma-Ata Declaration on Primary Health Care,*' 12 September 1978 in *Health for ALL Series No. 1*. Geneva: WHO, 1978.

Index

Tobacco Control (FCTC)
soft-law, 87. *See also* environmental treaties
South-North: 30–1, 106; health divide, 6,
65; origin of term, 133*n*; unequal share
of burden, 18, 27, 31, 40, 106
state sovereignty: and health, 36–7, 63,
79; promoting rights in other states, 39
Stiglitz, Joseph, 45, 148*n*
Structural Adjustment Programs (SAP),
40–3

Thai Cigarettes Case (*United States v.
Thailand*), 84
Theory of Justice. *See* Rawls, John
Thucydides, 14, 34, 135*n*, 143*n*
tobacco: 82–4, 113; and TB, 83. *See also*
FCTC
trade, and impeding public health diplomacy, 62; liberalization and tobacco, 84
traditional medicine, 9–10, 65, 90–101,
107–8, 113, 169–70*n*; devoid of scientific methodology, 90; examples of, 97;
scientification of, 101
transborder threat of disease. *See* transnational spread of disease
transnational spread of disease, 6, 8, 27,
47, 49, 50, 57–8, 63, 75, 110, 130,
155*n*
travel, 58

Treaty of Westphalia, 64, 126–7
tuberculosis (TB): 53–5, 57, 115–16; and
Canada, 55; drug-resistant strains, 54;
and HIV, 54; and immigration, 55; re-
emergence of, 53–5; and tobacco, 83.
See also GFATM

UN Development Programme (UNDP),
87–8, 114
UN Environment Programme (UNEP),
86–8
UNAIDS, 111
underdevelopment: and disease, 10, 27,
31, 81, 114; and malaria, 93

vulnerability of multilateralism, 60–89

West Nile Fever, 57
World Bank, 23, 41, 111, 113; and GEF,
87–8
World Health Assembly (WHA): 61, 66–
73, 82; as a microcosm, 67
World Health Organization (WHO): 14,
66–89; constitution, 66–8, 71–2;
endorsing traditional medicine, 100;
origins of, 52
World Trade Organization (WTO): 80,
166*n*; and tobacco, 83–4

yellow fever: 49, 76. *See also* IHR